Special Purchase
Our Price $8.00

The best of
Asian Cooking

This edition is produced by Arden Publications, Suite 15A, 257 Gloucester Road, Hongkong and Times Editions Pte. Ltd., 422 Thomson Road, Singapore 1129.

Design by PPA Design Ltd., Hongkong.

Copyright © 1985, John Mitchell
ISBN No. 0–517–60678–X
Printed in Singapore.
1986 edition published by Crescent Books,
distributed by Crown Publishers, Inc.

h g f e d c b a

The Best Of
Asian Cooking

JOHN MITCHELL

Crescent Books
New York

Contents

Isiyaki (facing page) is a Japanese meal of prime beef steak, cooked on a very hot, pre-heated rock and served with fresh vegetables.

Introduction

To write a comprehensive introduction to the many-splendored and varied flavors of Asian cuisine would result in another book entirely and even the most carefully thought-out précis would still end up a lengthy essay. My intention, then, is to let the recipes that follow act as their own introduction and here all I wish to do is to explain my method of selection and editing. For I have no doubt that there will be those, familiar with the food of the region, who claim that I have excluded a most important ingredient from their favorite recipe or, worse still, omitted that recipe altogether. However, while it is true to say there are a number of accepted 'standard' Asian dishes — written up in most Asian cook books, passed on from generation to generation of books, and eaten with enthusiastic regularity — there is not the strict adherence to conformity as there is in the classical cooking of France or even of other Western cuisines. The important thing to remember is that, within the bounds of certain religious and cultural customs and conventions, nearly all local eating habits are based on personal tastes and it's a fact that few Asian cooks, professional or amateur, allow themselves to become obsessed with exact weights and measures or precise instructions. 'Doing what comes naturally' would seem to be the accepted, and indeed very acceptable, attitude.

For example, when I started to sort through all the material I had gathered I found, in my files, no less than sixteen variations of recipes for the marinades and sauces used for Satay, that very popular Indonesian and Malaysian 'meat-on-a-stick', and as for the different sauces for the Sweet & Sour dishes so favored by the Chinese and for the Curries of India and South East Asia — it seemed the number was endless. Altogether I had a total of over fifteen hundred recipes from which to select and while I suppose it is only natural that personal preference played some part in the final choice, this was not intended and what I set out to do was to present a balanced 'diet' of recipes from many parts of Asia. I tried to find recipes that had not been published as often as others although, at the same time, I felt it necessary to include those so universally popular

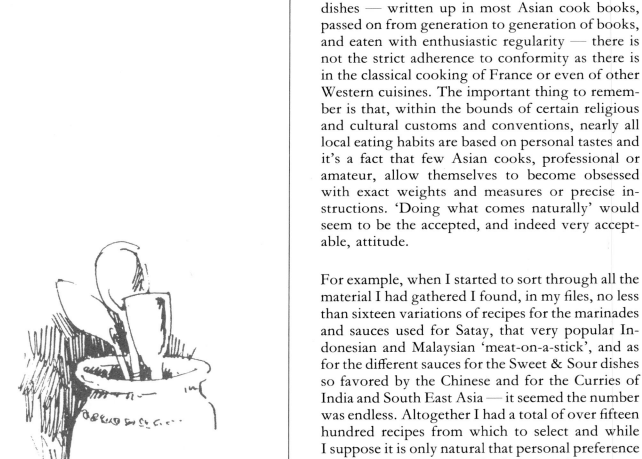

that their omission would probably have been disappointing to many readers.

Consistency and style always present problems when editing a cookbook and particularly so, as in this case, when the recipes come from such a diverse number of sources. As I explain below, I've deliberately made some changes and, while attempting to remain as 'orderly' as possible, have, at the same time, tried to present the recipes in a simple and easy to follow manner. It should be noted, however, that I have made certain deliberate assumptions and have not gone into any detail regarding the preparation of basic ingredients, there being many excellent books (already, I feel sure, a part of most readers' kitchen library) which graphically explain the gutting of chicken, the scaling of fish, the skinning of tomatoes and the shredding of meat. And, while I have not generally been very specific in giving the size and weight of vegetables, believing this to be more a matter for the cook's discretion, I have shown precise measurements for the many spices used throughout, although I realise that some adjustments may often prove necessary to cater for individual palates. Indeed, while 'one tasting spoon' and 'some willingness to ad-lib' are not actually listed as ingredients, both should be regarded as essential if the maximum reward is to be gained from cooking and eating in the Asian style.

Although the average Asian meal does not consist of a number of separate courses served consecutively, it still seemed to me that the most straightforward way to divide the book was by the types of food rather than by the different countries. For not only are there many dishes common to more than one country but there is also, for example, excellent Indian food to be found in Singapore and Hong Kong as well as Bombay and Delhi and, of course, Chinese restaurants abound throughout the region as they do throughout the Western world. The country named each time should therefore be taken as an indication of where I obtained the particular recipe rather than its national origin, although in most cases the two are the same. It may seem strange that China is not named as a source of any of the recipes but this is because my travels in that country have been very limited. It should be noted, however, that all the recipes from Hong Kong and Taiwan, many from Singapore and some from Malaysia fall within the category of ethnic Chinese cuisine.

Even having decided on the method and order of presenting the recipes, there still remained some confusion: Should the Soup Noodles be placed with the noodles (it is!) or with the soups; should the Hainanese Chicken Rice be placed in the rice section (it isn't!) or alongside the other chicken recipes. And you may find other similar, apparent, discrepancies. But then, that's what Asian food is all about; an incredible 'pot-pourri' of delicious flavors certain to satisfy even the most demanding and discerning of palates. I would add that the suggested number of servings (which can only be approximate at the best of times) are based on individual courses and quantity adjustments may prove necessary when serving a 'multi-dish' meal, Asian style.

I said previously that I intended the recipes to be regarded as their own introduction to Asian cuisine but I must point out that I have deliberately made some changes from the original recipes I collected, in spite of the fact that most of these were obtained from many of Asia's leading chefs. I have taken this liberty, firstly, to bring a standardization to the book and to direct the preparation more towards the domestic kitchen, particularly those kitchens outside the region: I believe now that most of the dishes can be successfully prepared anywhere, although in just a few cases I've had to include ingredients which may prove difficult to obtain in Western countries (See Glossary & Notes on pages 186–189). However, I also made changes simply because I believe the pleasure of cooking comes from experimenting and improvising and, with that in mind, I hope that you too will be prepared to add a personal measure of ingenuity and your own magic touch to the recipes. That way, I'm sure, you will succeed in delighting your family and friends with your very own **Best of Asian Cooking.**   *J.M.*

Snacks & Starters

Snacks alone might perhaps have been a more accurate way of introducing this section, for few of the recipes that follow would be served as starters in the sense that the word is used in Western cuisine. It is much more likely in an Asian home, or restaurant, that a plate of simple pickles, or a few fresh nuts, or perhaps just a thimble-size cup of fragrant tea, would precede the serving of the main course. For example, the Pakistani Starters (pages 13–15) are more likely to be served with an afternoon cup of tea rather than as a first course at dinner. And the Chinese Dim Sum (pages 24–27) make up a complete meal; a meal usually served from the very early morning up to, and including, lunch-time.

However, in spite of all this, I believe that the following recipes, together with many others which, alas, space has forced me to omit, do make excellent starters when a meal is being served in a Western (or course-by-course) manner. One word of warning though; I deliberately avoided using the word *Appetizers*, for all these 'little dishes' are so tasty that once sampled, and without the self-control which most of us lack, tend to 'take over' and leave a limited space for the varied delights to follow.

Lamb Tikka *Fried chunks of spicy lamb*	**Pork & Salad Rolls**	**Sambal Daging** *Spicy shredded beef*
Sheek Kebabs *Minced beef kebabs*	**Lumpia Ubod** *Spring rolls with heart of palm*	**Kaeb Moo** *Crispy fried pork*
Shami Kebabs *Lamb & lentil pasties*	**Onion Cakes**	**Cha Shui Bao** *Steamed buns with pork filling*
Samosas *Deep fried spicy pasties*	**Fried Lumpia** *Deep fried spring rolls*	**Won Ton** *Fried meat dumplings*
Kari Pap *Curry puffs*	**Chicken Pakoras** *Deep fried chicken in batter*	**Cha Shui** *Barbecued pork*
Cutlis *Meatballs*	**Bakwan Udang** *Shrimp fritters*	**Shui Mai** *Steamed shrimp dumplings*
Beef Pasties	**Shrimp Toast with Sesame Seeds**	**Woo Kok** *Fried taro dumplings*
Pork & Crabmeat Rolls	**Impanadas** *Fried chicken tortillas*	

     Previous pages: Recipe for **Szechuan Stir-Fried Shrimp** is on page 59.

Pakistan

LAMB TIKKA
(Fried Chunks of Spicy Lamb)

1½ lbs boneless lamb — leg or shoulder
1 cup yoghurt
3 tablespoons chili powder
2 tablespoons coriander powder
2 tablespoons garam masala
2 tablespoons salt
¼ cup fresh lime juice   serves 8

Cut the lamb into cubes of approximately 1 inch. Pour the yoghurt into a large flat dish and add all other ingredients. Add the lamb, stir to blend thoroughly, and set aside in the refrigerator for 6 hours. Remove the meat from the marinade and allow to drain slightly, then place on to skewers and cook over a charcoal fire for approximately 10 minutes. Cubes should be removed from skewers before serving.

Pakistan

SHAMI KEBABS
(Lamb & Lentil Patties)

1¼ pounds fresh lamb, finely ground
½ cup dal (lentils)
¼ cup ghee
3 tablespoons garam masala
2 teaspoons salt
3 eggs
oil for frying   makes 10

Grind the lamb and mix with the dal. Heat the ghee in a pan and cook the meat and dal for 10 minutes, stirring frequently to avoid sticking. Mix the garam masala and salt and add to the meat. Cook for another minute, then remove from the heat and allow to cool. Pass the mixture through a processor to produce a smooth paste. Beat the eggs and blend into the mixture then divide into ten portions, roll into balls, and flatten into thin patties, approximately ½ inch thick. Heat the oil in a frying pan and fry the patties for 3–4 minutes, turning once until golden brown. Serve immediately.

Pakistan

SHEEK KEBABS
(Ground Beef Kebabs)

1 kilo lean boneless beef*
4 brown onions
6 green chilies
1 inch knob fresh ginger
2 cloves garlic
¼ cup chili powder
2 tablespoons garam masala
3 tablespoons salt
2 tablespoons fresh lemon juice   makes 20

Grind the beef. Chop the onions, chilies, ginger and garlic very finely and mix with the meat. Add the spices, fresh lemon juice and an equal amount of cold water. Stir to blend thoroughly, then stick the mixture around the sides of skewers. (Kebabs should be approximately 4 inches long.) Cook over a charcoal fire for 5–6 minutes and remove from skewers before serving.

*Lamb or chicken may be substituted if preferred.

Pakistan

SAMOSAS
(Deep Fried Spicy Pasties)

2 cups all-purpose flour
½ teaspoon salt
2 tablespoons ghee
oil for deep frying

Filling:
½ pound lean ground lamb
1 brown onion
¾ inch knob fresh ginger
1 clove garlic
¼ cup ghee
1 teaspoon red chili powder
1 teaspoon coriander powder
½ teaspoon turmeric powder
1 teaspoon garam masala
½ teaspoon salt

makes 20

Sift the flour and salt into a mixing bowl. Melt the ghee and add to the bowl together with ⅓ cup of warm water. Knead well and, if necessary, add a little extra warm water to ensure that the dough does not crumble. After kneading, cover the bowl with a damp cloth and set aside for 30 minutes. On a lightly-floured surface, roll the dough into a large ball, then divide into 20 individual balls and flatten these into circles. Spoon a little of the prepared filling into the center of the circles of dough and fold into half-moon shapes. Crimp the edges with the fingers and seal with a little water. Heat the oil until it is almost smoking then deep-fry the samosas until golden brown. Drain off excess oil before serving.

To make the filling; grind the lamb and chop finely the onion, ginger and garlic. Heat the ghee in a pan and sauté the onion, ginger and garlic until soft, then add the chili, coriander and turmeric powders and continue to cook over a fairly high heat for 5 minutes, stirring continuously. Add the lamb, barely cover with cold water and bring to the boil. Lower heat and simmer until the lamb is three quarters cooked and most of the liquid has been absorbed, stirring frequently throughout. Add the garam masala and salt, stir to blend thoroughly and cook for another 5–6 minutes, until the mixture is thick but not too dry.

Malaysia

KARI PAP
(Curry Puffs)

1 pound finely ground round steak
2 potatoes
1 brown onion
3 fresh red chilies
2 cloves garlic
½ inch knob fresh ginger
1 stem lemon grass
½ teaspoon turmeric powder
½ teaspoon coriander powder
½ inch stick cinnamon
2 curry leaves
½ cup thick coconut milk
salt to taste
freshly ground black pepper
1 package puff pastry
oil for deep frying

makes 20

Have the steak reground until fine. Parboil the potatoes, allow to cool then cut into small dice. Chop the onion, chilies, garlic, ginger and lemon grass finely. Heat the oil in a frying pan and sauté the onions until golden brown, then add the chilies, garlic, ginger and lemon grass. Stir-fry for 2 minutes, then add the meat and all the spices, including the cinnamon stick and curry leaves. Pour in the coconut milk and bring to the boil. Add the potato, lower heat and simmer gently until the liquid has almost dried up, then remove the cinnamon stick and curry leaves and set aside to cool. Roll out the pastry and cut into circles, approximately 3 inches in diameter. Place 2 heaped teaspoons of the meat mixture onto each pastry round, fold over and flute the edges. Heat the oil until almost smoking and deep fry the pasties until golden brown.

CUTLIS
(Meatballs)

Sri Lanka

½ lb lean ground beef
1 teaspoon salt
¼ teaspoon black pepper
2 tablespoons vinegar
1 scant pound potatoes
1 brown onion
2 sprigs mint leaves
1 green chili
1 stalk celery
oil for frying
1 egg, beaten
½ cup breadcrumbs

serves 8

Season the ground beef with salt, pepper and vinegar. Boil and mash the potatoes and chop finely the onion, mint leaves, chili and celery. Heat ¼ cup of oil in a frying pan and stir-fry the beef for 3–4 minutes, then add the onion, mint, chili and celery and cook for another 5 minutes. Add the mashed potato and blend thoroughly. Allow the mixture to cool slightly and shape into balls or small patties, then dip in the beaten egg and coat with breadcrumbs. Heat the remaining oil and deep-fry the meatballs until well browned. Drain off excess oil before serving.

BEEF PASTIES

Sri Lanka

2 cups flour
¼ teaspoon salt
¼ cup butter
1 egg
2 tablespoons lemon juice
2 tablespoons fresh milk
oil for deep frying

Filling:
½ pound ground beef
1 brown onion
2 green chilies
1 tomato
1 potato, boiled
1 cardamom
1 clove
⅓ cup oil
3 curry leaves
¼ teaspoon salt
freshly ground black pepper
1 teaspoon coriander powder
1 teaspoon curry powder
½ teaspoon cumin powder
1 teaspoon vinegar
⅓ cup thick coconut milk
2 tablespoons lime juice

serves 8

Sift the flour and salt into a mixing bowl. Cut the butter into small pieces, add to the flour and knead well. Separate the egg and add the yolk to the flour together with the lemon juice. Add just sufficient cold water to produce a stiff dough and continue to knead. Allow the dough to stand for 30 minutes, then turn on to a lightly-floured board, roll out and cut into circles, about 2½ inches in diameter. Add the milk to the egg-white and beat lightly. Place a small quantity of spiced beef in the center of each circle of dough and dampen the edges with the beaten egg. Fold the dough to form half-moon pasties, crimp the edges securely with the fingers and brush with remaining egg-wash. Heat the oil until it starts to smoke and deep-fry the pasties until golden brown. Drain well before serving.

To make the filling; regrind beef, chop the onion, chilies and tomato, cut the potato into small cubes and crush the cardamom and cloves. Heat the oil, add the onion and curry leaves and stir-fry until the onion starts to brown, then add the beef, chili, cardamom, clove, salt, pepper, curry powder, cumin powder and vinegar and continue to cook for 5 minutes, stirring frequently. Add the tomato and potato and cook for 3 minutes, then pour in the coconut milk and bring to the boil. Lower heat and simmer for 5 minutes, then add the lime juice and stir well. Allow to cool slightly before placing on the dough.

Vietnam

PORK & CRABMEAT ROLLS

4 sheets rice paper wrappers*
6 dried Chinese mushrooms
1 large brown onion
2 spring onions
1/3 pound lean minced pork
1/3 pound shredded crabmeat
1 teaspoon sugar
salt to taste
freshly ground black pepper
oil for deep frying
4 lettuce leaves

Nuoc Mam Sauce:
3 fresh red chilies
2 cloves garlic
1 teaspoon sugar
1/2 teaspoon white pepper
1 lemon
2 tablespoons vinegar
1/2 cup nam pla (fish sauce)   serves 4

Place the rice papers on a flat surface and cover with a cloth. Lightly dampen another cloth and place this on top of the first. Allow to stand for 1 hour. Soak the mushrooms in warm water for 40 minutes, then remove and discard the hard stems and cut the caps into fine shreds. Chop finely the brown onion and spring onions. Mix the pork, crabmeat and vegetables and season with sugar, salt and freshly ground black pepper. Remove the cloth from the rice paper wrappers and place a portion of the mixture along the center of each. Roll and secure the ends by dampening and pressing with the fingers. Heat the oil in a wok until almost smoking and deep-fry the rolls until the outsides are crispy and golden. Remove from the oil, drain well, then wrap in lettuce leaves and serve with Nuoc Mam Sauce.

To make the sauce; split the chilies down the center, remove the seeds and chop finely. Chop the garlic finely and place in a mortar together with the chilies, sugar and white pepper. Pound well with a pestle. Peel the lemon, remove the seeds and chop up the flesh. Add this to the spice-paste and continue to pound. Finally, add the vinegar, fish sauce and 1/4 cup of cold water and blend thoroughly. Serve as a dip in a small side dish.

*Note: Rice paper wrappers are used frequently in many regional dishes of Indo-China and Thailand but may prove difficult to obtain outside these areas. If these are not available use Lumpia wrappers (see recipe opposite page)

Vietnam

PORK & SALAD ROLLS

4 sheets rice paper wrappers
1/3 pound lean pork
1/3 pound pork skin
1/4 cup vegetable oil
1 teaspoon sugar
1 teaspoon salt
1/2 teaspoon white pepper
4 lettuce leaves
sprig of mint
12 thin slices cucumber   serves 4

Prepare the rice paper wrappers as for above recipe. Mince the lean pork. Boil the pork skin until tender, then chop into tiny pieces. Heat the oil and stir-fry the pork meat for 5–6 minutes, then add the chopped pork skin and season with sugar, salt and white pepper. Stir well and cook for another 2 minutes, then set aside and allow to cool. Place a lettuce leaf on top of each wrapper and add a few mint leaves and the cucumber slices. Spread the pork evenly on top across the center of the wrapper, then roll and seal the edges. Serve with Nuoc Mam Sauce (see preceding recipe).

Philippines

LUMPIA UBOD
(Spring Rolls with Heart of Palm)

½ pound boiled pork
½ pound cooked shrimp
½ pound ubod (heart of palm)
2 carrots
1 brown onion
¼ pound cabbage
2 cloves garlic
¼ cup pork fat
salt to taste
freshly ground black pepper
12 lettuce leaves
12 lumpia wrappers

Lumpia wrappers:
1½ cups rice flour
1 tablespoon cornstarch
pinch of salt
2 eggs
⅔ cup fresh milk

Sauce:
3 cloves garlic
3 tablespoons sugar
2 tablespoons light soy sauce
2 tablespoons fresh lime juice
⅔ cup chicken stock
1 tablespoon cornstarch   serves 6

Chop the pork finely. Shell and de-vein the shrimp and chop into small pieces. Cut the ubod and carrots into julienne strips, chop the onion, shred the cabbage and crush the garlic. Heat the pork fat in a pan and sauté the onion and garlic for 2–3 minutes, then add the pork and shrimp and season to taste with salt and freshly ground black pepper. Cook over a medium heat for about 10 minutes, stirring frequently, then add the ubod, carrot and cabbage and continue to stir for another 4 minutes. To serve; place a lettuce leaf on top of each wrapper and a quantity of the mixture on top. Roll up and fold in at one end, leaving the lettuce protruding from the other, then pour a little sauce over the top.

To make the wrappers; sift the flour, cornstarch and salt into a mixing bowl and make a well in the center. Break in the eggs and slowly add the milk, stirring continuously until a smooth thin batter results. Pour a little batter into a preheated frying pan and tilt so that the wrapper is very thin and approximately 6 inches in diameter. Cook for about 45 seconds on each side. Remove and prepare the remaining wrappers in a similar manner.

To make the sauce; chop the garlic very finely and place in a saucepan. Add the sugar, soy sauce, lime juice and chicken stock, stir well and bring to the boil. Lower the heat and simmer gently for 3 minutes. Mix the cornstarch with a small quantity of cold water and stir into the sauce to thicken slightly.

Hong Kong

ONION CAKES

6 spring onions
2½ cups all-purpose flour
⅓ cup melted lard
1 teaspoon salt
½ teaspoon white pepper
3 tablespoons sesame oil
1 egg, beaten
peanut oil for frying   serves 10–12

Chop the spring onions finely. Sift the flour into a mixing bowl and add just sufficient boiling water to produce a thick, sticky dough. Add the salt, white pepper, melted lard and half the sesame oil and knead until the dough is smooth. Roll out on a lightly-floured surface and spread the chopped spring onion on top. Sprinkle the remaining sesame oil on top and shape the dough into a roll, approximately 2 inches in diameter. Cut into pieces and flatten slightly, then coat with the beaten egg. Heat the oil in a wok and fry the onion cakes until golden brown. Serve immediately.

FRIED LUMPIA
(Deep Fried Spring Rolls)

Philippines

½ pound roasted pork
½ pound cooked shrimp
4 mushrooms
2 brown onions
2 carrots
½ inch knob fresh ginger
2 tablespoons dark soy sauce
2 tablespoons sugar
salt to taste
freshly ground black pepper
lumpia wrappers (see recipe page 19)
2 eggs, beaten
oil for deep frying

serves 6

Shred the pork. Shell and de-vein the shrimp and chop into very small pieces. Shred the mushrooms, chop the onions finely and cut the carrots and ginger into julienne strips. Heat the oil in a pan and sauté the onion and ginger for 3–4 minutes, then add the pork, shrimp, mushroom, carrot, soy sauce and sugar and season to taste with salt and freshly ground black pepper. Stir well, then remove pan from the heat and allow the mixture to cool. Make the wrappers as for the Lumpia Ubod (page 19) but smaller in diameter, approximately 5 inches. Spoon the mixture on to the wrappers, roll up diagonally, fold in the ends and seal with the beaten egg. Heat the oil until almost smoking and deep-fry the lumpia until crispy and golden. Remove from the oil and drain thoroughly. Serve with side dishes of vinegar, soy sauce, mustard and hot chili sauce.

CHICKEN PAKORAS
(Deep Fried Chicken in Batter)

India

1 chicken, about 3 pounds
1 inch knob fresh ginger
2 cloves garlic
2 cloves
1 black cardamom seed
½ teaspoon cumin seeds
½ teaspoon coriander seeds
2 cups yoghurt
salt to taste
freshly ground white pepper
oil for deep frying

Batter:
2 cups besan (chick-pea flour)
¼ teaspoon salt
3 eggs
¼ teaspoon cumin powder
¼ teaspoon poppy seeds
2 tablespoons vinegar
2 tablespoons fresh lemon juice

serves 6

Skin and de-bone the chicken, chop the meat into bite-size pieces and place in a shallow dish. Chop the garlic and ginger and grind together with the cloves, cumin, coriander and cardamom seeds. Add the ground spices to the yoghurt, season to taste with salt and white pepper and pour over the pieces of chicken. Place in a refrigerator and allow to marinate for 12 hours. To cook; heat the oil in a large frying pan, dip the marinated chicken in the prepared batter and deep fry until golden brown and crispy. Serve immediately with sweet mango chutney.

To prepare the batter, sift the flour and salt into a mixing bowl, break in the eggs and stir well. Add the remaining ingredients and blend thoroughly until the batter is thick and smooth.

Indonesia

BAKWAN UDANG
(Shrimp Fritters)

½ pound fresh baby shrimp
2 shallots
1 leek
1 clove garlic
2½ cups vegetable oil
¾ cup flour
½ teaspoon salt
2 eggs
freshly ground black pepper   serves 4

Shell and de-vein the shrimp. Chop the shallots and leek and crush the garlic. Heat a little oil in a shallow pan and sauté the shrimp for 4–5 minutes. Remove and set aside. Clean the pan, add a little more oil, and sauté the shallot for 3 minutes, then add the leek and garlic and continue to stir-fry for another 3–4 minutes. Remove and set aside. Sift the flour and salt into a large bowl and make a well in the center. Break the eggs into the well and beat to produce a smooth, thick batter, using a little water if necessary. Add the shrimp and vegetables to the batter, season with freshly ground black pepper and stir to blend thoroughly. Heat the remaining oil until it starts to smoke, then drop in spoonfuls of the batter and deep fry until golden and crispy.

Taiwan

SHRIMP TOAST WITH SESAME SEEDS

1 generous pound fresh shrimp
1 egg white
2 teaspoons cornstarch
2 teaspoons light soy sauce
2 teaspoons Chinese wine
½ teaspoon salt
½ teaspoon white pepper
8 slices white bread
½ cup sesame seeds
oil for deep frying   serves 4–6

Shell and de-vein the shrimp and chop very finely. Beat the egg in a mixing bowl and add the shrimp, cornstarch, soy sauce, Chinese wine, salt and white pepper. Mix together thoroughly to form a thick, smooth paste. Cut the crusts off the bread, spread the mixture on evenly and sprinkle with sesame seeds. Heat the oil in a wok until it is almost smoking, then deep-fry the pieces until golden. Remove, drain off all excess oil and cut into quarters.

Philippines

IMPANADAS
(Fried Chicken Tortillas)

1 chicken breast
1 small brown onion
3 stems spring onion
1 green pepper
¼ cup butter
2 cups cream of rice
salt to taste
freshly ground black pepper
12 tortilla shells
oil for deep frying   makes 12

Place the chicken breast in a small saucepan and cover with 2 cups of cold water. Bring to the boil and simmer until the chicken is cooked. Remove and de-bone the chicken and retain the stock. Chop finely the brown onion, spring onion and the green pepper. Heat the butter in a shallow pan and sauté the chicken for 2 minutes, then add the onion, spring onion and pepper and continue to cook over a low heat for another 5 minutes. Add the paprika, pour in the chicken stock and bring to the boil. Add the cream of rice and season to taste with salt and freshly ground black pepper. Simmer until the mixture thickens, then remove from heat and allow to cool. When cool, place a little of the mixture in the center of the tortilla shells, fold and seal edges with a little water or milk. Heat the oil until almost smoking, then deep fry the impanadas until the shell is crispy and golden, approximately 3 minutes.

Malaysia

SAMBAL DAGING
(Spicy Shredded Beef)

1 pound beef steak
3/4 inch knob fresh ginger
8 dried red chilies
2 cloves garlic
8 shallots
1 cup thick coconut milk
3 tablespoons tamarind water
2 tablespoons sugar
1/2 teaspoon salt
freshly ground black pepper
pinch monosodium glutamate
3 tablespoons peanut oil
1/2 teaspoon coriander powder
1/2 teaspoon turmeric powder   serves 4

Chop the beef into chunks and boil until tender. Allow to cool, then shred finely. Pound together the ginger, dried chilies, garlic and half the shallots with a small quantity of cold water to form a smooth thick paste. Pour the coconut milk into a saucepan, together with the tamarind water, add the beef and spice-paste and bring to the boil. Add the sugar, salt, freshly ground black pepper and monosodium glutamate, lower the heat and simmer over a medium heat, stirring frequently, until all the liquid has been absorbed. Chop the remaining shallots. Heat the oil in a frying pan and sauté the shallots for 2 minutes, then add the coriander and turmeric powder and continue to cook over a medium heat for another 2–3 minutes. Add the spiced meat from the saucepan, stir to blend thoroughly and heat through. Then, allow to cool, by which time the beef should be quite dry and 'flaky'. A delicious snack with a glass of beer.

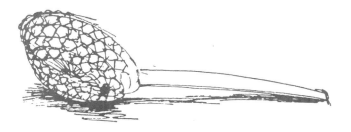

Thailand

KAEB MOO
(Crispy Fried Pork)

3/4 pound pork belly with skin
2 teaspoons salt
oil for deep frying
2 shallots
2 cloves garlic
1 inch knob fresh ginger
3 small tomatoes
2 fresh red chilies
2 fresh green chilies
1 teaspoon chopped coriander root
2 tablespoons dark soy sauce
2 tablespoons rice wine
1/4 cup chicken stock
freshly ground black pepper
2 teaspoons nam pla (fish sauce)   serves 4

With a sharp knife score the pork skin, approximately every 1/2 inch, and rub in the salt. Set aside for 30 minutes, then cut into strips. Heat the oil until it begins to smoke and deep-fry the pork until the skin is golden and crispy. Remove the pork, drain thoroughly and allow to cool, then cut into small dice. Chop the shallots, garlic, ginger and tomatoes. Finely chop 1 red and 1 green chili and cut the 2 remaining into fine julienne strips. Pour a small quantity of oil into a frying pan and sauté the shallot, garlic and ginger for 3–4 minutes. Then, add the chopped chili, tomato, coriander root, soy sauce, wine and stock and bring to the boil. Add the pork, season with freshly ground black pepper and stir to blend thoroughly. Allow to simmer for 15 minutes, then add the nam pla, stir again and cook for another 3–4 minutes. Transfer to a serving plate and garnish with the julienne strips of chili. Serve with steamed rice.

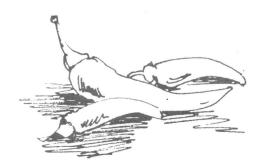

23

Overleaf: **Chinese Dim Sum Selection** (recipes pages 26 & 27)

Hong Kong

CHA SHUI BAO
(Steamed Buns with Pork Filling)

½ pound roasted pork
2 spring onions
2 tablespoons vegetable oil
2 teaspoons sugar
¼ cup oyster sauce
2 tablespoons light soy sauce
freshly ground black pepper
2 teaspoons cornstarch

Dough:
½ cup sugar
1 ounce fresh compressed yeast
5 cups all-purpose flour
¼ teaspoon salt   makes 8

Cut the pork into small dice and chop finely the spring onions. Heat the oil in a small pan, add the onions and sauté for 1 minute, then add the pork, sugar, oyster sauce, soy sauce and freshly ground black pepper and cook gently for another 2 minutes, stirring occasionally. Mix the cornstarch with a small quantity of cold water and stir into the mixture. Remove from the pan and set aside to cool. To cook; spoon a small quantity of the pork mixture on to a piece of dough and fold up the edges to form a bun, leaving a small opening at the top. Place the buns in a tightly sealed container and steam over boiling water for approximately 10 minutes.

To make the dough; dissolve the sugar in ½ cup of warm water, sprinkle in the yeast, mix well and allow to ferment for 5 minutes. Sift the flour and salt into a mixing bowl, make a well in the center and gradually add the fermented yeast. Stir with a wooden spoon to mix thoroughly, knead firmly for 10 minutes, then cover with a cloth and set aside for 45 minutes. Turn out the dough on to a lightly-floured surface and shape into a roll, 2 inches in diameter. Cut the roll into 1 inch pieces and flatten out with the hands.

Singapore

WON TON
(Fried Meat Dumplings)

12 won ton wrappers
¾ pound fresh pork ground fine
2 dried Chinese mushrooms
¼ cup bamboo shoot
1 spring onion
2 tablespoons lard
1 teaspoon light soy sauce
1 teaspoon Chinese wine
1 teaspoon sesame oil
2 teaspoons sugar
½ teaspoon salt
¼ teaspoon white pepper
pinch monosodium glutamate
1 egg, beaten
oil for deep frying   makes 12

Spread out the won ton wrappers on a flat, lightly-greased surface. Mince the pork. Soak the mushrooms in warm water for 40 minutes, then remove and discard the hard stems. Chop the mushroom caps, bamboo shoot and spring onion very finely. Heat the lard in a wok and sauté the meat and vegetables for 2–3 minutes. Add the soy sauce, Chinese wine, sesame oil, sugar, salt, white pepper and monosodium glutamate and continue to cook over a medium heat for another 2 minutes, stirring frequently. Remove the mixture from the pan and allow to cool, then spoon equal portions on to each of the won ton wrappers. Fold into triangle shapes, seal with the beaten egg and deep fry in very hot oil until golden brown.

Hong Kong

CHA SHUI
(Barbecued Pork)

2 pounds pork loin with skin
1/2 inch knob fresh ginger
2 cloves garlic
1/4 cup light soy sauce
1/4 cup Chinese wine
3 tablespoons sugar
pinch red food coloring
1 teaspoon salt
1/3 cup clear honey

serves 8

Remove the bone from the pork, score the skin with a sharp knife and cut the meat into strips, about 1 1/2 inches wide. Chop finely the ginger and garlic and combine with the soy sauce, Chinese wine, sugar, half the honey and coloring. Rub this mixture into the underside of the pork and rub the salt into the scored skin. Set aside for 30 minutes. Then, place on a spit and cook over a very hot charcoal fire for 25–35 minutes, turning at regular intervals and basting with the honey. When the meat is cooked, coat with the remaining honey and cut into thin slices.

Hong Kong

SHUI MAI
(Steamed Shrimp Dumplings)

12 won ton wrappers
1/2 pound fresh shrimp
2 dried Chinese mushrooms
2 canned water chestnuts
2 spring onions
1/4 cup bamboo shoot
1 teaspoon light soy sauce
1 teaspoon dark soy sauce
2 teaspoons Chinese wine
1 egg, beaten
2 teaspoons peanut oil
salt to taste
freshly ground black pepper

makes 12

Spread out the won ton wrappers on a flat, lightly-greased surface. Shell and de-vein the shrimp. Soak the mushrooms in warm water for 40 minutes, then remove and discard the hard stems. Peel the water chestnuts. Chop finely the shrimp, mushrooms caps, water chestnuts, spring onions and bamboo shoots and place in a small mixing bowl. Add the soy sauce and Chinese wine and season to taste with salt and freshly ground black pepper. Blend thoroughly and spoon equal portions of the mixture on to the wrappers. Fold into small dumplings and seal with the beaten egg. Place the dumplings on a rack, sprinkle with the peanut oil and steam over rapidly boiling water in a tightly sealed container for 12 minutes.

Taiwan

WOO KOK
(Fried Taro Dumplings)

1 pound taro root
4 dried Chinese mushrooms
1/2 pound fresh shrimp
1/2 pound lean pork meat
vegetable oil
2 teaspoons cornstarch
salt
freshly ground black pepper
1/4 cup all-purpose flour
1/2 cup melted lard

makes 16

Peel and cut the taro into slices. Place in a steamer and cook until tender, then mash while still hot. Soak the mushrooms in warm water for 40 minutes, discard the hard stems and dice the caps. Shell and de-vein the shrimp and chop finely. Chop the pork finely. Heat 1/3 cup of oil in a pan and stir-fry the pork and shrimp for 5 minutes. Mix the cornstarch with a little cold water and add to the pan. Season to taste with salt and freshly ground black pepper and continue to cook for another 2 minutes, then remove and drain off the excess oil. Sift the flour into a mixing bowl, add the lard, a pinch of salt and the mashed taro and knead well. Turn on to a lightly-floured surface and shape into a roll. Cut into slices, place the shrimp and pork mixture into the centers and fold. Pinch the edges with the fingers and seal with a little water. Heat the remaining oil in a large pan and deep fry the taro dumplings until crispy and golden brown. Serve immediately.

Soups

As I stated in the introduction, the order of serving dishes for an Asian meal does not generally follow such a rigid format as in the West. This is particularly true where soups are concerned. In Japan and some countries of South East Asia it is common practice to serve a bowl of clear soup together with another course to be used as a refresher and an aid to digestion, just as a glass of water might be. Then again, there are other soups that are so hearty and filling that they constitute a meal in themselves, such as the Chinese soup noodles (recipes for these appear in the noodle section) which are so often served at roadside stalls throughout the region, and the thick and spicy soups of Indonesia and Malaysia which, with a bowl of steamed rice, provide for many a simple, yet highly satisfying, meal.

With formal Chinese meals where, for once there is a distinct and meaningful order of serving, there are often two soup courses, a thick and substantial soup being served half way through the meal and a light clear broth, intended to clean the palate, being served towards the end. The first soup in such a meal is often chosen to 'give face' and is one way of indicating the host's regard for his guests. An excellent example of this is the **Shark's Fin with Abalone** (page 39) which is expensive and time-consuming to prepare — a compliment to any guest.

Dashi *Basic Japanese soup stock*	**Sop Kepiting** *Crab soup*	**Chicken & Lemon Soup**
Suimono *Clear soup with egg*	**Sinigang na Sugpo** *Sour clam soup*	**Chicken Yakhni** *Spicy chicken soup*
Akadashi *Red bean paste soup*	**Tom Yam Kung** *Hot & sour shrimp soup*	**Duck & Yam Soup**
Gyojiru *Japanese fish soup*	**Jemangiri Skorba** *Vegetable soup*	**Set Hnit Myo Hincho** *Twelve Varieties soup*
Mushroom & Crispy Rice Soup	**Parippu Soup** *Lentil soup*	**Soto Ayam** *Chicken soup*
Hot & Sour Szechuan Soup	**Bird's Nest with Quail Eggs**	**Shredded Beef & Egg Soup**
Won Ton Soup *Soup with Chinese dumplings*	**Shark's Fin with Abalone**	**Pig's Liver & Tomato Soup**
Shell Soup Filipina	**Fresh Fish Head Soup**	**Sop Lembu** *Oxtail soup*
Halaan Soup *Clam soup*	**Raw Fish & Vegetable Soup**	**Mulligatawny** *Light curry soup*
Abalone with Vegetable Soup	**Winter Melon Soup**	**Sop Kambing** *Lamb soup*

Japan

DASHI
(Basic Japanese Soup Stock)

8 cups cold water
2 squares kombu (dried black seaweed)
7 ounces katsuobushi (dried bonito flakes)

In a large saucepan bring the water to a rapid boil. Wash the kombu under cold running water and add to the pan. Lower the heat and allow to simmer for 2 minutes then remove the kombu and add the katsuobushi. Stir well and bring back to the boil. Immediately remove the pan from the heat and allow the flakes to settle to the bottom. Then, pour through a fine strainer or cheese-cloth into a bowl. Use immediately or store in a refrigerator up to 48 hours.

Japan

SUIMONO
(Clear Soup with Egg)

4 cups dashi
2 teaspoons cornstarch
salt to taste
2 eggs
1/2 cup chopped spring onion   serves 4

Pour the stock into a saucepan, add the cornstarch and stir to blend thoroughly. Bring to the boil and add salt to taste. Stir the stock well and, while swirling, break in the eggs. Cook for 1 minute then transfer to a tureen and garnish with chopped spring onion.

Japan

AKADASHI
(Red Bean Paste Soup)

4 cups dashi
1/4 cup red bean paste
4 squares tofu (bean curd)
salt to taste
1 spring onion   serves 4

Pour the stock into a saucepan and bring to the boil. Rub the bean paste through a fine sieve into the boiling stock, using a little of the stock to help press it through. Finely dice the tofu and add to the stock. Lower the heat, season with salt and simmer for 1 minute. Then, chop finely the spring onion, add to the soup and serve immediately.

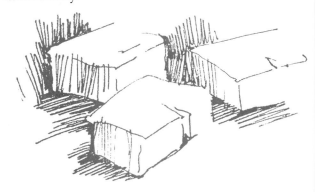

Japan

GYOJIRU
(Japanese Fish Soup)

1 pound red snapper fillets
2 teaspoons salt
3 inch square kombu (dried black seaweed)
1/4 cup chopped spring onion   serves 6

Ensure no bones remain in the fish and remove all the skin. Cut the fish into small pieces, place in a shallow dish and season with the salt, then set aside in the refrigerator for 5 hours. Afterwards, rinse well under cold running water. Place 4 cups of water in a saucepan and bring to the boil. Add the fish and the kombu and bring back to the boil. Lower the heat, cover and simmer over a very low heat for 2 hours. Transfer to a soup tureen and garnish with chopped spring onion.

HOT & SOUR SZECHUAN SOUP

4 dried Chinese mushrooms
¹/₂ cup bamboo shoot
¹/₂ cup cucumber, shredded
2 squares chili beancurd
2 fresh red chilies
³/₄ inch knob fresh ginger
¹/₄ pound shrimp
¹/₄ pound roasted pork
2 tablespoons vegetable oil
6 cups chicken stock
2 teaspoons light soy sauce
2 teaspoons dark soy sauce
2 tablespoons vinegar
2 tablespoons Chinese wine
1 teaspoon freshly ground white pepper
salt to taste
2 teaspoons cornstarch
1 egg
1 teaspoon chili oil   serves 6

Soak the mushrooms in warm water for 40 minutes, then discard the hard stems and shred the caps. Shred all the other vegetables. Shell and de-vein the shrimp and cut in half lengthways. Shred the pork. Heat the oil in a large pan, add the vegetables, shrimp and pork and stir-fry for 2 minutes, then pour in the stock and bring to the boil. Add soy sauce, vinegar, Chinese wine, freshly ground white pepper and salt to taste, lower the heat and simmer for another 3 minutes. Mix the cornstarch with a small quantity of cold water and add to the soup to thicken slightly. Beat the egg and stir into the soup just prior to transferring to a tureen. Heat the chili oil and sprinkle this over the soup, then serve immediately.

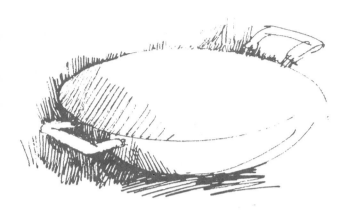

MUSHROOM & CRISPY RICE SOUP

8 dried black Chinese mushrooms
2 cups sticky rice
6 cups chicken stock
2 tablespoons Chinese wine
1 teaspoon dark soy sauce
1 teaspoon salt
¹/₂ teaspoon freshly ground white pepper
oil for deep frying
1 teaspoon chopped
Chinese parsley   serves 4

Place the mushrooms in a shallow dish and pour in just sufficient warm water to cover. Allow to soak for 40 minutes, then remove and discard the hard stems but retain the water. Slice the mushroom caps. Steam the rice in a large pan until it is overcooked and sticks to the bottom of the pan. Allow to cool slightly, then remove carefully and cut into bite-size pieces. Pour the stock into a large saucepan and bring to the boil. Add the mushrooms, reserved water, Chinese wine, soy sauce, salt and freshly ground white pepper. Boil rapidly for 2 minutes, then lower the heat and simmer for 35 minutes. Meanwhile, heat the oil in a wok and deep-fry the pieces of rice until they are crispy and golden. To serve; place the pieces of rice in a soup tureen and pour the boiling soup on top. Garnish with chopped Chinese parsley.

WON TON SOUP
(Soup with Chinese Dumplings)

Hong Kong

24 frozen won ton wrappers
¹/₂ pound fresh pork
¹/₄ pound fresh shrimp
6 water chestnuts
salt
white pepper
pinch monosodium glutamate
1 egg-white, beaten
1 quart chicken stock
¹/₂ small Chinese cabbage   serves 4

Place the won ton wrappers in a warming oven to thaw out, then lay out flat on a lightly-greased pastry board. Cut away excess fat from the pork, shell and de-vein the shrimp and skin the water chestnuts. Grind together the pork, shrimp and chestnuts and season with salt, white pepper and monosodium glutamate. Spoon a little of the mixture on to each wrapper, fold into triangle shapes and seal the edges with the beaten egg-white. In a large saucepan bring the stock to the boil. Cut the cabbage leaves into 3 in. lengths, add these to the stock and continue to boil rapidly for 2 minutes. Transfer the vegetable to individual serving bowls and add the won ton to the stock. When they rise to the surface, remove, drain and place in the serving bowls. Adjust the seasoning of the stock, continue to boil for another minute, then pour into the bowls.

SHELL SOUP FILIPINA

Philippines

¹/₂ pound large green clams
¹/₂ pound small clams
¹/₂ pound small oysters
¹/₂ pound mussels
2 brown onions
¹/₄ pound eggplant
1 cup string beans
1 clove garlic
¹/₃ cup vegetable oil
salt to taste
freshly ground white pepper
pinch monosodium glutamate
2 cups fish stock   serves 2

Place all the shells in a basin of cold water and scrub with a stiff brush, then change the water and repeat the process several times. Chop the onions, slice the eggplant, cut the beans into 1 in. lengths and crush the garlic. Heat the oil in a large pan and sauté the onion and garlic for 2–3 minutes. Then, add the eggplant and beans and season with salt, freshly ground white pepper and monosodium glutamate. Continue to stir over a medium heat for 2 minutes, then add all the shells and continue to cook, stirring frequently, until all the shells open, discarding any that fail to do so. Transfer all the shells, vegetables and oysters into soup bowls and pour the fish stock into the pan. Bring to the boil and reduce slightly, then pour over the shells and serve immediately.

Philippines

HALAAN SOUP
(Clam Soup)

3/4 pound fresh clams
1 brown onion
2 shallots
3/4 inch knob fresh ginger
1 stem lemon grass
2 cloves garlic
1/4 cup butter
2 cups light fish stock
2 fresh chili leaves
salt to taste
freshly ground white pepper
pinch monosodium glutamate   serves 4

Wash the clams thoroughly under cold running water. Chop the onion, shallots and ginger and crush the garlic. Melt the butter in a large saucepan and sauté all the vegetables including the garlic for 3–4 minutes, then add the clams and pour in the fish stock together with an equal quantity of cold water. Bring to the boil, add the chili leaves and cook over a high heat until the clams open, discarding any that remain closed. Lower the heat, season with salt, freshly ground white pepper and monosodium glutamate and simmer gently for another 2 minutes. Remove the chili leaves before transferring to a soup tureen.

Hong Kong

ABALONE WITH VEGETABLES

12 ounces canned abalone
4 dried black Chinese mushrooms
6 button mushrooms
4 straw mushrooms
2 sliced carrots
6 long green beans
1/2 inch knob fresh ginger
salt to taste
freshly ground black pepper
pinch monosodium glutamate   serves 4–6

Cut the abalone into thin slices. Soak the black mushrooms in warm water for 40 minutes and remove the hard stems. Slice the carrots, cut the beans into 3/4 in. lengths and finely chop the ginger. In a large saucepan bring 6 cups of water to the boil, add the abalone and all the mushrooms and boil rapidly for 2 minutes. Add the carrots, beans and ginger and season to taste with salt, freshly ground black pepper and monosodium glutamate. Boil for another 2 minutes, then cover the pan, lower the heat and simmer for 3 minutes. Do not overcook.

Indonesia

SOP KEPITING
(Crab Soup)

1 fresh crab, about 1 1/4 pounds
1 large onion
2 cloves garlic
1/2 inch knob fresh ginger
1 fresh red chili
2 stems lemon grass
2 carrots
2 sticks celery
1 leek
1/3 cup butter
salt to taste
freshly ground black pepper
6 cups fish stock
fresh parsley leaves   serves 6

Wash the crab, remove and crack the claws and cut the body into pieces. Slice the onion, chop the garlic, ginger, chili and lemon grass and cut the carrots, celery and leek into julienne strips. Heat the butter in a large pan and sauté the onion and garlic for 3 minutes, then add the pieces of crab and stir-fry for 5 minutes. Add the remaining vegetables and season to taste with salt and freshly ground black papper. Stir to mix well and allow to cook slowly for another 3 minutes. Meanwhile, heat the stock in a saucepan and when almost at the boil pour over the crab. Bring to the boil and cook for 4–5 minutes, stirring frequently. Pour into a soup tureen and garnish with fresh parsley leaves.

Philippines

SINIGANG NA SUGPO
(Sour Clam Soup)

1 pound fresh clams
2 brown onions
2 tomatoes
2 radishes
2 leeks
2 chili leaves
2 ounces kangkong leaves, or mustard leaves
1 cup green beans
¼ cup tamarind water
2 tablespoons patis (fish sauce)
salt to taste
freshly ground white pepper
pinch monosodium glutamate   serves 4–6

Wash the clams thoroughly under cold running water. Chop the onion, shallots and ginger and crush the garlic. Melt the butter in a large saucepan and sauté all the vegetables including the garlic for 3–4 minutes, then add the clams and pour in the fish stock together with an equal quantity of cold water. Bring to the boil, add the chili leaves and cook over a high heat until the clams open, discarding any that remain closed. Lower the heat, season with salt, freshly ground white pepper and monosodium glutamate and simmer gently for another 2 minutes. Remove the chili leaves before transferring to a soup tureen.

Thailand

TOM YAM KUNG
(Hot & Sour Shrimp Soup)

1½ pounds fresh shrimp
2 stems lemon grass
2 shallots
4 small green chilies
2 tablespoons oil
3 sweet basil leaves
salt to taste
2 tablespoons nam prik pow (salted fish paste)
¼ cup fresh lime juice
2 teaspoons freshly
chopped coriander leaves   serves 4–6

Shell and de-vein the shrimp, leaving the tails attached. Retain the heads. Cut the lemon grass into 1 inch lengths and pound lightly with the back of a kitchen knife. Cut the shallots into fine strips and the chilies into very thin rings. Heat the oil in a large saucepan, add the shrimp heads and stir-fry for 3–4 minutes then pour in 1½ quarts of water and bring to the boil. Add the lemon grass, sweet basil leaves and salt to taste. Cover the pan, lower the heat and simmer for 10 minutes, then strain through a fine sieve into a fresh saucepan. Bring back to the boil, add the shrimp and cook until they turn pink and are just firm. Moisten the nam prik pow with a little of the lime juice and add to the stock together with the shallots, chili and remaining lime juice. Stir to blend thoroughly and allow to simmer for another 2 minutes. Transfer to a soup tureen and garnish with freshly chopped coriander leaves.

Note: For this soup to be most appreciated, both the 'hot' and the sour tastes should react equally on the palate, so extra chili and/or lime juice should be added to individual bowls according to personal tastes.

Overleaf: **Tom Yam Kung**

India

JEMANGIRI SKORBA
(Vegetable Soup)

1 brown onion
3 tomatoes
2 cloves garlic
3/4 inch knob fresh ginger
1/4 cup butter
2 teaspoons turmeric powder
1/2 teaspoon curry powder
6 cups chicken stock
2 tablespoons fresh lemon juice
salt to taste
1/4 cup fresh cream   serves 4–6

Chop the onions and tomatoes into small dice. Chop the garlic and ginger and pound together with a small quantity of cold water to form a paste. Heat the butter in a saucepan and sauté the onion until golden brown. Add the garlic and ginger paste, turmeric powder and curry powder and cook for 3–4 minutes, stirring continuously. Add the tomato, pour in the stock and bring to the boil. Once at the boil, lower the heat and simmer gently for 1 hour. Strain into a fresh saucepan, add the lemon juice and salt and cook for another 2 minutes. To serve; pour into a tureen and stir in the cream.

Sri Lanka

PARIPPU SOUP
(Lentil Soup)

1 1/4 cups lentils
1 brown onion
2 tomatoes
1/4 cup oil
1/2 teaspoon curry powder
1/2 teaspoon cumin powder
6 cups chicken stock
1/2 cup thick coconut milk
salt to taste
freshly ground black pepper
freshly chopped parsley   serves 4–6

Soak the lentils for 4 hours, then drain thoroughly. Chop finely the onion and tomatoes. Heat the oil and sauté the onion until it becomes soft and transparent, then add the tomatoes and continue to cook for 3 minutes. Add the lentils, curry powder, cumin and stock and bring to the boil. Lower heat and cook slowly for approximately 1 hour, then add the coconut milk and season to taste with salt and pepper. Stir well and cook for another few minutes, then transfer to a soup tureen and sprinkle the freshly chopped parsley on top.

Hong Kong

BIRD'S NEST WITH QUAIL EGGS

2 ounces dried bird's nest
2 tablespoons Chinese wine
1 quart chicken stock
1 cup snow peas (mangetout)
2 spring onions
1/2 teaspoon salt
1/4 teaspoon white pepper
pinch monosodium glutamate
12 quail eggs
1/4 cup shredded cooked ham   serves 4–6

Soak the bird's nest in cold water for 4–5 hours, remove any feathers and impurities and place in a saucepan. Cover with approximately 1/2 cup of cold water and bring to the boil. Lower the heat, add the Chinese wine and simmer gently for 30 minutes. Drain and set aside. Bring the stock to the boil and season with salt, pepper and monosodium glutamate. Cut the spring onions into 1 in. lengths and add to the boiling stock together with the snow peas. Lower the heat and simmer for 5 minutes, then add the bird's nest and continue to cook over a medium heat for another 2–3 minutes. Meanwhile, break the eggs into small dishes, add a small quantity of shredded ham to each and poach until the eggs are set. To serve; pour the soup into a tureen and float the poached quail eggs on top.

Hong Kong

SHARK'S FIN WITH ABALONE

3/4 pound dried shark's fin
3 ounces smoked ham
1/4 pound fresh chicken meat
4 spring onions
1 inch knob fresh ginger
6 cups chicken stock
2 tablespoons Chinese wine
2 tablespoons light soy sauce
2 teaspoons dark soy sauce
salt to taste
freshly ground black pepper
5 ounces canned abalone
2 tablespoons vegetable oil
finely chopped Chinese parsley serves 6–8

Place the shark's fin in a large saucepan, cover with cold water and soak overnight. Drain thoroughly, then place back in the pan, cover with fresh water and bring to the boil. Lower heat and simmer for about 2 hours, then rinse under cold running water for 5 minutes. (To test if the shark's fin is ready for cooking, press gently between the fingers and it should break easily. If it fails to do so, cover with fresh water and boil for a longer period of time.) Meanwhile, shred the ham and chicken meat and chop finely the spring onion and ginger. Pour the stock into a double-boiler and bring to the boil. Add the ham, chicken, spring onion, ginger, Chinese wine, soy sauce, salt and pepper and cover with a tightly fitting lid. Place over boiling water and steam for 2–3 hours. Finally, cut the abalone into thin slices and sauté in hot oil for 1 minute. To serve; divide the shark's fin into individual bowls, add a few slices of abalone and pour the boiling stock on top. Garnish with finely chopped Chinese parsley.

Hong Kong

FRESH FISH HEAD SOUP

1/3 pound fresh fish head
3/4 cup bamboo shoot
1 inch knob fresh ginger
2 tablespoons Chinese wine
2 tablespoons vinegar
1/2 teaspoon salt
freshly ground black pepper
2 fresh red chilies
2 fresh green chilies
2 tablespoons vegetable oil
5 cups fish stock
2 tablespoons dark soy sauce   serves 4

Scale and thoroughly wash the fish head, cut into small pieces and place in a shallow dish. Cover the bamboo shoot with cold water, bring slowly to the boil and simmer for 25 minutes. Chop the bamboo shoot and ginger and add to the fish head together with the Chinese wine, vinegar, salt and freshly ground black pepper. Allow to stand for 30 minutes, turning the pieces of fish head once or twice. Chop the chilies. Heat the oil in a wok, add the chilies and stir-fry for 1 minute then add the fish head, together with the marinade, and cook over a medium heat for 5 minutes, stirring continuously. Bring the stock to the boil separately, then pour over the fish head. Add the soy sauce, place a lid over the wok and simmer for another 5 minutes.

RAW FISH & VEGETABLE SOUP

Taiwan

1 pound fish fillets
6 lettuce leaves
½ inch knob fresh ginger
4 pieces kale (Chinese broccoli)
2 spring onions
oil for frying
½ teaspoon sesame oil
salt to taste
freshly ground white pepper
pinch monosodium glutamate
2¼ cups fish stock
*1 teaspoon freshly chopped
    Chinese parsley*

serves 4

Remove the skin from the fish, ensuring that no bones remain, and cut into thin slices. Tear the lettuce leaves into strips. Cut the ginger into julienne strips and chop the kale and the spring onions. Heat the oil in a small pan and stir-fry the ginger and kale for 3–4 minutes, then remove and drain. Arrange the lettuce leaves in the bottom of a soup tureen and add the kale, ginger, spring onion and slices of fish. Sprinkle the sesame oil on top and season to taste with salt, freshly ground pepper and monosodium glutamate. Bring the stock to a rapid boil and pour over the fish and vegetables. Garnish with freshly chopped Chinese parsley and serve immediately.

WINTER MELON SOUP

1 large winter melon, approximately 2 pounds
8 dried Chinese mushrooms
6 water chestnuts
¼ pound fresh shrimp
2 ounces crabmeat
¼ pound fresh lean pork
¼ pound white chicken meat
2 ounces duck meat
1 inch knob fresh ginger
1 clove garlic
6–7 cups chicken stock
salt to taste
freshly ground black pepper
2 teaspoons light soy sauce
½ teaspoon sesame oil   serves 6

Remove the top quarter of the melon and cut the base so that the melon will stand upright in the steamer. Scoop out the seeds and sufficient pulp to allow the stock to be poured in, taking care not to break the outside skin. Soak the mushrooms in warm water for 40 minutes, then remove the hard stems. Peel the water chestnuts and chop finely. Shell, de-vein and chop the shrimp, flake the crabmeat and dice the pork, chicken and duck. Finely chop the ginger and garlic. Bring the stock to the boil, add the mushrooms, water chestnuts, pork, chicken, duck, ginger and garlic and season to taste with salt and freshly ground black pepper. Simmer for 15 minutes, then pour into the melon. Place in a steamer, cover the melon with its own 'lid' and cover the pan. Cook gently for approximately 4 hours, then add the shrimp, crabmeat, soy sauce and sesame oil and continue to cook for another 30 minutes. When serving, scoop out the flesh of the melon and add to each individual bowl.

Cambodia

CHICKEN & LEMON SOUP

³/₄ pound chicken meat
¹/₂ teaspoon salt
¹/₂ teaspoon white pepper
1 clove garlic
2 small green chilies
2 spring onions
few sweet basil leaves
¹/₄ cup vegetable oil
¹/₄ cup fresh lemon juice   serves 4

Chop the chicken meat and season with salt and freshly ground white pepper. Crush the garlic, slice the green chilies into very thin rings and chop the spring onions and basil leaves. Heat the oil in a saucepan, add the garlic and sauté for 3–4 minutes, until soft and transparent, then add the chicken meat and continue to cook for another 5 minutes, stirring frequently. Add 6 cups of cold water and bring to the boil. Lower the heat and simmer for 15 minutes, then add the lemon juice, adjust seasonings to taste and leave to simmer for another 10–15 minutes. Finally, add the chili and spring onion, stir for 1 minute, then transfer to a soup tureen and garnish with sweet basil leaves.

Pakistan

CHICKEN YAKHNI
(Spicy Chicken Soup)

chicken carcass
2 cloves garlic
³/₄ inch knob fresh ginger
15 black peppercorns
6 cloves
¹/₄ teaspoon aniseed powder
1 teaspoon salt
fresh coriander leaves   serves 6–8

Place the bones in a large saucepan, cover with 8 cups of cold water and bring to the boil. Chop the garlic and ginger and add to the stock, together with the peppercorns, cloves and aniseed powder. Lower the heat and simmer for 1¹/₂ hours, then add salt and cook for another 10 minutes. Pour through a strainer into a soup tureen and garnish with chopped coriander leaves.

Singapore

DUCK & YAM SOUP

1 duck, about 3 pounds
4 carrots
4 tomatoes
4 brown onions
4 shallots
1 inch knob fresh ginger
6 cloves garlic
20 fresh black peppercorns
1 teaspoon salt
¹/₂ cup canned salted soya beans
1¹/₄ pounds yams
2 tablespoons vegetable oil   serves 4–6

Prepare the duck and, with a sharp knife, remove most of the meat. Chop the meat into small pieces and place the carcass into a large stock pot. Chop coarsely the carrots, tomatoes, half the onions and shallots and shred half the ginger and garlic. Add these to the stock pot together with half the peppercorns and cover with 8 cups of cold water. Bring to the boil, add 1 teaspoon of salt and boil rapidly for 2 minutes. Lower the heat, remove the scum from the surface and place a tightly-fitting lid on the pot. Simmer gently for about 2¹/₂ hours, then pass through a fine sieve and allow to cool. Chop finely the remaining onions, shallots, ginger and garlic and pound together with the remaining peppercorns and the salted soya beans to form a smooth paste. Peel the yam and cut into ¹/₂ inch cubes. Heat the oil in a deep saucepan and stir-fry the pounded spice mixture for 5 minutes. Add the duck meat and the yam and pour in the prepared stock. Bring to the boil and adjust seasonings to taste. Cover the pan and lower the heat to simmer gently for another 45–50 minutes.

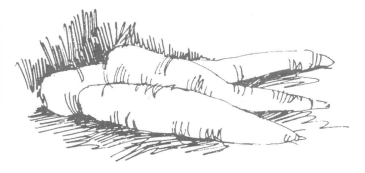

SET HNIT MYO HINCHO
(Twelve Varieties Soup)

Burma

½ pound chicken meat
⅓ pound chicken livers
4 dried Chinese mushrooms
1 large brown onion
2 cloves garlic
4 spring onions
3 stalks celery
½ pound Chinese cabbage
1 small choko
4 coriander leaves
2 inch square bean curd
1½ cups bean sprouts
¼ cup vegetable oil
6 cups chicken stock
2 tablespoons ngan pye-ye (fish sauce)
salt to taste
freshly ground black pepper
2 eggs　　　　serves 4–6

Slice the chicken meat and the livers. Soak the mushrooms in warm water for 40 minutes and discard the hard stems. Slice the onion and garlic and chop finely the spring onion, celery, cabbage, choko, coriander leaves and bean curd. Trim the bean sprouts and cut into short lengths. Heat the oil and sauté the onion and garlic for 3–4 minutes, then add the chicken meat and liver and stir-fry for another 5 minutes. Add the stock, season with fish sauce, salt and pepper and bring to the boil, then add all the vegetables and the bean curd and allow to simmer for 20 minutes. Just prior to serving, beat the eggs lightly and stir into the soup.

Malaysia

SOTO AYAM
(Chicken Soup)

1 fresh chicken, about 2½ pounds
4 spring onions
1 brown onion
¾ inch knob fresh ginger
½ inch knob fresh galangal (optional)
2 stems lemon grass
2 curry leaves
2 teaspoons salt
10 black peppercorns
6 shallots
3 cloves garlic
½ teaspoon blachan (shrimp paste)
¼ cup peanut oil
1 teaspoon coriander powder
½ teaspoon turmeric powder
2 tablespoons lemon juice
½ cup crispy fried onion　　serves 4–6

Joint the chicken, place in a large saucepan and cover with 8 cups of cold water. Chop the spring onions, brown onion, ginger, galangal and lemon grass. Add these to the pan together with the curry leaves, salt and black peppercorns. Bring to the boil, then lower the heat, cover the pan and simmer until the chicken is tender, approximately 1 hour. Allow to cool, then remove the chicken, cut the meat from the bones and slice finely. Pour the stock through a fine strainer and set aside. Chop the shallots and crush the garlic and the blachan. Heat the oil in a clean saucepan and sauté the shallots until golden brown. Add the garlic and blachan and continue to stir over a medium heat for 3 minutes. Add the coriander and turmeric powder, lemon juice and stock and bring to the boil. Lower the heat, cover the pan and simmer very slowly for 20 minutes, removing the lid and stirring occasionally. Finally, add the slices of chicken, adjust seasonings to taste and simmer, uncovered, for another 5–10 minutes. To serve; pour into individual soup bowls and sprinkle the crispy fried onion on top.

Overleaf: **Soto Ayam and Sop Lembu**

Singapore

SHREDDED BEEF & EGG SOUP

¹/₃ pound lean beef
¹/₂ teaspoon salt
freshly ground black pepper
1 teaspoon cornstarch
¹/₂ teaspoon baking soda
2 tablespoons light soy sauce
2 tablespoons peanut oil
¹/₂ teaspoon sesame oil
5 cups stock
3 egg-whites
2 spring onions, chopped
chopped Chinese parsley   serves 4

Shred the beef and season with the salt and freshly ground black pepper. Combine the cornstarch, baking soda, soy sauce and peanut oil, and pour over the beef. Sprinkle the sesame oil on top and allow to marinate for 20 minutes. Remove the beef and strain, retaining the marinade juices. In a large saucepan bring some water to the boil, add the beef and boil rapidly for 3 minutes, stirring continuously. Pour off the water and add the stock to the pan. Bring back to the boil and allow to simmer for 10 minutes, then pour in the reserved marinade and continue to simmer for another 5 minutes. Beat the egg-whites and gradually stir into the soup. When the egg begins to set, transfer to a soup tureen and garnish with the chopped spring onions and parsley.

Hong Kong

PIG'S LIVER & TOMATO SOUP

¹/₂ pound pork liver
1 spring onion
1 inch knob fresh ginger
2 tablespoons sugar
¹/₄ teaspoon white pepper
salt to taste
2 tablespoons dark soy sauce
2 tablespoons vegetable oil
5 cups chicken stock
¹/₂ pound fresh tomatoes   serves 4

Slice the liver into 1 inch pieces, and place into a shallow dish. Chop the spring onion and ginger, and place in the dish with the liver. Add the sugar, pepper, salt and soy sauce, and allow to stand for 30 minutes. Heat the oil in a wok or frying pan, add the liver and marinade ingredients, and stir-fry for 5 minutes over a medium heat. In a large pan bring the stock to the boil, and when simmering add the liver. Slice the tomatoes, place into the wok and cook for 2–3 minutes. Then, transfer all the ingredients from the wok into the stock, cover and simmer over a low heat for another 5–7 minutes.

Malaysia

SOP LEMBU
(Oxtail Soup)

1³/₄ pounds oxtail
1 teaspoon salt
¹/₂ teaspoon white pepper
¹/₄ cup all-purpose flour
2 small brown onions
2 shallots
2 carrots
1 stick celery
1 leek
¹/₂ cup butter
6 cups clear beef stock
2 teaspoons fresh lemon juice
1 teaspoon chopped parsley   serves 4–6

Wash and joint the oxtail. Dry thoroughly, then season with salt and pepper and coat lightly with the flour. Chop the onions and shallots, cut the carrots and celery into small dice and slice the leek. Heat three-quarters of the butter in a large saucepan and sauté the onion for 4–5 minutes, then add the carrot, celery, leek and the oxtail and cook for another 3 minutes, stirring frequently. Add the stock and cook over a low heat until the meat is tender, approximately 2 hours. In the meantime, heat the remaining butter in a small pan and fry the chopped shallot until golden and crispy, then remove from the pan, drain thoroughly and set aside. Remove the oxtail from the stock, cut off all the meat and cut into dice. Pour the stock through a strainer into a fresh saucepan and add the meat. Bring back to the boil, add the fresh lemon juice and adjust seasonings to taste. Serve in individual soup bowls and sprinkle a little crispy fried shallot and chopped parsley on top.

Singapore

MULLIGATAWNY SOUP
(Light Curry Soup)

2 brown onions
2 carrots
1 cooking apple
¼ cup butter
½ cup all-purpose flour
3 tablespoons curry powder
6 cups chicken stock
2 bay leaves
2 sprigs parsley
2 sprigs thyme
2 tablespoons tomato paste
salt to taste
freshly ground white pepper
¼ cup mango chutney
½ cup cooked rice
5 tablespoons fresh cream   serves 4–6

Dice the onions, carrots and apple. Melt the butter in a large saucepan, add the onion and carrot and sauté for 2–3 minutes until the onion becomes soft. Add the flour and curry powder and stir-fry over a moderate heat for 2 minutes, then pour in the stock, stir well and bring to the boil. Make a bouquet-garni of the bay leaves, parsley and thyme and add to the stock together with the tomato paste and diced apple. Season to taste with salt and freshly ground white pepper, cover the pan, lower the heat and simmer gently for 1 hour. Then, remove from the heat, discard the bouquet-garni and allow the soup to cool. Pour through a coarse sieve into a fresh saucepan, pressuring the vegetables with a wooden spoon. Just prior to serving, return the soup to the stove and bring back to the boil. Chop the chutney into tiny pieces and add this to the pan together with the cooked rice. Stir well and let simmer for another minute, then stir in the cream and immediately transfer to a soup tureen.

Indonesia

SOP KAMBING
(Lamb Soup)

1 pound fresh lamb chops
½ inch knob fresh ginger
3 shallots
3 cloves garlic
8 ounces canned chili bean-curd
¼ cup vegetable oil
2 ounces dried seaweed
1 teaspoon salt
½ teaspoon white pepper
¼ teaspoon five-spice powder
¼ teaspoon dom kwee powder*
1 teaspoon fresh lime juice   serves 4

Leaving on the bone, chop the lamb into pieces approximately ¾ inch in length. Chop finely the ginger and shallots and crush the garlic. Drain the bean curd and cut into quarters. Soak the seaweed in cold water for 30 minutes, then drain thoroughly. Heat the oil in a large saucepan and quickly stir-fry the lamb for 2–3 minutes to seal in the flavor. Add the ginger, shallot, garlic and bean-curd and continue to stir for another 2 minutes. Add the seaweed, salt, white pepper, five-spice powder, dom kwee powder and fresh lime juice and pour in 6 cups of cold water. Bring to the boil, stir well, then cover the pan, lower the heat and simmer gently until the meat is tender, approximately 1 hour.

*Note: Dom kwee powder is scraped from the root of the same name which is more likely to be obtained from a Chinese medicine shop rather than a food store. It may be difficult to obtain in some places outside Asia and its use may be regarded as optional. However, it adds to the soup a very distinctive flavor and should be used whenever possible.

47

Seafoods

While the heading might be considered a slight misnomer, in so much as it encompasses fish found up-stream and in inland lakes, it is a fact that most of the main ingredients used in this section's recipes come from the seas surrounding Asia. They provide a very high proportion of the food consumed by Asians of all creeds and nationalities for, unlike various meats, fish carries no religious taboos and is acceptable to all but the strictest vegetarian. Also, most varieties of 'soft' fish are strongly recommended for weight-reducing diets. Where specific varieties of Asian fish are mentioned, substitute your local varieties.

Thakkali Isso *Prawn & tomato curry*	**Hoi Lai Pad Prik** *Clams with hot sauce*	**Fish Mustard Curry**
Kakuluwo *Curried crab*	**Orr Chien** *Oyster omelette*	**Smoked Pomfret**
Fried Salt & Pepper Crabs	**Spicy Fried Cockles**	**Stuffed Red Snappers**
Laing *Spicy crab*	**Fried Mussels in Black Bean Sauce**	**Fish Head Curry**
Braised Crab with Ginger	**Shredded Abalone with Vegetables**	**Fried Fish Curry**
Poo Cha *Stuffed crab shells*	**Po Tak** *Sour seafood pot*	**Tod Man Pla** *Fried fish cakes with hot sauce*
Crab with Pork & Egg	**Hoh Mok Hoy** *Steamed mussels*	**Ikan Acar Kuning** *Fish with yellow pickle sauce*
Pad Priew Wan Goong *Sweet & sour shrimp*	**Tinuktok** *Seafoods in cabbage leaves*	**Deep Fried Fish with Sweet & Sour Sauce**
Jhinga Curry *Shrimp curry*	**Zarzuela de Pescado** *Mixed seafoods in wine*	**West Lake Fish**
Goong Pad *Fried shrimp with chili paste*	**Mixed Seafoods in Coconut Shell**	**Gulai Ikan**
Sautéed Shrimp with Garlic	**Sautéed Eel**	**Steamed Garoupa with Ginger**
Shrimp in Hot Garlic Sauce	**Unagi Unatma** *Eel with eggs*	**Saengson Chim** *Fish & vegetable stew*
Sweet & Sour Shrimp	**Kakejiru** *Grilled eels*	**Deep Fried Garoupa**
Karee Udang *Shrimp curry*	**Cumi-Cumi Isi** *Stuffed squid*	**Miris Malu** *Sour spicy fish*
Spicy Shrimp	**Cumi-Cumi Panir** *Deep fried squid*	**Pla Pad King** *Sea bass with fresh ginger*
Spiced Shrimp with Okras	**Deep Fried Cuttlefish**	**Steamed Pomfret Rolls**
Steamed Shrimp	**Sotong Ayam** *Stuffed cuttlefish*	**Steamed Garoupa with Ham & Vegetables**
Szechuan Stir-Fried Shrimp	**Pla Mueg Pad Prik** *Fried squid with hot sauce*	**Sliced Fish in Wine Sauce**
Gaeng Karee Goong *Lobster & shrimp curry*	**Sautéed Cuttlefish with Oyster Sauce**	**Saengson Chun** *Fried fish fillets*
Goong Musaman Karee *Shrimp curry*	**Rellenong Bangus** *Stuffed milkfish*	**Ikan Asam Padeh** *Fish in sour sauce*
Sautéed Lobster	**Ikan Bantut** *Spicy fish in aluminium foil*	**Kinulot** *Shark meat with coconut milk*
Lobster Curry 'Pulau Tioman'	**Fish Curry Goa Style**	**Fried Pomfret with Vegetables**
Lobster Omelette	**Gaeng Kua Nuer** *Fish & vegetable curry*	**Achar Ikan** *Deep fried snapper with vegetables*
Lobster with Chinese Wine	**Pla Dook Foo** *Deep fried smoked catfish*	
Lobster Masala	**Machli Curry** *Curried fillets of pomfret*	
Tempura *Deep-fried seafood & vegetables*		
Tahong Filipina *Mussels in spicy sauce*		

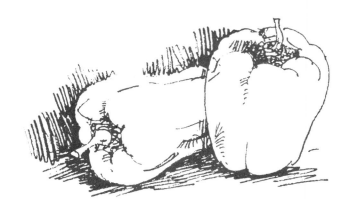

Sri Lanka

THAKKALI ISSO
(Prawn & Tomato Curry)

1 pound fresh shrimp
1 brown onion
4 cloves garlic
³⁄₄ inch knob fresh ginger
1 fresh red chili
³⁄₄ inch stem lemon grass
2 cloves
2 cardamoms
2 large tomatoes
¹⁄₄ cup oil
3 fresh curry leaves
1 teaspoon chili powder
1 teaspoon turmeric powder
1 teaspoon fenugreek powder
1 teaspoon paprika
³⁄₄ inch stick cinnamon
¹⁄₂ cup thin coconut milk
¹⁄₂ cup thick coconut milk
salt to taste
1 teaspoon fresh lime juice
1 teaspoon curry powder   serves 4

Shell and de-vein the shrimp, then rinse under running water and pat dry. Chop the onion, garlic and ginger, slice the chili and lemon grass and crush the cloves and cardamoms. Cut the tomatoes into wedges. Heat the oil until very hot, add the onion, garlic, ginger, lemon grass and curry leaves and stir-fry for 2 minutes. Then, add the shrimp, tomatoes, chili, clove, cardamom, spice powders and cinnamon stick and stir well. Cook over a medium heat, shaking the pan frequently. Pour in the thin coconut milk, stir to blend, and bring to the boil. Lower heat and allow to simmer for 5 minutes, then add the thick coconut milk and salt to taste. Stir well and bring back to the boil, then lower heat and simmer gently for another 10 minutes. Finally, remove cinnamon stick, transfer to a serving dish and sprinkle the lime juice and curry powder on top.

Sri Lanka

KAKULUWO
(Curried Crab)

3 medium-size crabs
2 shallots
2 green chilies
3 cloves garlic
1 inch knob fresh ginger
¹⁄₂ teaspoon turmeric powder
¹⁄₂ teaspoon fenugreek powder
¹⁄₂ teaspoon chili powder
2 teaspoons paprika
2 tablespoons curry powder
2 inch stick cinnamon
4 fresh curry leaves
4 fresh coriander leaves
1 cup thin coconut milk
³⁄₄ cup thick coconut milk
¹⁄₄ cup grated coconut
2 teaspoons ground rice
2 teaspoons fresh lime juice
salt to taste   serves 4–6

Clean the crabs and place in rapidly boiling water for 5 minutes, then remove and break into bite-size pieces, crushing the shell a little, so that the meat can later be more easily removed. Slice the shallots and chilies and grind the garlic and ginger. Place the crab in a pan, add the shallot, chili, garlic, ginger, spice powders, cinnamon stick, curry leaves, coriander leaves and thin coconut milk and bring to the boil. Lower heat and simmer gently for 5–10 minutes. Mix together the thick coconut milk, grated coconut, ground rice, lime juice and salt and add to the crab. Cook slowly for another 10 minutes, stirring occasionally. Remove the cinnamon stick before serving.

Vietnam

FRIED SALT & PEPPER CRABS

2 medium-size crabs
2 shallots
2 cloves garlic
³/₄ inch knob fresh ginger
¹/₂ cup peanut oil
3 tablespoons salt
2 tablespoons freshly ground white pepper
2 teaspoons sugar
2 tablespoons Chinese wine
1 teaspoon finely chopped parsley   serves 4

Clean the crabs and place in rapidly boiling water for 6–8 minutes, then remove, break off the claws and cut the bodies into bite-size pieces. Smash the shells slightly to enable the meat to be more easily removed. Chop finely the shallots, garlic and ginger. Heat the oil in a pan until it begins to smoke, then add the shallot, garlic and ginger and sauté for 3 minutes. Next, add the crab and cook for another 5 minutes, stirring continuously. Then, add the salt, pepper, sugar and Chinese wine, stir to blend well and cover pan with a tightly fitting lid. Retain over a medium heat until the crabs are cooked, then transfer to a serving dish and spoon a little of the cooking oil on top. Garnish with finely chopped parsley.

Philippines

LAING
(Spicy Crab)

2 medium-size crabs
1 brown onion
¹/₂ inch knob fresh ginger
3 tablespoons blachan (dried shrimp paste)
6 cloves garlic
1¹/₄ cups thick coconut oil
12 taro leaves
2 tablespoons fresh lime juice
salt to taste
freshly ground black pepper
2 tablespoons peanut oil   serves 4

Clean the crabs and place in rapidly boiling, salted water until they turn bright red (approximately 20 minutes), then carefully remove all the meat from the bodies and claws. Slice the onion, shred the ginger and blachan and crush 4 cloves of garlic and place these in an earthenware pot, together with the crab meat. Finely chop the remaining garlic and place to one side. Pour the coconut oil into the pot and bring to the boil. Retain over a high heat until the mixture starts to become oily, then shred the taro leaves by hand and add to the pot. Next, lower heat, allow to simmer for 6–8 minutes, then add fresh lime juice and season to taste with salt and pepper. Stir to blend well and allow to simmer for another minute before transferring to a serving dish. Finally, heat the oil, sauté the chopped garlic until it becomes crispy and sprinkle it on top of the crab.

Hong Kong

BRAISED CRAB WITH GINGER

2 fresh crabs, about 1¹/₄ pounds each
2 tablespoons cornstarch
1 inch knob fresh ginger
2 shallots
2 spring onions
oil for deep frying
1 cup chicken stock
2 tablespoons Chinese wine
2 teaspoons sesame oil
2 teaspoons sugar
salt to taste
freshly ground white pepper   serves 4

Thoroughly clean the crabs, cut into serving-size pieces and dust with half the cornstarch. Grate the ginger and chop finely the shallots and spring onions. Heat the oil in a wok and deep-fry the crab pieces for 3–4 minutes, then remove, drain and pour away most of the oil. Add the ginger, shallot and spring onion to the wok and sauté for 2 minutes, then add the stock, Chinese wine, sesame oil, sugar, salt and pepper and bring to the boil. Replace the crab, cover the wok with a tightly fitting lid and continue to cook over a medium heat until the crabs are fully cooked, approximately 6–8 minutes. Finally, mix the remaining cornstarch with a small quantity of cold water, add this to the pan and stir until the sauce thickens slightly.

POO CHA
(Stuffed Crab Shells)

Thailand

4 medium size crabs
¼ pound lean pork, ground
1 small brown onion
2 cloves garlic
¾ inch knob fresh ginger
1 fresh red chili
2 coriander leaves
1 teaspoon chopped coriander root
1 egg
salt to taste
freshly ground black pepper
oil for deep frying   serves 4

Clean the crabs and cook in rapidly-boiling water for approximately 15 minutes. Allow to cool, then carefully remove the back shells and place these in a warming oven. Extract all the meat from the body and claws, shred finely and place in a large bowl. Grind the pork, chop finely the onion, garlic, ginger, chili and coriander leaves and add these to the bowl together with the chopped coriander root. Beat the egg lightly and add to the mixture, then season to taste with salt and black pepper and blend thoroughly. Spoon the mixture into the warm shells and place these on a rack in a steamer. Cover the pan with a tightly-sealed lid and cook over boiling water for 25–30 minutes. Then, remove the shells and allow to cool. Finally, heat the oil until it starts to smoke and deep-fry the crab-shells until the tops are golden.

CRAB WITH PORK & EGG

Hong Kong

2 crabs, about 1¹/₂ pounds each
1 teaspoon salt
2 tablespoons vinegar
6 thin slices cooked pork
4 eggs
3 shallots
2 spring onions
1 inch knob fresh ginger
2 cloves garlic
1 tablespoon fermented soy beans
1 teaspoon finely chopped dried orange peel
2 tablespoons Chinese wine
2 tablespoons light soy sauce
freshly ground black pepper
¹/₄ cup white breadcrumbs
2 teaspoons sesame oil   serves 4–6

Thoroughly clean the crabs and cook in rapidly-boiling water for approximately 15 minutes. Allow to cool, then carefully remove the back shells and place these in a warming oven. Extract all the meat from the body and claws, shred finely and place in a large bowl. Grind the pork, chop finely the onion, garlic, ginger, chili and coriander leaves and add these to the bowl together with the chopped coriander root. Beat the egg lightly and add to the mixture, then season to taste with salt and black pepper and blend thoroughly. Spoon the mixture into the warm shells and place these on a rack in a steamer. Cover the pan with a tightly-sealed lid and cook over boiling water for 25–30 minutes. Then, remove the shells and allow to cool. Finally, heat the oil until it starts to smoke and deep-fry the crab-shells until the tops are golden.

Thailand

PAD PRIEW WAN GOONG
(Sweet and Sour Shrimp)

1½ pounds fresh shrimp
½ teaspoon salt
freshly ground white pepper
2 teaspoons white sugar
2 tablespoons fresh lime juice
2 tablespoons rice wine
1 clove garlic
1 large brown onion
1 green pepper
2 tomatoes
½ small cucumber
¼ cup vegetable oil
2 teaspoons palm sugar
2 tablespoons tomato paste
2 teaspoons nam pla (fish sauce)
2 tablespoons light soy sauce
⅓ cup chicken stock
¾ cup canned pineapple pieces
2 teaspoons cornstarch
freshly chopped coriander leaves   serves 4

Shell and de-vein the shrimp and place in a shallow bowl. Season with salt and pepper and sprinkle the white sugar on top. Pour half the lime juice and rice wine over the shrimp and set to one side for 15 minutes. Mince the garlic and chop the onion, green pepper, tomatoes and cucumber. Heat the oil in a large pan and sauté the garlic and onion for 2–3 minutes, until the onion is soft and translucent. Add the shrimp and stir fry for 3 minutes, then add the green pepper, tomato, cucumber, palm sugar, tomato paste, nam pla, soy sauce, stock and remaining lime juice and wine. Stir well and bring to the boil, then lower heat, add the pineapple pieces and cook over a moderate heat for another 3–4 minutes. Finally, mix the cornstarch with a small quantity of cold water, add to the sauce and stir to thicken slightly. Transfer to a serving dish, sprinkle the finely chopped coriander leaves on top and serve with steamed rice.

Pakistan

JHINGA CURRY
(Shrimp Curry)

1½ pounds fresh shrimp
1 brown onion
2 tomatoes
¾ inch knob fresh ginger
3 cloves garlic
½ cup vegetable oil
1 teaspoon red chili powder
½ teaspoon coriander powder
½ teaspoon turmeric powder
salt to taste
2 tablespoons fresh lime juice   serves 4

Shell and de-vein the shrimp. Chop the onion, tomatoes, ginger and garlic. Heat the oil in a pan and fry the shrimp lightly, then remove and set aside. Add the onion, ginger and garlic to the pan and sauté for 2 minutes, then add the spices and stir-fry for 3 minutes. Add the tomatoes and continue to cook for another 5 minutes, stirring frequently. Replace the shrimp, add the lime juice and salt and pour in ¾ cup of water. Stir to blend thoroughly and bring to the boil. Lower heat and allow to simmer for 10–20 minutes until the sauce thickens slightly.

Thailand

GOONG PAD
(Fried Shrimp with Chili Paste)

1 pound fresh shrimp
1 shallot
1 clove garlic
³/₄ inch knob khaa (Siamese ginger)
2 fresh red chilies
¹/₂ inch stem lemon grass
1 teaspoon chopped coriander root
¹/₄ teaspoon chopped nutmeg
1 teaspoon grated blachan (shrimp paste)
2 teaspoons fresh lime juice
¹/₂ teaspoon salt
freshly ground black pepper
1 cup thick coconut milk
2¹/₂ cups rice flour
oil for deep frying   serves 4

Shell and de-vein the shrimp, leaving the tails intact. Chop the shallot, garlic, ginger, chilies and lemon grass and place into a large bowl. Add the coriander, nutmeg, blachan, lime juice, salt, pepper and coconut milk and stir to blend thoroughly. Place the shrimp in the spice marinade, stir well and set aside for 30 minutes. Then remove the shrimp, drain well and dust with the rice flour. Heat the oil in a large pan until it starts to smoke, then add the shrimp and cook until they turn a deep pink color. Drain off all excess oil from the shrimp and serve with steamed rice or freshly cooked green vegetables.

Philippines

SAUTEED SHRIMP WITH GARLIC

24 fresh jumbo shrimp
3 cloves garlic
¹/₄ cup olive oil
salt to taste
freshly ground white pepper
¹/₄ cup dry sherry
¹/₂ teaspoon paprika   serves 4

Shell and de-vein the shrimp. Chop the garlic very finely. Heat the oil in a frying pan until it starts to smoke and sauté the shrimp over a very high heat for 30 seconds. Add the garlic, season to taste with salt and pepper and stir-fry for another 3–4 minutes, then pour in the sherry, and flame. As soon as the flame dies, transfer the shrimp to a serving dish and sprinkle the paprika on top.

Taiwan

SHRIMP IN HOT GARLIC SAUCE

1 pound fresh shrimp
1 egg-white
2 tablespoons Chinese wine
1 tablespoon cornstarch
¹/₂ teaspoon salt
¹/₄ teaspoon white pepper
1 brown onion
2 spring onions
3 fresh red chilies
1 inch knob fresh ginger
2 cloves garlic
vegetable oil for deep frying
¹/₂ cup fish stock
2 tablespoons black bean paste
2 tablespoons light soy sauce
1 teaspoon sugar
¹/₂ teaspoon sesame oil   serves 4

Shell and de-vein the shrimp and cut in half lengthways. Lightly beat the egg-white, add the Chinese wine, half the cornstarch, the salt and white pepper and mix well. Add the shrimp and place in the refrigerator for 30 minutes. Finely chop the onions, chilies and ginger and crush the garlic. Heat the oil in a wok, spoon in the coated shrimps and fry for 2–3 minutes until the shrimp turn pink. Remove, drain thoroughly and set aside in a warm place. Pour off most of the oil from the wok, add the onions, chili, ginger and garlic and cook over low heat for 5 minutes, stirring continuously. Add the stock, bean paste, soy sauce and sugar and bring to the boil. Replace the shrimp and simmer gently for another 2–3 minutes. Mix the remaining cornstarch with a small quantity of cold water, add to the pan and stir well until the sauce thickens slightly. Transfer to serving dish and sprinkle with sesame oil.

SWEET & SOUR SHRIMP

Hong Kong

1³/₄ pounds fresh medium-size shrimp
1 egg
¹/₄ cup vinegar
2 teaspoons Chinese wine
2 tablespoons light soy sauce
2 tablespoons ketchup
2 tablespoons sugar
¹/₂ teaspoon salt
freshly ground black pepper
¹/₂ cup cornstarch
1 large brown onion
1 green pepper
2 spring onions
2 fresh red chilies
¹/₂ inch knob fresh ginger
¹/₂ cup vegetable oil
1 cup canned pineapple chunks   serves 6

Shell and de-vein the shrimp, rinse under cold running water and place in a shallow dish. Beat the egg lightly, mix with the vinegar, Chinese wine, soy sauce, ketchup, sugar, salt and pepper and pour over the shrimp. Allow to stand for 15 minutes, then remove shrimp and dust with the cornstarch. Retain the marinade. Slice the brown onion, cut the pepper into medium-size pieces and finely chop the spring onions, chilies and ginger. Heat the oil in a wok and stir-fry the shrimp for 4–5 minutes, then remove and set aside. Pour away half the oil from the wok, then add the onion and sauté until it starts to brown. Next, add the green pepper, spring onion, chili and ginger and retain over a fairly high heat for 3–4 minutes, stirring frequently. Finally, replace the shrimp, add the pineapple chunks and reserved marinade and adjust seasonings to taste. Stir well and allow to simmer for another 2 minutes before transferring to a serving dish.

KAREE UDANG
(Shrimp Curry)

Indonesia

1³/₄ *pounds fresh medium-size shrimp*
4 fresh red chilies
2 shallots
1 clove garlic
³/₄ inch knob fresh ginger
¹/₂ inch knob fresh langkuas (local ginger)
4 candlenuts
1 teaspoon coriander powder
1 teaspoon cumin powder
1 teaspoon turmeric powder
¹/₂ teaspoon salt
¹/₄ cup vegetable oil
2¹/₂ cups thick coconut milk
1 teaspoon chopped
celery leaves   serves 4–6

Shell and de-vein the shrimp, leaving the tails intact. Boil the chilies for a few minutes, then chop finely. Chop the shallots, garlic, ginger and langkuas and grind these together with the chili, candlenuts, spice powders and salt and add a little of the oil to form a smooth paste. Heat the remaining oil in a pan and stir-fry the spice-paste for 5–6 minutes, then add the shrimp and pour in 1 cup of water. Bring to the boil and cook, over a fairly high heat, for 15 minutes, then add the coconut milk and bring back to the boil. Lower heat and allow to simmer for another 15–20 minutes, until the sauce thickens. Transfer to a serving dish and sprinkle the chopped celery leaves on top.

57

Malaysia

SPICY SHRIMP

1 pound large fresh shrimp
2 teaspoons salt
1/2 teaspoon saffron powder
3/4 inch knob fresh ginger
4 cloves garlic
2 curry leaves
1 stem lemon grass
1 teaspoon mustard seeds
3/4 inch cinnamon stick
4 cloves
2 large tomatoes
4 fresh green chilies
1/4 cup vegetable oil
10 dried red chilies
2 tablespoons cumin seeds
2 tablespoons black peppercorns
2 tablespoons coriander seeds
3/4 cup thin coconut milk
3/4 cup thick coconut milk
1/2 cup finely chopped celery   serves 4–6

Shell and de-vein the shrimp, leaving the tails intact. Rub the salt and saffron over the shrimp. Chop the ginger and garlic and pound together to form a smooth paste. Wrap the curry leaves, lemon grass, mustard seeds, cinnamon stick and cloves in a piece of muslin and secure well. Slice the tomatoes and chop the green chilies. Heat the oil in a pan and stir-fry the pounded ginger and garlic for 2 minutes. Add the shrimp and the spice bag, cover the pan and cook over a low heat for 15 minutes. Grind together the dried chilies, cumin seeds, black peppercorns and coriander seeds and mix with the thin coconut milk. Remove the cover from the pan and pour this mixture on to the shrimp. Stir well and bring to the boil. Add the sliced tomatoes and green chili, lower heat and simmer for another 10 minutes. Then pour in the thick coconut milk, adjust seasonings to taste and continue to simmer until the oil rises to the surface. Remove the spice bag, transfer to a serving dish and sprinkle the finely chopped celery on top.

India

SPICED SHRIMP WITH OKRAS

1 pound fresh shrimp
1 teaspoon salt
1/4 teaspoon turmeric powder
1/4 teaspoon chili powder
2 brown onions
3/4 pound okras
6 fresh red chilies
4 cloves garlic
2 teaspoons coriander seeds
1/4 teaspoon cumin seeds
1/2 cup grated coconut
2 tablespoons vinegar
1/3 cup vegetable oil
2 tablespoons tamarind water
2 teaspoons garam masala   serves 4

Shell and de-vein the shrimp and place into a saucepan containing 1 1/2 cups of boiling water. Add the salt, turmeric powder and chili powder and cook for 3–4 minutes. Remove from the heat and drain the shrimp, retaining the water. Chop the onions and the okras. Remove the seeds from the chilies and chop finely. Crush the garlic. Pound together the chili, garlic, coriander seeds, cumin seeds, grated coconut and vinegar to form a smooth spice-paste. Heat the oil in a pan and sauté the onion until soft and golden, then add the spice-paste and continue to cook for 3–4 minutes, stirring frequently. Add the okras and pour in 1/2 cup of the reserved water. Bring to the boil, then lower heat, place a lid on the pan and simmer for 15 minutes. Remove the lid, add the tamarind water and garam masala and stir to blend thoroughly. Allow to simmer for another 2–3 minutes, then add the shrimp and heat through. Serve immediately.

Singapore

STEAMED SHRIMP

1¼ pounds fresh jumbo shrimp
1 inch knob fresh ginger
2 tablespoons Chinese wine
2 teaspoons sesame oil
¼ teaspoon five-spice powder
½ teaspoon salt
¼ teaspoon white pepper
2 egg-whites
2 teaspoons chili oil
½ cup finely chopped spring onion   serves 6

Shell and de-vein the shrimp. Cut in half, lengthways, and arrange on an heatproof plate. Cut the ginger into julienne strips and place on top of the shrimp. Sprinkle the Chinese wine and sesame oil on top and season with the five-spice powder, salt and freshly ground white pepper. Beat the egg-whites lightly and pour over the shrimp. Boil a little water in the bottom of a wok and place the shrimp on a wooden rack above the level of the water. Place a tightly fitting lid on the wok and steam for 5–6 minutes. Before serving, sprinkle a little chili oil over the shrimp and garnish with finely chopped spring onions.

Taiwan

SZECHUAN STIR-FRIED SHRIMP

1 pound fresh jumbo shrimp
2 shallots
2 spring onions
¾ inch knob fresh ginger
1 clove garlic
oil for deep frying
1 teaspoon hot bean paste
¼ cup tomato ketchup
2 tablespoons Chinese wine
2 teaspoons sugar
salt to taste
freshly ground black pepper
pinch monosodium glutamate
2 teaspoons cornstarch   serves 4–6

Shell and de-vein the shrimp. Chop finely the shallots, spring onions, ginger and garlic. Heat the oil in a wok until almost smoking and deep-fry the shrimp for 2 minutes, then remove, drain and set aside. Pour away most of the oil from the wok (leaving 2 tablespoons only), then add the shallot, spring onion, ginger and garlic and sauté for 3 minutes. Add the bean paste, tomato ketchup and Chinese wine and bring to the boil, then add the shrimp and stir-fry over a moderate heat for 2 minutes. Add the sugar, salt, freshly ground black pepper and monosodium glutamate and pour in ⅓ cup of cold water. Bring back to the boil and cook for another 3 minutes, stirring continuously. Mix the cornstarch with a small quantity of cold water and add to the pan to slightly thicken the sauce. Serve immediately.

Thailand

GAENG KAREE GOONG
(Lobster and Shrimp Curry)

4 fresh rock-lobster tails
4 fresh jumbo shrimp
1 green pepper
2 fresh red chilies
⅓ cup vegetable oil
3 tablespoons curry paste
2 tablespoons nam pla (fish sauce)
2 tablespoons sugar
8 cherry tomatoes
12 seeded red dates
1¼ cups thick coconut milk
2 teaspoons chopped coriander   serves 4–6

Carefully remove all the lobster meat and cut into slices. Shell and de-vein the shrimp and cut in half, lengthways. Cut the green pepper into small chunks and slice the chili finely. Heat the oil in a large frying pan until it is very hot, then add the lobster and shrimp and stir-fry for 2–3 minutes until the meat turns a deep pink. Remove the seafood and set aside. Add the curry paste to the pan and cook for 3 minutes, stirring continuously, then add the nam pla, sugar, pepper, chili, tomatoes, dates and coconut milk. Stir well and bring to the boil, then replace the seafood, lower heat and cook slowly for 5–6 minutes, stirring occasionally. Transfer to a serving dish and sprinkle the finely chopped coriander on top.

GOONG MUSAMAN KAREE
(Shrimp Curry)

1½ pounds fresh shrimp
2 shallots
2 cloves garlic
1 inch knob fresh khaa (Siamese ginger)
¾ inch stem lemon grass
2 teaspoons chopped coriander root
10 dried red chilies
½ teaspoon chopped lime peel
3 teaspoons roasted coriander seeds
1 teaspoon roasted cumin seeds
2 roasted cardamom seeds
½ teaspoon ground nutmeg
2 cloves
¼ teaspoon ground mace
½ teaspoon cinnamon powder
2 large brown onions
½ cup vegetable oil
2 tablespoons tamarind water
1 cup thick coconut milk
2 tablespoons sugar
salt to taste
freshly ground black pepper
fresh coriander leaves
for garnish

serves 4–6

Shell and de-vein the shrimp. Chop finely the shallots, garlic, ginger and lemon grass and pound these together with the coriander root, dried chilies, lime peel, coriander, cumin, cardamom, cloves, nutmeg, mace and cinnamon, then add a small quantity of cold water to produce a smooth paste. Slice the onions. Heat the oil in a large pan, add the shrimp and sauté for 3–4 minutes, then remove and set aside. Add the spice-paste to the oil and stir-fry for 4–5 minutes, then add the coconut milk and bring to the boil. Add the tamarind water and sugar and season to taste with salt and black pepper. Bring back to the boil, add the onion and replace the shrimp, then lower heat and cook for another 10 minutes. Transfer to a large serving dish and garnish with fresh coriander leaves.

SAUTEED LOBSTER

Hong Kong

1 fresh lobster, about 5 pounds
1 teaspoon cornstarch
½ teaspoon white pepper
1 inch knob fresh ginger
2 spring onions
1 small green pepper
1 clove garlic
¾ cup peanut oil
2 tablespoons Chinese wine
2 teaspoons light soy sauce
1 teaspoon sugar
¾ cup fish stock
sprigs of Chinese parsley for garnish serves 4

Place the lobster into a pan of rapidly boiling water. Immediately bring the water back to the boil and cook for approximately 25 minutes (5–6 minutes per pound). Allow to cool, then remove the meat and cut into bite-size chunks. Sprinkle the cornstarch over the meat and season with salt and white pepper. Chop finely the ginger, spring onions and green pepper and crush the garlic. Heat the oil in a wok and sauté the lobster for 2–3 minutes, then remove and pour away most of the oil. Add the ginger and garlic to the remaining oil and sauté for 3 minutes, then add the onion and green pepper and replace the lobster. Stir-fry for another minute, then add the Chinese wine, soy sauce, sugar and stock and bring to the boil. Lower heat, adjust seasonings to taste and cook slowly for 3 minutes more, then transfer to a serving plate and garnish with sprigs of Chinese parsley.

Malaysia

LOBSTER CURRY 'PULAU TIOMAN'

1 medium-size lobster
1/2 pound small shrimp
2 brown onions
4 red chilies
2 green chilies
2 cloves garlic
1/2 cup clarified butter
1 3/4 cups curry sauce (see right)
3/4 cup grated coconut
3/4 cup crispy fried onion
salt to taste
freshly ground black pepper
1/2 cup small pineapple chunks

Sauce:
4 shallots
1/2 inch knob fresh ginger
1 stem lemon grass
1 clove garlic
2 teaspoons peanut oil
2 teaspoons curry powder
1/2 teaspoon anise powder
1/2 teaspoon cumin powder
1/2 teaspoon saffron powder
3/4 cup thick coconut milk
1 1/4 cups fish stock
1/2 teaspoon salt
1/4 teaspoon white pepper
1/2 inch cinnamon stick
2 cloves
3 cardamom seeds   serves 4–6

Remove the lobster meat from the shell and cut into chunks. Shell and de-vein the shrimp. Slice the onions, chop the chilies coarsely and crush the garlic. Melt the butter in a large pan and sauté the onion and garlic for 2–3 minutes, then add the lobster meat and the shrimp and cook for 5 minutes, stirring frequently. Remove the seafood and reduce the sauce in the pan by half, then pour in the curry sauce, add the chilies and adjust seasoning to taste with salt and freshly ground black pepper. Bring to the boil, replace the lobster and shrimp, lower heat and simmer gently for approximately 20 minutes. Remove the seafood and arrange on a serving platter. Add the grated coconut and crispy fried onion to the sauce, stir to blend and pour on top. Garnish with small chunks of pineapple.

To make the sauce; chop the shallots, ginger, lemon grass and garlic. Place in a bowl, add one quarter of the peanut oil and pound to a smooth paste. Heat the remaining peanut oil in a pan and stir-fry the spice-paste for 3–4 minutes. Then, add the curry powder, anise, cumin and saffron. Pour in the coconut milk and fish stock, season with the salt and white pepper and bring to the boil. Lower heat, add the cinnamon stick, cloves and cardamom seeds and simmer for 20 minutes. Before pouring the sauce over the seafoods remove the cinnamon, cloves and cardamom.

Singapore

LOBSTER OMELETTE

3/4 pound cooked lobster meat
salt
freshly ground white pepper
2 spring onions
1 small green pepper
1 inch knob fresh ginger
1 clove garlic
oil for frying
2 tablespoons Chinese wine
2 tablespoons light soy sauce
10 eggs
1 teaspoon sesame oil
1 teaspoon chopped Chinese parsley   serves 4

Chop the lobster into small chunks and season with salt and freshly ground white pepper. Chop the spring onion, green pepper, ginger and garlic. Heat some of the oil in a wok and sauté the ginger and garlic for 3–4 minutes, then add the lobster, spring onion, green pepper, Chinese wine and soy sauce and bring to the boil. Lower heat and allow to simmer for 2 minutes, then transfer to a large bowl. Beat the eggs lightly with a fork and pour into the bowl, add the sesame oil and finely chopped parsley, adjust seasonings to taste and stir to blend thoroughly. Heat the remaining oil in the wok, tilt to make sure that all the cooking surface is well greased, then pour in the omelette mixture and cook over a fairly low heat, until the egg sets. Turn and break up slightly during the cooking time. Serve immediately.

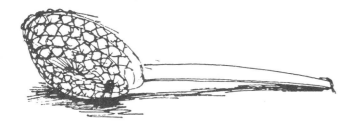

India

LOBSTER MASALA

1 pound cooked lobster meat
2 brown onions
3 tomatoes
2 cloves garlic
1¹/₂ inch knob fresh ginger
2 cloves
1 teaspoon red chili powder
¹/₂ teaspoon coriander powder
¹/₄ teaspoon cinnamon powder
¹/₄ teaspoon cardamom powder
pinch saffron
salt to taste
¹/₄ cup fresh lemon juice
¹/₄ cup peanut oil
1 teaspoon freshly chopped
coriander leaves   serves 4

Cut the lobster meat into bite-size chunks. Chop the onions and tomatoes. Chop the garlic and ginger finely, then grind these together with the cloves, all the spice powders and the fresh lemon juice to produce a thick spice-paste. Heat the oil in a pan and sauté the onion for 2–3 minutes until soft. Add the masala (spice-paste) and continue to cook over a moderate heat for another 5 minutes, stirring frequently. Add the tomato, lobster, and ¹/₂ cup of cold water and bring to the boil. Stir to blend thoroughly, then lower heat and simmer for 3 minutes. Adjust seasonings to taste and serve immediately.

Hong Kong

LOBSTER WITH CHINESE WINE

1 fresh medium-size lobster
2 teaspoons vinegar
1 teaspoon salt
¹/₂ teaspoon white pepper
pinch monosodium glutamate
2 brown onions
1 clove garlic
oil for deep frying
1 cup clear fish stock
3 tablespoons Chinese wine
2 tablespoons tomato sauce
2 tablespoons sugar
2 teaspoons cornstarch
1 teaspoon chopped Chinese parsley serves 4

Place the lobster into a large pan of rapidly boiling water, add the vinegar and cook for 15–20 minutes. Discard the head and tail and chop the body of the lobster into 16 pieces. Season with salt, freshly ground white pepper and monosodium glutamate. Chop the onions and crush the garlic. Heat the oil in a wok and when it starts to smoke add the pieces of lobster and deep-fry for 40 seconds, turning frequently with a slotted spoon, then remove, drain off excess oil and set aside. Pour away most of the oil from the wok, leaving about 3 tablespoons. Reheat, add the onion and garlic and sauté for 3–4 minutes, then pour in the stock and bring to the boil. Add the Chinese wine, tomato sauce and sugar and adjust seasonings according to taste. Bring back to the boil, then add the lobster pieces, lower heat and allow to simmer for 5 minutes. Finally, mix the cornstarch with a small quantity of cold water and stir into the sauce to thicken slightly. Transfer to a large dish and garnish with freshly chopped Chinese parsley.

63

TEMPURA
(Deep Fried Seafood and Vegetables)

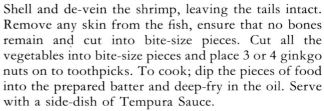

12 medium-size fresh shrimp
1 pound fish fillets
8 fresh mushrooms
2 brown onions
4 spring onions
1 small eggplant
4 asparagus spears
small can bamboo shoots
small can ginkgo nuts
vegetable oil for deep frying

Batter:
1 egg
pinch baking soda
2 cups all-purpose flour

Tempura Sauce:
⅓ cup mirrin
⅓ cup Japanese soy sauce
⅔ cup dashi (see page 30)
¼ teaspoon salt
pinch monosodium glutamate
¼ cup finely grated white radish   serves 4

Shell and de-vein the shrimp, leaving the tails intact. Remove any skin from the fish, ensure that no bones remain and cut into bite-size pieces. Cut all the vegetables into bite-size pieces and place 3 or 4 ginkgo nuts on to toothpicks. To cook; dip the pieces of food into the prepared batter and deep-fry in the oil. Serve with a side-dish of Tempura Sauce.

Note: It is important that the oil be kept at an even temperature, approximately 375°F, during the whole period of cooking. Only a few pieces should be cooked at a time and the oil continually brought back to the desired temperature. While cooking, the food should be turned occasionally with long wooden chopsticks and, when cooked, should be placed on sheets of absorbent paper arranged on serving plates.

To make the batter; break the egg into a bowl and add 1½ cups of ice-cold water. Add the baking soda and the flour and mix thoroughly until the batter is perfectly smooth and thin. If the batter appears too thick, add a little more ice-cold water.

Note: It is important that the batter be of the correct consistency and also be freshly made just prior to using. It should never be stored, even for a short period.

To make the sauce; heat the mirrin in a small saucepan until it is warm (but not too hot), then remove from the heat and light with a match. Shake the pan slightly until the flame dies then add the soy sauce and dashi, return to the heat and bring to the boil. Season with salt and monosodium glutamate and allow to cool. Finally, add the finely grated white radish and stir to blend thoroughly.

Philippines

TAHONG FILIPINA
(Mussels in Spicy Sauce)

2 pounds mussels
2 brown onions
2 red chilies
3 cloves garlic
1 bay leaf
1/4 cup corn oil
salt to taste
freshly ground black pepper　　　serves 4

Place the mussels in a bowl of cold water and scrub with a stiff brush, then rinse and repeat the process. Finely chop the onions, chilies and garlic and pound the bay leaf. Heat the oil in a pan and stir-fry the onion, chili and bay leaf for 2–3 minutes, then season with salt and freshly ground black pepper. Add the mussels and cook until the shells all open, discarding any that fail to do so. After the shells open stir well to ensure that the juice from the mussels gets into the sauce. Discard the top shells and arrange the mussels on serving plates. Add the garlic to the pan and cook until crispy and golden, then pour over the mussels and serve immediately.

Thailand

HOI LAI PAD PRIK
(Clams with Hot Sauce)

1 pound small clams
2 shallots
3/4 inch knob khaa (Siamese ginger)
4 fresh red chilies
1 clove garlic
1/3 cup vegetable oil
1 teaspoon chopped coriander root
2 teaspoons nam pla (fish sauce)
2 tablespoons chili sauce
1 1/4 fish stock
salt to taste
freshly ground black pepper
2 teaspoons cornstarch
fresh coriander leaves　　　serves 4

Scrub the clams with a stiff brush and rinse well in cold water. Chop the shallots, ginger, chilies and garlic. Heat the oil in a pan, add the shallot, ginger and garlic and sauté for 3–4 minutes, then add the chilies, coriander root, nam pla and chili sauce. Cook over a moderate heat for 2 minutes, then add the clams and fish stock and bring to the boil. Cook until all the clams open (discarding any that fail to do so), then transfer the clams to a serving dish. Mix the cornstarch with a small quantity of cold water and add to the sauce. Season to taste with salt and freshly ground black pepper and stir well until the sauce thickens. Pour the sauce over the clams and garnish with coriander leaves.

Singapore

ORR CHIEN
(Oyster Omelette)

1/2 pound small fresh oysters
2 teaspoons Chinese wine
freshly ground black pepper
1 spring onion
1 fresh red chili
1 clove garlic
few celery leaves
1/2 cup rice flour
1/4 teaspoon salt
3 eggs
vegetable oil
2 teaspoons light soy sauce
1 teaspoon dark soy sauce　　　serves 4

Wash the oysters under cold running water, then allow to drain. Season the oysters with Chinese wine and freshly ground black pepper and set aside for 20 minutes. Chop the spring onion, chili, garlic and celery leaves very finely. Mix the flour and salt with 1/2 cup of warm water. Beat the eggs in a separate bowl. Heat the oil in a wok until it is very hot, then add the batter and egg. Stir to blend and allow to set slightly, breaking the mixture up with a spatula, then remove to the side of the wok. Add the oysters, onion, chili, garlic and celery leaves and stir-fry for 3–4 minutes. Add the soy sauce and adjust seasonings to taste, then bring the egg mixture back to the center of the wok, stir to blend thoroughly and continue to cook until the egg is set.

Malaysia

SPICY FRIED COCKLES

1 pound cockles
4 fresh red chilies
4 cloves garlic
¼ cup peanut oil
1 teaspoon dark soy sauce
1 teaspoon black bean sauce
2 teaspoons tomato sauce
2 teaspoons satay sauce
salt to taste
freshly ground black pepper
pinch monosodium glutamate
1 teaspoon cornstarch   serves 4

Wash the cockles and pry open with a knife. Chop the chilies and crush the garlic. Heat the oil until very hot then sauté the chili and garlic for 2 minutes. Add all the sauces and pour in 1 cup of cold water, then season to taste with salt, freshly ground black pepper and monosodium glutamate and bring to the boil. Lower heat and simmer gently for 2 minutes, then add the cockles and continue to cook over a medium heat for another 2–3 minutes. Finally mix the cornstarch with a small quantity of cold water, add to the sauce and stir to thicken.

FRIED MUSSELS IN
BLACK BEAN & CHILI SAUCE

2 pounds fresh mussels
½ cup vegetable oil
3 tablespoons preserved soy beans
½ green pepper
3 fresh red chilies
¾ inch knob fresh ginger
2 cloves garlic
2 tablespoons sugar
1 teaspoon salt
freshly ground black pepper
1 cup chicken stock
1 heaping tablespoon cornstarch
1 teaspoon finely chopped parsley   serves 4

Wash the mussels under cold running water and scrub with a stiff brush. Leave to soak in cold water for 20 minutes, then rub dry. Heat ⅓ cup of oil in a frying pan and stir-fry the mussels until the shells open, discarding any that fail to do so. Set the mussels aside and clean the pan. Crush the soy beans and mix with a little cold water. Cut the green pepper, red chilies and ginger into thin strips and crush the garlic. Heat the remaining oil in the pan and sauté the garlic for 2 minutes. Add the soy bean, green pepper, chili and ginger and continue to cook over a moderate heat for another 2 minutes. Add the mussels, sugar, salt and pepper and pour in the chicken stock. Bring to the boil, then lower heat and simmer for 2 minutes. Mix the cornstarch with a small quantity of cold water, add to the pan and stir until sauce thickens slightly. Serve in individual clay pots and garnish with chopped parsley.

Hong Kong

SHREDDED ABALONE
WITH VEGETABLES

1 pound canned abalone
½ teaspoon salt
freshly ground black pepper
2 sticks celery
1 inch knob fresh ginger
2 spring onions
¼ cup lard
2 tablespoons Chinese wine
2 tablespoons light soy sauce
¼ cup chicken stock
2 teaspoons sugar
2 tablespoons oyster sauce   serves 4

Drain the abalone, cut into thin slices and season with salt and pepper. Chop finely the celery, ginger and spring onions. Heat the lard in a wok and sauté the ginger for 2 minutes, then add the celery, spring onion, Chinese wine, soy sauce, stock and sugar and bring to the boil. Lower heat, add the oyster sauce and stir to blend thoroughly. Finally, add the slices of abalone and cook for another minute. Serve immediately.

Note: Abalone must not be overcooked or it will toughen. If using fresh abalone, soften and tenderise beforehand but do not cook for a longer period.

PO TAK
(Sour Seafood Pot)

Thailand

8 fresh mussels
1 small crab
4 large fresh shrimp
1 small squid
¹/₂ pound fillet of seabass
4 cups chicken stock
2 pickled Chinese plums, with juice
50 ml nam pla (fish sauce)
salt to taste
freshly ground white pepper
pinch monosodium glutamate
5 small fresh red chilies
2 tablespoons fresh lemon juice
freshly chopped coriander leaves   serves 2

Scrub the mussels with a wire brush and rinse in salted water. Cook the crab in rapidly boiling water for 6–8 minutes, then cut into 4 pieces. Shell and de-vein the prawns, leaving the tails intact. Clean the squid and cut into 4 pieces. Remove skin from the seabass, ensure all small bones have been removed and cut into bite-size pieces. Pour the chicken stock into a large pan and bring to the boil. Add the pickled plums with juice, the nam pla, salt, freshly ground white pepper and monosodium glutamate. Lower heat and simmer gently for 10 minutes, then add all the seafood. Smash the chilies with the back of a knife and add to the stock, together with the lemon juice. Continue to keep over a moderate heat until the seafood is completely cooked and the mussels have opened (discard any that fail to do so), then transfer to a clay serving pot and garnish with freshly chopped coriander leaves.

HOH MOK HOY
(Steamed Mussels)

Thailand

2 pounds fresh mussels
1 shallot
1 clove garlic
4 fresh red chilies
¹/₃ cup vegetable oil
1 teaspoon chopped coriander root
1 teaspoon chopped khaa (Siamese ginger)
1 teaspoon chopped lemon grass
¹/₂ teaspoon chopped lime peel
2 teaspoons blachan (shrimp paste)
1 cup coconut cream
1 duck egg, beaten
¹/₄ cup rice flour
salt to taste
freshly ground black pepper
sweet basil leaves   serves 4

Scrub the mussels with a stiff brush and rinse in cold water. Cook in a steamer until they open, discarding any that fail to do so. Remove the mussels from the shell, retaining the larger shells. Chop the shallot, garlic and chilies. Heat the oil in a pan and sauté the shallot and garlic for 3–4 minutes, then add the chilies, coriander, ginger, lemon grass, lime peel and blachan. Continue to cook, stirring frequently, until the mixture gives off a fragrant aroma, then remove from the pan and place in a mixing bowl. Add the coconut cream, egg, flour, salt and freshly ground black pepper and stir to combine thoroughly. Blanch the basil leaves in boiling water and arrange in the bottom of the retained shells. Place three mussels in each shell and spoon a little sauce on top of each. Place in a steamer and cook until heated through, then serve immediately.

Philippines

TINUKTOK
(Seafoods in Cabbage Leaves)

3/4 pound fresh shrimp
1/2 pound white fish fillets
1 young coconut
1 brown onion
1 inch knob fresh ginger
2 tablespoons fresh lime juice
1 1/2 cups thick coconut milk
salt to taste
freshly ground black pepper
16 cabbage leaves   serves 4

Shell and de-vein the shrimp and chop finely. Chop the fish, onion and ginger. Open the coconut, discard the water and chop the meat. Place all these ingredients into a mortar, add the lime juice, a little coconut milk, salt and freshly ground black pepper and pound to produce a smooth paste. Divide the mixture, place into the center of the leaves and fold into triangles. Heat the remaining coconut milk in a large saucepan and bring to the boil. Add the stuffed leaves, place a lid on the pan, lower heat and simmer until most of the liquid has been absorbed, then serve immediately.

Philippines

ZARZUELA DE PESCADO
(Mixed Seafoods in Wine)

1 1/4 pounds fillets of firm white fish
12 mussels
12 shrimp
2 brown onions
4 tomatoes
1 clove garlic
2 tablespoons vegetable oil
1/2 cup dry white wine
2 teaspoons fresh lemon juice
salt to taste
freshly ground white pepper
1 teaspoon finely chopped parsley   serves 6

Remove any skin from the fish fillets and cut the flesh into small pieces. Boil the mussels in water until they open, discarding any that fail to do so, then remove from the shell. Shell and de-vein the shrimp. Chop the onions and tomatoes into fairly small pieces and crush the garlic. Heat the oil in a pan, add the onion and garlic and sauté for 2–3 minutes until golden. Add the tomato, mussels and shrimp and continue to cook slowly for another few minutes, stirring frequently, then add the white fish, pour in the wine and bring to the boil. Lower the heat and simmer for 3–4 minutes, then add the fresh lemon juice, season to taste with salt and freshly ground white pepper and stir to blend thoroughly. Serve immediately with boiled rice.

Philippines

MIXED SEAFOODS IN COCONUT SHELL

1/3 pound fresh shrimp
1/4 pound mussels
1/4 pound clams
1/4 pound squid
1/3 pound fish fillets
1 brown onion
2 shallots
2 spring onions
2 tomatoes
1 red pepper
1/2 inch knob fresh ginger
1 clove garlic
1/4 cup vegetable oil
salt to taste
freshly ground white pepper
1 young coconut   serves 2

Shell and de-vein the shrimp. Boil the mussels and clams until they open, (discarding any that fail to do so), then discard the shells. Cut the squid and fish into small pieces. Chop the brown onion, shallots, spring onions, tomatoes, red pepper and ginger and crush the garlic. Heat the oil in a pan and sauté the brown onion, shallot, ginger and garlic for 3–4 minutes, then add the shrimp and squid and continue to cook until the squid is brown. Lower the heat slightly, add all the remaining seafood and vegetables and season to taste with salt and freshly ground white pepper. Cook slowly for 10–15 minutes, stirring frequently. Cut the coconut in half and discard the water. Fill the coconut halves with the seafood mixture and bake in a pre-heated moderately hot oven for a few minutes. Serve in the shells.

Hong Kong

SAUTEED EEL

1 pound fresh eel
2 cloves garlic
1 inch knob fresh ginger
2 spring onions
2 tablespoons vegetable oil
2 tablespoons Chinese wine
2 tablespoons light soy sauce
2 teaspoons dark soy sauce
1/3 cup fish stock
freshly ground white pepper
2 teaspoons cornstarch
2 teaspoons sesame oil   serves 4–6

Soak the eel in cold water for 1 hour, then remove the skin and cut into thin slices. Chop the garlic and ginger very finely and cut the spring onions into short pieces. Heat the oil in a wok and sauté the garlic and ginger for 3–4 minutes, then add the eel and continue to cook, stirring continuously, for another 5 minutes. Add the wine, soy sauce and stock, season with freshly ground white pepper and bring to the boil. Lower heat, add the spring onion and allow to simmer for 3–4 minutes. Mix the cornstarch with a little cold water and stir into the sauce to thicken slightly. Transfer to a serving dish and sprinkle heated sesame oil on top.

Japan

UNAGI UNATAMA
(Eel with Egg)

4 small eels
1/4 cup oil
2 cups kake-tare sauce (see following recipe)
8 cups cooked rice
2 2/3 cups cold water
2 tablespoons sake
2 teaspoons sugar
pinch monosodium glutamate
2 eggs   serves 4

Prepare and cook the eels as described in recipe below, using approximately half the kake-tare for glazing. Arrange the eels on four beds of cooked rice. Pour the remaining sauce into a pan, add the water, sake, sugar and monosodium glutamate and bring to a rapid boil, stirring continuously. Break the eggs into the sauce and whisk with a fork until the egg begins to set. Pour the sauce over the eel and serve immediately.

Japan

KAKEJIRU
(Grilled Eels)

4 small eels
1/4 cup oil
3 cups kake-tare sauce
6 cups cooked rice

Kake-tare sauce:
2 cups mirin
2 cups Japanese soy sauce
1/2 cup brown sugar   serves 4

Cut off the heads and tails from the eels, slit along the underside and remove the backbone, then clean thoroughly and spread out on a flat surface. Cut the eels in half, crossways, and skewer each piece with 4 evenly-spaced skewers, taking care not to pierce the meat on either side. Brush with the oil and cook under a fairly hot grill for 15 minutes; the skin-side for 10 minutes and the underside for 5 minutes. Remove from the grill and brush with the prepared kake-tare sauce, then return to the grill and cook for another 2–3 minutes. Repeat this process a few times until the eel is cooked and well-glazed, then remove the skewers carefully, taking care not to tear the meat. To serve; place a bed of steaming-hot cooked rice into four serving bowls, arrange 2 pieces of eels on top of each and pour the remaining sauce over the eel.

To prepare the sauce; combine all the ingredients in a saucepan and bring to a rapid boil. Lower heat and allow to simmer, stirring frequently, until the sugar has dissolved and the mixture attains a smooth, syrupy consistency. Then, remove from heat and, using a wooden ladle, agitate in an up-and-down movement for about 10 minutes.

Overleaf: **Unagi Unatama & Kakejiru**

麻布 山

CUMI-CUMI ISI
(Stuffed Squid)

1 pound fresh squid
3/4 pound snapper fillets
1 clove garlic
2 egg-whites
1/2 teaspoon salt
1/4 teaspoon white pepper
dash of nutmeg
2 shallots
2 fresh red chilies
3 candlenuts
2 stems lemon grass
oil for frying
1 cup thin coconut milk   serves 4

Wash the squid under cold running water and dry thoroughly. Remove the skin from the snapper (ensure no bones remain) and cut the meat into tiny pieces. Crush the garlic. Beat the egg-whites lightly, add the snapper and garlic and season with salt, white pepper and nutmeg. Stir to blend thoroughly, then stuff the mixture into the squid. Chop the shallots, chilies, candlenuts and lemon grass, then sauté in very hot oil for 3–4 minutes. Add the coconut milk and bring to the boil, then lower heat and add the stuffed squid. Allow to simmer until the squid is very tender, approximately 1 hour, then transfer to a serving dish and pour the sauce on top.

CUMI-CUMI PANIR
(Deep Fried Squid)

1 1/4 pounds fresh squid
2 tablespoons fresh lime juice
2 teaspoons sesame oil
2 tablespoons soy sauce
1/4 teaspoon salt
1/4 teaspoon white pepper
2 eggs
1/2 cup breadcrumbs
oil for deep frying   serves 4

Wash the squid under cold running water and dry thoroughly. Cut the squid down the center, open out into flat pieces and make criss-cross incisions in the flesh. Sprinkle on the lime juice, sesame oil and soy sauce and season with salt and white pepper, then set aside for 30 minutes. Beat the eggs lightly, pour over the squid and allow to stand for another 5 minutes, then coat with breadcrumbs. Heat the oil until it begins to smoke, then deep fry the squid until tender, about 5–6 minutes. Serve with rice and green vegetables.

DEEP FRIED CUTTLEFISH

1 1/4 pounds small cuttlefish
3 red chilies
2 cloves garlic
1 teaspoon bicarbonate of soda
4 cups vegetable oil
1/4 cup peanut oil
2 teaspoons sugar
1/4 cup tomato sauce
2 teaspoons Worcestershire sauce
salt to taste
freshly ground black pepper
lettuce leaves
1 teaspoon finely chopped parsley   serves 4

Clean the cuttlefish and remove the head and backbone. Cut the chilies into julienne strips and crush the garlic. Bring a pan of water to the boil, add the bicarbonate of soda and boil the cuttlefish for 10 minutes, then pour into a colander, drain and pat dry with a paper towel. Heat the vegetable oil in a wok until it is smoking and deep fry the cuttlefish for 2–3 minutes until the outside skin is crispy, then remove and drain off all excess oil. Clean the wok and heat the peanut oil, then add the chili and garlic and stir-fry for 3 minutes. Add the sugar, tomato sauce, Worcestershire sauce, salt and freshly ground black pepper and stir to blend thoroughly. Finally, return the cuttlefish and cook for another minute, stirring frequently. To serve; arrange crispy lettuce leaves on a serving plate, place the cuttlefish on top and garnish with finely chopped parsley.

Singapore

SOTONG AYAM
(Stuffed Cuttlefish)

8 medium size cuttlefish
1 pound cooked chicken meat
2 shallots
2 spring onions
2 fresh red chilies
1 teaspoon blachan (shrimp paste)
2 teaspoons peanut oil
2 teaspoons sugar
salt to taste
pinch monosodium glutamate
1 cup thick coconut milk
2 teaspoons sesame oil   serves 4

Clean the cuttlefish and remove the head and the backbone. Chop the chicken meat finely, season to taste and stuff into the cuttlefish. Chop the shallots, spring onions, chilies and blachan and pound these together. Heat the oil in a small pan and fry the pounded ingredients for 3 minutes, then add the sugar, salt and monosodium glutamate and stir to blend thoroughly. Add the coconut milk, bring to simmering point and stir well for another 2–3 minutes. Finally, add the stuffed cuttlefish, cover the pan and simmer over a moderate heat until fully cooked, approximately 25 minutes. Transfer to a serving plate and sprinkle hot sesame oil on top.

Thailand

PLA MUEG PAD PRIK
(Fried Squid with Hot Sauce)

2 pounds fresh squid
2 shallots
2 cloves garlic
2 fresh red chilies
2 spring onions
¼ cup vegetable oil
2 teaspoons nam pla (fish sauce)
2 teaspoons oyster sauce
¼ cup rice wine
salt to taste
freshly chopped coriander leaves
freshly ground white pepper   serves 4–6

Prepare the squid and cut into bite-size pieces. Par-boil for 3 minutes, then set aside to drain thoroughly. Chop the shallots, garlic, chilies and spring onions. Heat the oil in a pan and sauté the shallot and garlic until brown and crispy, then, add the squid, chili, spring onion, nam pla, oyster sauce and wine and season to taste with salt and freshly ground white pepper. Stir-fry over a moderate heat until the squid is fully cooked, about 5–6 minutes then add the chopped coriander leaves, stir for another minute and transfer to a serving dish. Serve with steamed rice.

Malaysia

SAUTEED CUTTLEFISH WITH OYSTER SAUCE

1 pound small fresh cuttlefish
2 small red onions
½ inch knob fresh ginger
2 cloves garlic
¼ cup vegetable oil
¼ cup oyster sauce
2 teaspoons light soy sauce
1 teaspoon dark soy sauce
2 tablespoons Chinese wine
½ teaspoon vinegar
1 teaspoon sugar
freshly ground black pepper
1 teaspoon sesame oil   serves 4

Clean the cuttlefish thoroughly, discarding the head section and the ink sac. Bring to the boil about 4 cups of water, drop in the cuttlefish and cook for 3 minutes, then remove and drain. Finely chop the red onions and ginger and crush the garlic. Heat the oil in a wok and sauté the onion, ginger and garlic for 2 minutes, then add the cuttlefish and continue to cook over medium heat for another 2 minutes, stirring frequently. Pour off most of the oil from the wok and add the oyster sauce, soy sauce, Chinese wine, vinegar, sugar, and freshly ground black pepper. Bring back to the boil, stir to dissolve the sugar and simmer for another 2 minutes, then transfer to a serving dish. Finally, heat the sesame oil and sprinkle over the cuttlefish.

RELLENONG BANGUS
(Stuffed Milkfish)

Philippines

*1 bangus (milkfish), about 1½ pounds
(or any firm white fish)
¼ cup fresh lime juice
¼ cup light soy sauce
½ teaspoon white pepper
1 brown onion
2 tomatoes
2 cloves garlic
2 tablespoons lard
¾ cup cooked peas
½ cup seedless raisins
salt to taste
freshly ground black pepper
3 eggs
½ cup all-purpose flour
oil for deep frying*

serves 2

Scale and gut the fish and wash thoroughly. Make a slit completely along the back of the fish, cut the backbone at both ends and remove all the flesh and bones. Very carefully remove all the bones from the fish and flake the meat. Soak the skin of the bangus for about 15 minutes in a mixture of the lime juice, soy sauce and white pepper, then set aside. Cut the onion and tomatoes into small dice and crush the garlic. Heat the lard in a frying pan and sauté the onion, tomato and garlic for 2–3 minutes, then add the flaked fish and season to taste with salt and freshly ground black pepper. Stir to blend thoroughly and continue to cook for another 4–5 minutes, then remove from the heat and transfer to a mixing bowl. Beat the eggs and add to the mixture together with the peas and raisins. Mix together well, then stuff the mixture into the bangus skin, secure with thread and dredge with the flour. Heat the oil until almost smoking and deep-fry the fish for 2–3 minutes until the skin is crispy and golden. Drain off all excess oil, transfer to a serving platter and garnish with sprigs of parsley, sliced cucumber and lemon wedges.

IKAN BANTUT
(Spiced Fish Wrapped in Aluminum Foil)

Malaysia

1 ikan bawal (pomfret), about 2 pounds
2 cups coconut flesh
1 fresh red chili
1 stem lemon grass
1 teaspoon salt
¼ teaspoon white pepper
1 teaspoon turmeric powder
pinch monosodium glutamate
2 fresh turmeric leaves
aluminum foil
1 teaspoon fresh lemon juice   serves 2

Clean and scale the fish, remove the backbone but leave the head and tail intact. Pound together the coconut flesh, red chili, lemon grass, salt, white pepper, turmeric powder and monosodium glutamate and rub some of the mixture into the stomach of the fish. Spread the remaining mixture over the fish and place the fresh turmeric leaves on top. Wrap completely in aluminium foil and bake in a moderate oven for approximately 30 minutes until the fish is cooked. Unwrap the fish, arrange on a serving dish and sprinkle with the fresh lemon juice. Garnish with lemon wedges and sprigs of fresh parsley.

India

FISH CURRY GOA STYLE

2 pounds fish fillets
1 teaspoon salt
¹/₂ teaspoon white pepper
2 large brown onions
2 tomatoes
3 fresh green chilies
³/₄ inch knob fresh ginger
1 clove garlic
12 dried red chilies
1 cup freshly grated coconut
¹/₄ teaspoon coriander seeds
¹/₄ teaspoon turmeric powder
¹/₂ teaspoon cumin seeds
2 tablespoons peanut oil
¹/₂ cup tamarind water
4 slices raw mango　　　serves 6

Remove the skin from the fish and cut into medium-size pieces. Season with salt and white pepper and set aside for 30 minutes. Slice the onions and tomatoes and finely chop the green chilies, ginger and garlic. Grind together the dried red chilies, grated coconut, coriander seeds and turmeric powder together with ¹/₄ cup of cold water. Then, add the cumin seeds, ginger and garlic and continue to grind until a smooth masala (spice paste) results. Heat the oil in a large saucepan and add the onion and tomato. Fry for 2 minutes, then add the masala and the tamarind water. Stir well and bring to the boil. Add the raw mango slices, lower heat and simmer for 5 minutes. Add the fish and pour in just sufficient cold water to cover the fish. Bring back to the boil, then lower heat and simmer until the fish is cooked. Remove slices of mango before serving.

Note:　This is a sour dish and it must be noted that the mango used is raw and green. If not available, omit completely but under no circumstances use a ripe fruit.

Thailand

GAENG KUA NUER
(Fish and Vegetable Curry)

1¹/₂ pounds fillets of blackfish
2 shallots
2 cloves garlic
2 fresh red chilies
2 small green chilies
¹/₄ cup vegetable oil
2 teaspoons blachan (shrimp paste)
¹/₄ pound green beans
small cauliflower
¹/₄ pound bamboo shoots
12 small fresh mushrooms
1 teaspoon nam pla (fish sauce)
salt to taste
freshly ground white pepper
fresh coriander leaves　　　serves 4–6

Grill the fish and remove the skin and all the bones. Take ¹/₄ pound of the fish and mash with a fork and cut the remainder into small bite-size pieces. Chop the shallots, garlic and chilies and sauté these in very hot oil for 2 minutes. Then, add the shrimp paste and continue to cook, stirring frequently, for another 4 minutes. Remove from the oil and combine with the mashed fish to produce a smooth spicy-paste. Cut the beans into short lengths, break the cauliflower into florets and trim the bamboo shoots. In a large saucepan, bring 2 cups of water to a rapid boil, add the prepared spice-paste and stir well. Remove any surface scum from the water, then add the vegetables, putting in first the ones that are slowest to cook. When all the vegetables are cooked, add the nam pla and season to taste with salt and freshly ground white pepper. Add the chunks of grilled fish and bring back to the boil. Lower heat and allow to simmer for another 2 minutes before transferring to a serving dish. Garnish with fresh coriander leaves.

Thailand

PLA DOOK FOO
(Deep Fried Smoked Catfish)

1 smoked catfish
½ teaspoon white pepper
oil for deep frying
2 shallots
¼ cup nam pla (fish sauce)   serves 4

Take care to remove all the bones and skin from the catfish and flake the meat. Season the fish with white pepper and place in a frying basket. Heat the oil until it begins to smoke and deep fry the fish until it is crispy and golden brown. Remove from the oil, drain well and serve on a platter covered with large leaves. Chop the shallots, mix with the nam pla and serve separately as a dip. Serve hot with a glass of icy-cold beer.

Pakistan

MACHLI CURRY
(Curried fillets of Pomfret)

1 pomfret, about 1¾ pounds
2 brown onions
2 tomatoes
2 fresh red chilies
¼ coconut
½ cup vegetable oil
1 teaspoon coriander powder
salt to taste
freshly ground white pepper   serves 4

Clean the fish, remove the skin and bones, and cut into serving-size fillets. Chop the onions, tomatoes and chilies and scrape the flesh from the coconut. Heat 2 tablespoons oil in a pan and sauté the onion until soft and golden. Remove the onion, wipe the pan clean, add another 2 tablespoons oil and fry the coconut for 3–4 minutes, stirring frequently. Place the onion, coconut, chili and coriander powder into a mortar, add a little of the oil from the pan and pound to a smooth paste. Again, clean the pan and add the remaining oil, then stir-fry the spice-paste for 5 minutes. Add ⅔ cup of cold water and bring to the boil. Add the fish, season to taste with salt and freshly ground white pepper and lower heat. Simmer until the fish is cooked, about 15–20 minutes, then add the tomato, stir to blend thoroughly, and continue to cook for another 5 minutes. Serve immediately.

Sri Lanka

FISH MUSTARD CURRY

1 pound firm white fish
2 shallots
3 cloves garlic
2 cardamom seeds
2 cloves
2 teaspoons mustard powder
2 tablespoons fresh lime juice
¼ cup oil
¼ teaspoon turmeric powder
salt to taste
½ inch cinnamon stick
⅔ cup thin coconut milk
½ cup thick coconut milk   serves 2

Cut the fish into bite-size pieces. Chop finely the shallots and garlic, crush the cardamom and cloves and blend together the mustard and lime juice. Heat the oil in a pan and sauté the shallot and garlic for 2 minutes, then add the fish, cardamom, clove, turmeric, salt, cinnamon stick and thin coconut milk and bring to the boil. Cook over a moderate heat until the liquid has reduced by half. Blend together the thick coconut milk and the mustard and pour into the pan. Bring back to the boil and cook for another 2–3 minutes, then remove the cinnamon stick and transfer to a serving dish.

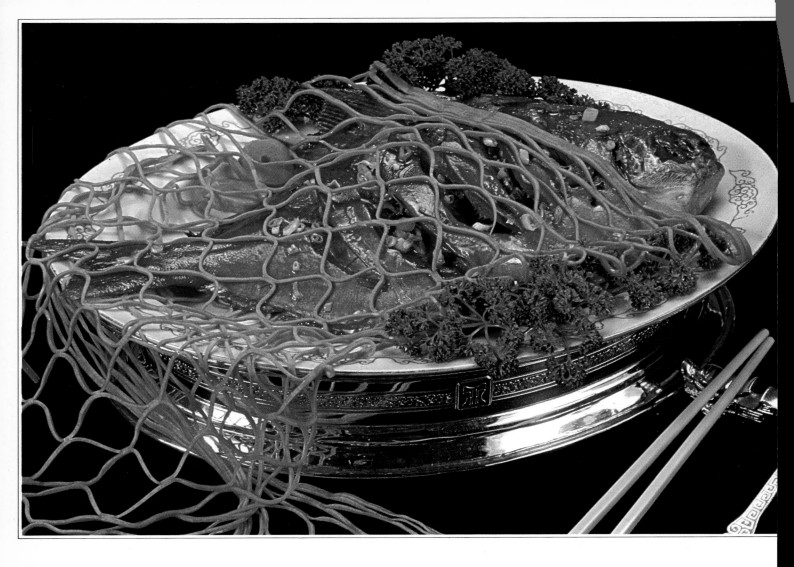

SMOKED POMFRET

Taiwan

1 whole pomfret, about 1¹/₄ pounds
1 inch knob fresh ginger
3 spring onions
2 tablespoons Chinese wine
2 tablespoons light soy sauce
pinch monosodium glutamate
1 teaspoon anise powder
1 teaspoon sugar
1¹/₂ cups rice
³/₄ cup flour
¹/₂ cup dry tea leaves (green or black)
2 teaspoons sesame oil   serves 2

Clean the fish and, with a sharp knife, score in a criss-cross fashion along both sides. Chop the ginger and spring onion very finely and mix half of this with the Chinese wine, soy sauce and monosodium glutamate. Rub the mixture into the flesh of the fish and allow to stand for 30 minutes, then place in a steamer and cook for 5 minutes. Mix together the remaining ginger and spring onion, anise powder, sugar, rice, flour and tea leaves. Place the mixture into a wok and cook over a high heat. When it starts to smoke, place the fish on a perforated rack into the wok (and above the mixture). Cover the wok with a tightly-fitting lid and smoke for approximately 2 minutes. Transfer to a serving dish, sprinkle with hot sesame oil and garnish with sprigs of Chinese parsley.

Note: The fish in the picture is decorated with a 'net' made from a large carrot. This is just one example of the fine vegetable carvings that play a major part in the presentation of Chinese food in some of the finer restaurants.

STUFFED RED SNAPPERS

Japan

4 small red snappers
½ cup sake (Japanese rice wine)
2 teaspoons salt
¾ cup tofu (bean curd)
1 carrot
3 Japanese mushrooms
2 stems spring onion
½ cup dashi (soup stock)
2 tablespoons Japanese soy sauce
2 teaspoons sugar
2 eggs
12 ginkgo nuts

For basting:
2 tablespoons Japanese soy sauce
2 tablespoons mirin
2 teaspoons sugar

serves 4

Cut the fish along the dorsal fin and remove bones. Clean thoroughly and rub the sake and salt into the cavities of the fish. Chop the bean curd, carrot, mushrooms and spring onion and place into a small saucepan. Add the dashi, soy sauce and sugar and bring to the boil. Lower heat and simmer until the vegetables are cooked, then beat the eggs and add to the stock. Continue to cook over a low heat, beating continuously, until the mixture thickens. Remove from heat and allow to cool slightly, then stuff the mixture into the fish cavities. Bake the dish in a pre-heated moderate oven for 7–8 minutes, basting occasionally with a mixture of the Japanese soy sauce, mirin and sugar. Serve garnished with ginkgo nuts.

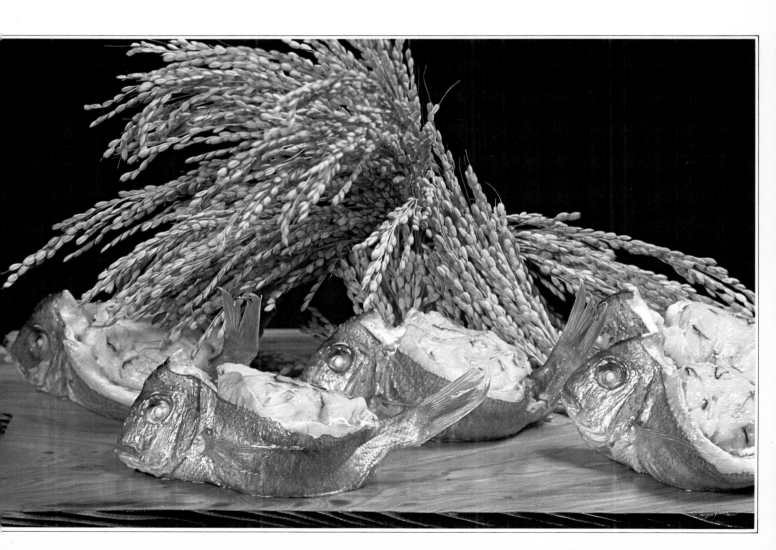

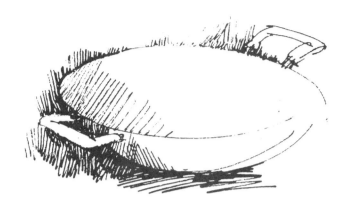

FISH HEAD CURRY

Singapore

1 large fish head
2 large brown onions
2 large tomatoes
4 fresh red chilies
2 fresh green chilies
1 inch knob fresh ginger
2 cloves garlic
1/4 cup vegetable oil
2 tablespoons curry powder
2 sprigs curry leaves
2 tablespoons tamarind water
1 2/3 cups thin coconut milk
salt to taste   serves 2

Wash the fish head under cold running water and pat dry. Slice the onions, quarter the tomatoes and finely chop the chilies, ginger and garlic. Mix the curry powder with a small quantity of cold water to form a smooth paste. Heat the oil in a large pan and fry the onion, ginger and garlic for 2–3 minutes, then add the chilies and continue to cook for another 3 minutes, stirring frequently. Next, add the curry powder and the curry leaves, cover the pan and cook over a moderate heat for 2 minutes, then remove the lid and slowly pour in the tamarind water and the coconut milk, stirring to blend thoroughly. When simmering, add the fish head and the tomatoes and season to taste with salt. Cook for 8–10 minutes over a moderate heat until the fish is completely cooked. Transfer the fish head to a serving plate and keep warm. Increase heat under the pan and reduce the sauce by one quarter, then pour this over the fish and serve immediately with plain rice.

Note: In many 'Western' kitchens the fish head is used only for stock, or indeed may often be wastefully discarded, yet here is to be found some of the tastiest meat on the fish. So even though fish fillets could simply be substituted by the unadventurous for a similar result the recipe is highly recommended in its original form.

FRIED FISH CURRY

Singapore

1 1/3 pounds pomfret or sole fillets
1/2 teaspoon red chili powder
1/2 teaspoon English mustard powder
1 teaspoon salt
1/2 teaspoon white pepper
1/4 cup fresh lime juice
1 cup all-purpose flour
4 shallots
1 inch knob fresh ginger
1 small green chili
2 cloves garlic
2/3 cup ghee
1 teaspoon curry powder
1 cup thick coconut milk   serves 4

Remove any skin from the fish, cut into bite-size pieces and place in a shallow dish. Sprinkle the chili powder, mustard, salt and white pepper over the fish and pour the lime juice on top. Set aside for 20 minutes, then coat the marinated fish with the flour. Chop the shallots, ginger and chili and crush the garlic. Heat two thirds of the ghee in a pan and fry the pieces of fish until they are golden brown, then remove from the pan and drain off excess oil. Clean the pan, add the remaining ghee and place over a high heat. When the ghee is very hot, add the shallot, ginger and garlic and sauté for 3–4 minutes, then add the green chili, curry powder and coconut milk and bring to the boil. Finally, replace the fish, lower heat, and simmer gently for 5–6 minutes.

Thailand

TOD MAN PLA
(Fried Fish Cakes with Hot Sauce)

²/₃ pound fish fillets
2 teaspoons chili paste
2 teaspoons light soy sauce
¹/₄ cup thick coconut milk
1 egg
¹/₄ cup cornstarch
salt to taste
freshly ground black pepper
¹/₄ pound long green beans
oil for frying
cucumber & tomato wedges

Hot sauce:
2 red chilies
1 clove garlic
¹/₂ inch knob fresh ginger
1 teaspoon chopped coriander root
2 tablespoons crushed roasted peanuts
25 g sugar
2 tablespoons fresh lime juice
2 tablespoons light soy sauce
¹/₄ cup chicken stock   serves 4

Broil the fish and allow to cool. Remove the skin and ensure no small bones remain, then flake the meat and place in a mixing bowl. Add the chili paste, soy sauce and coconut milk and mix well. Beat the egg lightly with the cornstarch and add to the bowl. Season with salt and freshly ground black pepper. Chop the beans into tiny pieces and add to the fish, then stir well to combine the mixture thoroughly, and shape into small patties. Heat the oil and fry the fish cakes, turning once so that they are a crispy golden-brown on both sides. Arrange on a serving dish, spoon a little sauce on top and garnish with tomato and cucumber wedges.

To make the sauce; chop the chilies, garlic and ginger into very tiny pieces and place in a mixing bowl, together with the coriander root and crushed peanuts. Dissolve the sugar in the lime juice and add to the bowl, together with the soy sauce and chicken stock. Stir to blend thoroughly and spoon over the fish patties.

Indonesia

IKAN ACAR KUNING
(Fish with Yellow Pickle Sauce)

2 small mackeral-tuna, about 1 pound each
¹/₄ cup fresh lemon juice
1 teaspoon salt
¹/₂ teaspoon white pepper
oil for deep frying

Sauce:
4 shallots
1 inch knob fresh ginger
2 cloves garlic
2 stems lemon grass
2 salem leaves (substitute curry leaves)
2 candlenuts
1 teaspoon turmeric powder
2 fresh red chilies
1 carrot
1¹/₄ inch piece cucumber
¹/₄ cup vegetable oil
2 tablespoons sugar
salt to taste
¹/₄ cup vinegar
1²/₃ cups thick coconut milk   serves 4

Clean the fish and place in a shallow dish. Sprinkle the lemon juice on top, season with salt and freshly ground white pepper and set aside in the refrigerator for 1 hour. Heat the oil until almost smoking and deep-fry the fish, then remove, drain off excess oil, and arrange on a serving plate. Pour the prepared sauce over the fish and serve immediately.

To prepare the sauce; chop the shallots and ginger and crush the garlic. Chop the lemon grass, salem leaves and candlenuts and place in a mortar together with the turmeric powder and 2 tablespoons of cold water. Pound to produce a thick paste. Cut the chilies, carrot and cucumber into julienne strips. Heat the oil in a pan and sauté the shallot, ginger and garlic for 3 minutes, then add the spice-paste and cook for another 3 minutes, stirring continuously. Add the sugar and salt, pour in the vinegar and coconut milk and stir to blend thoroughly. Bring to the boil, then lower heat and simmer for 10 minutes. Finally, add the vegetable julienne, stir well and continue to simmer for another 5 minutes.

DEEP FRIED FISH WITH SWEET & SOUR SAUCE

Hong Kong

1 pomfret, about 1¹/₄ pounds
¹/₂ teaspoon salt
¹/₂ teaspoon black pepper
2 eggs
2 tablespoons cornstarch
1 brown onion
1 green pepper
2 fresh red chilies
¹/₂ inch knob fresh ginger
1 clove garlic
oil for deep frying
2 tablespoons Chinese wine
2 tablespoons light soy sauce
2 tablespoons vinegar
¹/₃ cup fish stock
¹/₄ cup sugar
³/₄ cup canned pineapple chunks   serves 2

Scale and clean the fish but do not remove the head or tail. With a sharp knife score the skin in about six places and rub in the salt and black pepper. Beat the eggs and mix with three-quarters of the cornstarch. Pour the mixture over the fish and set on one side for 20 minutes. Chop the onion, green pepper, chilies, ginger and garlic. Heat the oil in a wok until it starts to smoke, then deep-fry the fish for 6–8 minutes, until it is cooked and the skin is golden and crispy. Remove the fish from the pan, drain off excess oil and keep warm. Pour away most of the oil from the wok, add the onion, green pepper, chili, ginger and garlic and sauté for 3–4 minutes, then add the Chinese wine, soy sauce, vinegar and sugar, adjust seasonings to taste and stir until the sugar has completely dissolved. Then, add the pieces of pineapple and simmer gently for another 2 minutes. Finally, mix the remaining cornstarch with a small quantity of cold water, add to the sauce and stir to thicken slightly. To serve; arrange the fish on a serving plate and pour the sauce on top.

WEST LAKE FISH

Hong Kong

1 whole freshwater fish, about 1³/₄ pounds
3 spring onions
2 small brown onions
1 red pepper
1 green pepper
1 inch knob fresh ginger
2 cloves garlic
3 lettuce leaves
¹/₄ cup vegetable oil
2 tablespoons Chinese wine
¹/₂ teaspoon salt
¹/₄ teaspoon white pepper
pinch monosodium glutamate
1 teaspoon sesame oil
2 tablespoons vinegar
2 tablespoons tomato sauce
¹/₄ cup sugar
1 tablespoon cornstarch   serves 4

Clean and scale the fish, leaving the head and tail intact. Chop the spring onions, brown onions, red and green peppers and ginger. Crush the garlic and shred the lettuce leaves. Heat half the vegetable oil in a wok and stir-fry the spring onion, pepper, ginger and garlic for 3–4 minutes, then add the Chinese wine, salt, white pepper, monosodium glutamate, sesame oil and 4 cups of water, and bring to the boil. Place the fish in the boiling liquid, cover the wok with a tight-fitting lid and remove from the heat. Allow to stand for 15 minutes, then transfer the fish and vegetables to a serving plate. Heat the remaining oil in a fresh pan, add the brown onion and sauté for 3–4 minutes, then add the vinegar and tomato sauce. Mix the cornstarch with a small quantity of cold water and add to the pan, together with the lettuce. Stir well, cook for another minute, then spoon over the fish.

Malaysia

GULAI IKAN

1 whole pomfret, about 1¼ pounds
2 brown onions
4 shallots
6 fresh red chilies
½ inch knob fresh ginger
½ knob fresh galangal (optional)
2 cloves garlic
2 stems lemon grass
¼ cup vegetable oil
½ teaspoon cumin powder
½ teaspoon coriander powder
½ teaspoon turmeric powder
2 cups thin coconut milk
2 tablespoons fresh lime juice
salt to taste
freshly ground black pepper   serves 4

Prepare the fish for cooking but leave whole. Finely chop the brown onions, shallots, chilies, ginger, galangal, garlic and lemon grass, then grind these to a fine paste. Heat the oil in a pan and fry the spice-paste for 5 minutes, stirring frequently. Add the cumin, coriander and turmeric and pour in the coconut milk. Bring to the boil, stir well and simmer for 5 minutes. Add the fish, pour in the lime juice and season to taste with salt and freshly ground black pepper. Allow to simmer until the fish is cooked, about 6–8 minutes. Remove the fish, cut into serving-size pieces and arrange in a serving dish. Boil the sauce rapidly for another minute then pour over the fish.

Singapore

STEAMED GAROUPA WITH GINGER

1 whole garoupa, about 1¼ pounds
½ teaspoon salt
¼ teaspoon white pepper
¾ inch knob fresh ginger
3 spring onions
2 tablespoons light soy sauce
2 tablespoons peanut oil   serves 2

Clean and scale the fish but do not remove the head or tail. With a sharp knife, make an incision along the underside and remove the backbone. Season the fish with salt and white pepper and set aside for 30 minutes. Chop the ginger and spring onions very finely, mix with the soy sauce and stuff into the prepared pocket of the fish. Place on a steamer rack. Heat the peanut oil and pour over the fish, then place the rack over boiling water, cover and cook for approximately 20 minutes.

Korea

SAENGSON CHIM
(Fish & Vegetable Stew)

1 pound fish fillets
4 large white mushrooms
4 carrots
1 large brown onion
1 small red pepper
1 inch knob fresh ginger
2 spring onions
2 ounces lean beef
2 tablespoons sugar
2 teaspoons sesame seeds
freshly ground black pepper
2 tablespoons sesame oil
⅓ cup light soy sauce
2 teaspoons chopped chives
⅓ cup chicken stock   serves 4–6

Remove the skin from the fish and make sure no bones remain. Slice the mushrooms, carrots, and brown onion. Cut the red pepper and ginger into julienne strips. Chop the garlic and spring onions finely and mince the beef. Mix together the beef, garlic, spring onions, sugar, sesame seeds, freshly ground black pepper, sesame oil and one third of the soy sauce. Place this mixture in the bottom of a pan or casserole, then place a layer of sliced vegetables on top and after that a layer of fish fillets. Sprinkle the chopped chives over the fish, then cover with the remaining sliced vegetables and the julienne of red pepper and ginger. Add the remaining soy sauce and the stock and cook over a low heat until cooked, approximately 30 minutes.

Hong Kong

DEEP FRIED GAROUPA

1 pound fillets of garoupa
2 spring onions
1/2 inch knob fresh ginger
1/4 cup Chinese wine
1 teaspoon sesame oil
1 teaspoon sugar
1/2 teaspoon salt
1/4 teaspoon white pepper
pinch monosodium glutamate
2 eggs
1 1/4 cups all-purpose flour
1 teaspoon baking soda
oil for deep frying   serves 4

Make certain the fillets are completely free of bones, then cut into pieces, about 2 in. x 1 in. and place in a shallow dish. Chop the spring onions and ginger very finely, mix with the Chinese wine, sesame oil, sugar, salt, white pepper and monosodium glutamate and pour over the fish, then set aside for 30 minutes. Break the eggs into a mixing bowl, add the flour, baking soda and sufficient cold water to make a thin, smooth batter. Heat the oil in a wok until it begins to smoke. Remove the fish from the marinade, coat with the batter and deep-fry until the outside is golden and crispy. Serve with green vegetables.

Sri Lanka

MIRIS MALU
(Sour Spicy Fish)

1 pound fish fillets
1/2 teaspoon salt
1/4 teaspoon white pepper
1/4 teaspoon turmeric powder
1/2 inch knob fresh ginger
2 cloves garlic
2 teaspoons chopped tamarind
1/4 cup vinegar
1 teaspoon chili powder
1 teaspoon paprika
3/4 inch cinnamon stick
6–8 curry leaves   serves 4

Cut the fish into bite-size pieces, season with salt, pepper and turmeric powder and set aside for 20 minutes. Chop the ginger very finely and crush the garlic. Combine the vinegar with an equal quantity of warm water and soak the tamarind for a few minutes, then strain the liquid through a fine sieve and discard the pulp. Place the fish in a saucepan, pour in sufficient water to barely cover, then add the ginger, garlic, chili powder, paprika, cinnamon stick, curry leaves and tamarind water. Bring to the boil, then cover the pan, lower heat and simmer for 5–6 minutes. Remove the lid, adjust seasonings to taste and continue to simmer until the fish is cooked, then remove the cinnamon stick and curry leaves and transfer to a serving dish.

Thailand

PLA PAD KING
(Sea Bass with Fresh Ginger)

3/4 pound fillets of white sea bass
1 inch knob fresh ginger
2 fresh red chilies
2 fresh green chilies
2 cloves garlic
2 spring onions
4 dried black mushrooms
1/2 cup vegetable oil
3 tablespoons preserved yellow peas
2 tablespoons nam pla (fish sauce)
2 teaspoons sugar
freshly ground white pepper
sprigs of fresh coriander   serves 4

Cut the fish into thick slices. Slice the ginger, cut the chilies into fine julienne strips, chop the garlic and cut the spring onions into 1/2 inch lengths. Soak the mushrooms in warm water for 40 minutes, then discard the hard stems and slice the caps. Heat the oil in a large frying pan and sauté the ginger and garlic for 3–4 minutes, then add the fish, mushrooms and preserved peas and retain over a medium heat until the fish is almost cooked, stirring occasionally. Add the chilies, spring onion, nam pla, sugar and freshly ground white pepper and stir to blend thoroughly. Continue to cook for another 2 minutes, then transfer to a serving dish and garnish with sprigs of fresh coriander.

STEAMED POMFRET ROLLS

1 pomfret, about 1¹/₄ pounds
¹/₂ teaspoon salt
¹/₄ teaspoon white pepper
4 ounces cooked ham
³/₄ inch knob fresh ginger
4 spring onions
fresh coriander leaves
1 teaspoon peanut oil   serves 4

Scale and clean the fish. Carefully remove the fillets and extract all the small bones but leave the backbone, head and tail intact. Slice the fillets of fish into 1¹/₂ in. lengths, flatten slightly with the side of a knife and season with salt and white pepper. Cut the ham, ginger and 3 of the spring onions into julienne strips and chop the remaining spring onion and the fresh coriander leaves. Next, place one strip each of ham, ginger and spring onion on top of each fish fillet and roll up leaving a little of the stuffing showing at both ends. When all the rolls have been completed arrange them attractively on the carcass of the pomfret and sprinkle the peanut oil on top. Place the fish in a steamer and cook over a medium heat for 7–8 minutes. When cooked transfer to a serving dish and garnish with the chopped spring onion and coriander.

STEAMED GAROUPA WITH HAM & VEGETABLES

Hong Kong

2 pounds garoupa fillets
12 dried Chinese mushrooms
¼ pound sliced Chinese ham
4 spring onions
⅓ cup vegetable oil
12 small pieces Chinese kale (broccoli)
¼ teaspoon salt
2 teaspoons crushed ginger
2 tablespoons Chinese wine
½ cup chicken stock
2 teaspoons sesame oil
freshly ground black pepper   serves 4–6

Cut the fish diagonally into thin slices. Soak the mushrooms in warm water for 40 minutes, then discard the hard stems and cut the caps in half. Slice the spring onions and place on the bottom of a large oven-proof plate. On top, arrange alternate slices of fish, ham and mushrooms. Set the plate on a bamboo rack, place in a steamer and cook over boiling water for approximately 12 minutes. Meanwhile, heat half the oil in a wok, add the kale and stir-fry for 1 minute, then add salt, pour in ½ cup of water and bring to the boil. Cook for another 3–4 minutes, then remove kale and keep warm. Heat the remaining oil in a fresh wok, add the crushed ginger and sauté for 2 minutes, then add the Chinese wine, chicken stock, sesame oil and black pepper and bring to the boil. Stir well and cook for another 2 minutes. To serve; arrange the kale on the plate with the fish, ham and mushrooms and pour the sauce on top.

Hong Kong

SLICED FISH IN WINE SAUCE

1¼ pounds fresh fish (bream, sole or bass)
freshly ground black pepper
salt to taste
pinch monosodium glutamate
1 egg
1 tablespoon cornstarch
6 dried Chinese mushrooms*
vegetable oil for deep frying
2 tablespoons Chinese wine
2 teaspoons light soy sauce
1 teaspoon dark soy sauce
1 teaspoon sugar
½ cup fish stock
1 teaspoon sesame oil   serves 4–6

Clean and fillet the fish and cut into slices. Season with freshly ground black pepper, salt to taste and monosodium glutamate. Beat the egg, mix with half the cornstarch and pour over the fish. Place in a refrigerator and leave for 30 minutes. Soak the Chinese mushrooms in warm water for 40 minutes, remove and discard the hard stems, and cut the caps into quarters. Heat the oil in a wok and fry the fish until it is half cooked, approximately 3 minutes. Remove the fish from the pan and drain thoroughly. Pour off most of the oil from the pan, add the Chinese wine, soy sauce and sugar, replace the fish and cook over a low heat for another 2–3 minutes. Mix the remaining cornstarch with the cold stock and pour into the pan. Bring to the boil and simmer until the sauce thickens slightly and becomes translucent, then transfer to a serving dish. Heat the sesame oil and sprinkle over the fish immediately prior to serving.

*Note: The original of this recipe called for the use of a dried Chinese fungus but as this may not be readily available dried mushrooms have been substituted.

Korea

SAENGSON CHUN
(Fried Fish Fillets)

1 pound white fish fillets
2 spring onions
½ inch knob fresh ginger
2 teaspoons roasted sesame seeds
10 black peppercorns
2 teaspoons sesame oil
¼ cup light soy sauce
vegetable oil for shallow frying   serves 4

Remove the skin from the fillets and slice into medium-size pieces. Chop the spring onion and ginger very finely and crush the sesame seeds and peppercorns. Mix these together with the sesame oil and soy sauce and pour over the fish. Set aside for 5 minutes then coat the fish with flour. Heat the oil in an iron pan and fry the fish until it is fully cooked and the skin is golden and crispy.

Indonesia

IKAN ASAM PADEH
(Fish in Sour Sauce)

1½ pounds fish fillets
2 shallots
1 inch knob fresh ginger
2 cloves garlic
2 fresh red chilies
½ teaspoon turmeric powder
½ teaspoon tamarind
2 tablespoons dark soy sauce
2 tablespoons vegetable oil
salt to taste
freshly ground black pepper   serves 4

Remove all skin from the fish fillets, ensure that no bones remain and cut into serving-size pieces. Chop, very finely, the shallots, ginger, garlic and chilies and pound these together with the turmeric powder, tamarind and soy sauce. Heat the oil in a shallow pan and stir-fry the spice-paste for 4–5 minutes, then add the fish, cover with approximately 1 cup of cold water and bring to the boil. Lower heat, season to taste with salt and freshly ground black pepper and cook over a very low heat. Serve with fresh vegetables and rice.

Philippines

KINULOT
(Shark Meat with Coconut Milk)

*1 pound baby shark-meat
2 brown onions
3/4 inch knob fresh ginger
2 cloves garlic
1 cup thick coconut milk
salt to taste
freshly ground black pepper
10 malunggay (horseradish) leaves* serves 4

Place the shark-meat in a saucepan and cover with cold water. Bring to the boil and cook until the meat is tender, then remove, drain thoroughly and cut into small slices. Slice the onions and the ginger and crush the garlic and place together in an earthenware pot. Pour the coconut milk on top of the vegetables, bring to the boil and season to taste with salt and freshly ground black pepper. Boil until the mixture becomes oily, then lower the heat, add the shark meat and simmer for 6 minutes. Add the leaves to the pan, stir well and continue to simmer for another minute, or more, but remove from heat before the leaves start to lose their bright green color.

Singapore

FRIED POMFRET WITH VEGETABLES

*1 1/4 pounds pomfret fillets
1/2 teaspoon salt
1/4 teaspoon white pepper
vegetable oil for deep frying
1/4 pound Chinese cabbage
1/2 cup carrots
1/2 cup canned golden mushrooms
1/2 cup canned bamboo shoot
2 cloves garlic
2 tablespoons peanut oil
2 tablespoons light soy sauce
2 tablespoons oyster sauce
2 tablespoons sugar
2 teaspoons cornstarch* serves 4

Make sure the fillets are completely free of bones, then season with salt and white pepper. Heat the oil in a wok and deep fry the fish until cooked, then remove, drain and set aside. Shred the cabbage and carrots, cook for 3–4 minutes in boiling water, drain and set aside. Shred the mushrooms and bamboo shoot and crush the garlic. Heat the peanut oil in a pan and sauté the garlic for 3–4 minutes, then add the vegetables and cook for another 2 minutes, stirring frequently. Add the soy sauce, oyster sauce and sugar and pour in 1/2 cup of cold water. Bring to the boil, add the fish and cook for 1 minute. Mix the cornstarch with a small quantity of cold water and stir into the sauce to thicken and serve immediately.

Malaysia

ACHAR IKAN
(Deep Fried Snapper with Vegetables)

*1 pound snapper fillets
1 teaspoon salt
1 teaspoon turmeric powder
1 cucumber
1 large brown onion
1 inch knob fresh ginger
2 cloves garlic
6 fresh red chilies
4 fresh green chilies
oil for deep frying
1/2 cup vinegar
2 tablespoons sugar* serves 4

Cut the fish into serving-size pieces and season with salt and half the turmeric. Slice the cucumber and onion, chop the ginger and garlic and cut the chilies, lengthways, into narrow strips. Heat the oil in a large pan and deep fry the fish, then remove, drain thoroughly and place in a serving dish. Pour most of the oil from the pan and add the cucumber, onion, ginger, garlic and chilies. Stir-fry for 2–3 minutes, then add the remaining turmeric powder and cook for another minute. Pour in the vinegar and bring to the boil, then add sugar and adjust seasonings to taste. Lower heat, allow to simmer for 5 minutes, then pour over the fish and serve immediately.

Poultry

Excluding rice (the cornerstone of most Asian meals), chicken must surely be the most popular source of food throughout the region. Like fish, it carries no major religious taboos and has the advantage of being plentiful, easy to raise and therefore, generally speaking, cheaper to purchase. And extra economy results from the fact that almost every part is edible, even the feet which are served in a variety of ways in South East Asian countries, and the skin which is used as a main ingredient in one form of the Japanese **Yakitori** (page 122). A whole chicken can be cooked as a 'special occasion' dish, such as **Beggar's Chicken** (pages 93 and 95) or just a few pieces can be used as a nutritious addition to a low priced meal of soup or noodles. And, because the meat is fairly bland it's ideal for preparing with a wide variety of marinades, spices and sauces.

However, the ubiquitous chicken must take second place to the duck when it comes to providing perhaps the best known of all Asian dishes: **Peking Duck** (page 114) can be a meal in itself with the first course being slices of the crispy skin (carved at the tableside in a ritualistic manner by the chef) and wrapped in pancakes, followed by the meat and finally a soup made from the carcass and bones. Pigeon and goose are also popular but their richer and stronger flavors make them less suitable for cooking with spices or 'hot' sauces. Game birds are served in Asian restaurants and sold in the local markets but they are not generally regarded as highly as in the West.

Kari Kering Hati Ayam *Dried chicken liver curry*	**Rellenong Manok** *Whole stuffed chicken*	**Chicken Biriyani**
Rendang Pedas Hati Ayam *Chicken liver & heart curry*	**Ayam Bumbu Rujak** *Spiced chicken in coconut milk*	**Chicken Badun**
Chicken Livers Baked in Salt	**Chicken Vindaloo**	**Baked Stuffed Pigeons**
Beggar's Chicken	**Chicken Almond Curry**	**Minced Pigeon in Lettuce Leaves**
Paper Wrapped Chicken	**Korma Ayam**	**Pigeons Baked in Salt**
Tom Kem Gai *Chicken casserole*	**Gaeng Phed Gai** *Curried chicken*	**Steamed Pigeon in Bamboo Cups**
Ayam Golek *Chicken in spiced coconut sauce*	**Drunken Chicken** *Marinated in Chinese wine*	**Sliced Pigeon with Bamboo Shoots**
Ayam Bakakak Bumbu Bali *Balinese style barbecued chicken*	**Chicken Jalfrazi** *Spicy chicken with tomatoes*	**Hin's Smoked Duck**
Chicken & Cashew Nuts in Yam Ring	**Chicken with Dried Red Chilies**	**Duck in Lemon Sauce**
Almond Chicken with Pineapple Sauce	**Hainanese Chicken Rice**	**Peking Duck**
Chicken Adobo	**Khaukswe** *Spicy sautéed chicken with noodles*	**Itek Bersantan** *Duckling in coconut milk*
		Bebek Betutu *Steamed stuffed duckling*
		Gaeng Phed *Duck & vegetables*

KARI KERING HATI AYAM
(Dried Chicken Liver Curry)

1 pound chicken livers
2 shallots
1 inch knob fresh ginger
2 cloves ginger
1/4 cup vegetable oil
2 cloves
1 inch stick cinnamon
1 teaspoon anise powder
1 teaspoon cumin powder
1 teaspoon white pepper
salt to taste
1 cup thick coconut milk   serves 4

Wash the chicken livers. Chop the shallots, ginger and garlic. Heat the oil in a pan, add the shallot, ginger and garlic and stir-fry for 3 minutes, then add the cloves, cinnamon stick, spice powders and salt to taste and continue to cook over a fairly high heat for another 3 minutes. Add the chicken livers, lower heat slightly and cook until the livers are tender, approximately 20 minutes. Pour in the coconut milk, increase heat and boil until the liquid has been completely absorbed. Remove the cloves and cinnamon stick before serving.

Malaysia

RENDANG PEDAS HATI AYAM
(Chicken Liver & Heart Curry)

3/4 pound chicken livers
1/2 pound chicken heart
2 brown onions
1 small cucumber
3 cloves garlic
4 fresh red chilies
1 inch knob fresh ginger
2 stems lemon grass
2 teaspoons curry powder
1 teaspoon turmeric powder
10 black peppercorns
2 tablespoons tamarind water
1/4 cup coconut oil
3 basil leaves
salt to taste   serves 4–6

Clean the livers and heart and chop into small pieces. Chop the onion, cucumber and garlic. Chop the chilies, ginger and lemon grass, then pound together with the curry powder, turmeric powder, peppercorns and tamarind water to form a smooth paste. Heat the coconut oil and sauté the onion and garlic for 3 minutes. Add the spice-paste and cook for 5 minutes, stirring frequently, then add the liver, heart, cucumber and basil leaves and pour in the coconut milk. Season to taste with salt. Bring to the boil, then lower heat and simmer for 35 minutes. Remove basil leaves before serving.

Hong Kong

CHICKEN LIVERS BAKED IN SALT

1 pound chicken livers
1 small brown onion
2 spring onions
1/2 inch knob fresh ginger
2 cloves garlic
1/4 cup Chinese wine
2 tablespoons dark soy sauce
1 teaspoon sugar
salt to taste
1/4 teaspoon white pepper
2 pounds rock salt   serves 4

Wash and trim the chicken livers and dry thoroughly. Chop finely the brown onion, spring onion and ginger and crush the garlic. Combine these with the Chinese wine, soy sauce, sugar, salt and white pepper and sprinkle over the livers. Set aside for 30 minutes. Heat the rock salt until it is very hot, then spread a 3/4 inch layer in the bottom of a wok. Arrange the livers on top and cover with the remaining hot salt. Place a tightly fitting lid on the wok and bake for 15–20 minutes.

Note: If personal preference dictates a longer cooking period, re-heat the salt before proceeding.

Taiwan

BEGGAR'S CHICKEN

1 fresh chicken, about 3 pounds
1 teaspoon salt
6 dried Chinese mushrooms
1/4 pound fat pork
3/4 cup pickled cabbage
3/4 cup beetroot
1 large brown onion
1 spring onion
1/2 inch knob fresh ginger
2 tablespoons light soy sauce
2 tablespoons Chinese wine
1 teaspoon sesame oil
1 teaspoon sugar
freshly ground black pepper
lotus leaves* (optional)
1 pound pastry dough*   serves 4–6

Clean and prepare the chicken and rub inside and out with the salt. Soak the mushrooms in warm water for 40 minutes, then drain, discard the hard stems and shred the caps finely. Dice the pork, shred the cabbage and beetroot and chop the onions and ginger. Fry the pork in a wok until it starts to become crispy, then add the mushroom, cabbage, beetroot, onion and ginger. Season with soy sauce, Chinese wine, sesame oil, sugar and freshly ground black pepper and stir over medium heat for 3–4 minutes. Remove mixture from the wok, drain off any excess oil and stuff inside the chicken. Wrap the stuffed chicken in lotus leaves and completely seal with the pastry dough. Bake in a very hot oven for 1½ hours, then reduce heat and continue cooking for another 45 minutes. To serve break away the pastry and remove the lotus leaves.

*Note: Traditionally the chicken is enclosed in clay rather than pastry but the latter is simpler and more usually acceptable for the domestic kitchen. Also note that if lotus leaves are not readily available they may be omitted when using pastry although this will most certainly result in some loss of the original flavor.

Singapore

PAPER WRAPPED CHICKEN

1 fresh chicken, about 3 pounds, with liver and gizzard
1 inch knob fresh ginger
3 spring onions
2 cloves garlic
2 tablespoons Chinese wine
2 tablespoons light soy sauce
2 tablespoons oyster sauce
1 teaspoon sesame oil
1 teaspoon sugar
salt to taste
freshly ground white pepper
pinch monosodium glutamate
oil for deep frying   serves 4–6

Prepare and de-bone the chicken and cut into bite-size pieces. Chop finely the liver and gizzard. Chop the ginger and spring onion and crush the garlic. Place all the above in a shallow dish and add the Chinese wine, soy sauce, oyster sauce, sesame oil, sugar, salt, pepper and monosodium glutamate. Set in the refrigerator and allow to marinate for 1 hour, occasionally turning the pieces of chicken. Cut out squares of greaseproof paper and place a piece of chicken in the center of each. Wrap up like an envelope, folding in the end flap to secure completely. Heat the oil in a wok and when it begins to smoke, add the chicken-parcels and deep-fry for 5–7 minutes, stirring frequently with a slotted spoon. To serve; drain off excess oil and transfer to a serving plate (the chicken should remain wrapped until the last minute before eating).

TOM KEM GAI
(Chicken Casserole)

Thailand

8 chicken legs
4 dried Chinese mushrooms
1 small brown onion
1 clove garlic
½ inch knob fresh ginger
½ teaspoon chopped coriander root
½ teaspoon salt
½ teaspoon black pepper
¼ cup vegetable oil
¼ cup brown sugar
2 tablespoons light soy sauce
4 hard boiled eggs   serves 4

Remove the skin from the chicken legs. Soak the mushrooms in warm water for 40 minutes and discard the hard stems. Chop the onion, garlic and ginger and pound together with the coriander root, salt and pepper. Heat the oil in a large casserole dish and cook the spice-paste for 5 minutes to give flavor to the oil. Then, discard the spice-paste leaving only the oil. Add the sugar and cook over a low heat, stirring continuously, until the mixture becomes syrupy. Add the soy sauce, together with 1 cup of cold water and bring to the boil, then add the chicken legs and the mushrooms and place a cover on the dish. Lower heat and simmer for 30–45 minutes, then add the hard boiled eggs and continue to cook slowly for another 3 minutes. Serve with steamed rice.

AYAM GOLEK
(Chicken in Spiced Coconut Sauce)

Malaysia

1 chicken, about 3 pounds
1 teaspoon salt
½ teaspoon white pepper
oil for deep frying
2 teaspoons cumin seeds
2 teaspoons anise seeds
10 candlenuts
4 tomatoes
2 shallots
2 spring onions
2 stalks celery
¼ cup ghee
¼ cup vinegar
⅔ cup thick coconut milk

serves 4–6

Prepare the chicken, rub the salt and white pepper over the outside and inside and allow to stand for 1 hour. Heat the oil in a large pan until it starts to smoke, then deep-fry the chicken for 4–5 minutes, until the skin is golden. Remove the chicken and drain off excess oil. Finely chop the tomatoes, shallots, spring onions and celery and grind together the cumin seeds, anise seeds and candlenuts. Heat the ghee in a pot and stir-fry the ground spices for 2 minutes, then add the chopped vegetables and cook slowly for another 3 minutes, stirring frequently. Add the vinegar and coconut milk, adjust seasonings to taste and bring to the boil. Stir well until the mixture starts to thicken, then lower heat, add the chicken and cook slowly for approximately 1¼ hours, until the chicken is tender and most of the liquid has been absorbed.

97

Indonesia

AYAM BAKAKAK BUMBU BALI
(Balinese Style Barbecued Chicken)

4 small spring chickens
1 teaspoon salt
freshly ground black pepper
¼ cup tamarind water
¼ cup coconut oil
2 shallots, thinly sliced

Sauce:
1 large brown onion
2 large tomatoes
3 cloves garlic
2 fresh red chilies
¾ inch knob fresh ginger
2 stems lemon grass
1 teaspoon coriander powder
2 tablespoons sweet soy sauce
1 teaspoon blachan (shrimp paste)
1 teaspoon chopped dried lemon peel
¼ cup vegetable oil
2 cups chicken stock
salt to taste
freshly ground black pepper   serves 4

Slit the chickens from the underside but do not cut through the backbone. Flatten out and place on brochettes. Season with salt, freshly ground black pepper and tamarind water and set aside for 20 minutes. Coat lightly with coconut oil, then cook over a charcoal fire, basting occasionally with the prepared sauce. When the chickens are cooked, transfer to a serving dish and pour the remaining sauce on top. Garnish with slices of raw shallots.

To make the sauce; chop the onion, tomato and garlic very finely. Chop the chilies, ginger and lemon grass and place into a stone mortar. Add the coriander powder, soy sauce, blachan and dried lemon peel and pound to produce a smooth paste. Heat the oil and sauté the onion and garlic for 3 minutes, then add the tomato and the spice-paste and cook for another 3 minutes, stirring frequently. Pour in the stock, season to taste with salt and freshly ground black pepper and bring to the boil. Boil rapidly for 5 minutes, then lower heat and allow to simmer until the sauce becomes quite thick.

Malaysia

CHICKEN & CASHEW NUTS IN YAM RING

1 pound chicken meat
½ inch knob fresh ginger
2 fresh red chilies
¼ teaspoon baking powder
2 tablespoons Chinese wine
2 tablespoons light soy sauce
salt to taste
freshly ground black pepper
pinch monosodium glutamate
½ pound yams
2 teaspoons sugar
oil for deep frying
finely chopped coriander leaves
¾ cup shelled cashew nuts   serves 4–6

Cut the chicken into small pieces and chop finely the ginger and chilies. Place the chicken, ginger and chilies in a dish, add the baking powder, Chinese wine, soy sauce, salt, freshly ground black pepper and monosodium glutamate and set aside for 15 minutes. Peel the yam, cut into small cubes and cook in a double boiler over rapidly-boiling water until soft then add the sugar and mash with a wooden spoon. Roll out and shape into a ring approximately 8 inches in diameter, then place on rack and set aside. Next, heat a small quantity of the oil in a wok, add the chicken and all the marinade and stir-fry for 3–4 minutes. Add the cashew nuts and continue to cook over medium heat, stirring frequently, until the chicken is tender, then remove and set aside. Add the remaining oil to the wok, bring to the boil and deep-fry the yam ring for a few minutes, until it is golden and crispy. Then, remove, drain off excess oil and place on a serving dish. Fill the center of the ring with the chicken and cashew nuts and garnish with finely chopped coriander leaves.

Singapore

ALMOND CHICKEN WITH PINEAPPLE SAUCE

4 chicken breasts
4 chicken thighs
2 eggs
1 teaspoon salt
1/2 teaspoon white pepper
2 teaspoons light soy sauce
2 teaspoons Chinese wine
4 tablespoons cornstarch
1/2 pound almonds
oil for deep frying

Sauce:
13/4 cups chicken stock
1/2 cup canned pineapple juice
1 teaspoon honey
4 ounces canned pineapple chunks
1 teaspoon sugar
1/4 teaspoon salt   serves 6

De-bone the pieces of chicken and flatten with a knife. Beat the eggs, add the salt, white pepper, soy sauce, Chinese wine and 2 tablespoons cornstarch and mix thoroughly. Marinate the chicken in the mixture for 30 minutes. Shell the almonds and chop coarsely. Remove the chicken from the marinade and place, skin downwards, on a flat surface. Sprinkle the chopped almonds on top and with the hands press firmly into the flesh of the chicken, then coat with the remaining cornstarch. Heat the oil in a wok and deep fry the chicken until cooked and golden, then remove and drain off all excess oil. To serve; cut the chicken into bite-size pieces, arrange on a large plate and pour the pineapple sauce on top.

To make the sauce; bring the stock to the boil, reduce slightly, then add all the other ingredients and stir to blend. Simmer over a low heat for 2 minutes before serving.

Philippines

CHICKEN ADOBO

1 fresh chicken, about 21/2 pounds
4 chicken livers
3/4 cup vinegar
2 tablespoons light soy sauce
2 teaspoons dark soy sauce
2 shallots
4 cloves garlic
1 bay leaf
salt to taste
freshly ground black pepper
13/4 cups chicken stock
1/2 cup vegetable oil   serves 4–6

Clean and prepare the chicken and cut into bite-size pieces. Wash the chicken livers and cut into thin slices. Place both into a saucepan, add the vinegar and soy sauce and set aside for 20 minutes. Then, chop the shallots very finely and crush the garlic and add these to the pan, together with the bay leaf, salt and freshly ground pepper. Pour in the stock, stir to blend thoroughly and bring to the boil. Lower heat and allow to simmer until the chicken is half cooked (approximately 15 minutes), then pour the liquid through a strainer into a fresh pan. Heat the oil in a frying pan and cook the chicken for 3–4 minutes until the outside is golden. Replace the chicken in the stock and bring back to the boil. Adjust seasonings to taste, place a lid on the pan, lower heat and allow to cook slowly until the chicken is tender. Finally, remove the lid, increase the heat to very high and boil until most of the liquid has evaporated then remove the bay leaf and transfer to a serving dish. Serve immediately with plain rice or allow to cool and serve with a mixed salad.

RELLENONG MANOK
(Whole Stuffed Chicken)

Philippines

1 chicken, about 3 pounds
1 teaspoon salt
1/2 teaspoon white pepper
1/4 cup fresh lime juice
margarine

Stuffing:
1 pound pork meat
1/4 pound chorizo sausage
1/4 pound cooked ham
1/4 pound Edam cheese
3 brown onions
1 red pepper
1/2 cup sweet-pickle relish
1 cup cooked peas
1/2 cup seedless raisins
salt to taste
freshly ground black pepper
pinch monosodium glutamate
4 eggs

serves 6–8

Clean and prepare the chicken and de-bone carefully. Season inside and out with the salt and white pepper and pour the lime juice over the chicken. Allow to stand for at least 30 minutes, then fill the cavity with the prepared stuffing and secure openings with thread. Wrap thin strips of aluminum foil around the chicken in order to maintain the shape. Cover the chicken evenly with the margarine, place in a baking dish and cook in a pre-heated moderate oven until tender, approximately 1 1/4 hours. Serve hot with vegetables or cold with a fresh salad.

To make the stuffing; cut up the pork, sausage and ham, grate the cheese, chop the onion and red pepper and mix these together with the sweet relish. Process the mixture to a paste, then add the peas and raisins and season with salt, freshly ground black pepper and monosodium glutamate. Finally, beat the eggs lightly, add to the mixture and stir well to achieve a smooth consistency.

AYAM BUMBU RUJAK
(Spiced Chicken in Coconut Milk)

Indonesia

1 fresh chicken, about 4 pounds
12 red chilies
8 shallots
4 cloves garlic
1 teaspoon blachan (shrimp paste)
1/2 teaspoon turmeric powder
1 teaspoon sugar
salt to taste
1/2 cup vegetable oil
1 1/4 cups thick coconut milk   serves 4

Prepare the chicken and cut into eight pieces. Boil the chilies for a few minutes until they soften. Slice the chilies, shallots and garlic and grind, together with the blachan, turmeric, sugar, salt and a small quantity of the oil. Heat the remaining oil in a large pan and stir-fry the spice-paste for 10 minutes, then add the chicken and the coconut milk, together with a similar quantity of hot water. Bring to the boil and stir well, then lower heat and cook for 40–45 minutes, stirring frequently, until the sauce has thickened and reduced considerably.

Sri Lanka

CHICKEN VINDALOO

1 fresh chicken, about 3 pounds
2 large brown onions
3 potatoes
2 shallots
6 cloves garlic
1 inch knob fresh ginger
6 dried red chilies
1 inch stick cinnamon
2 cloves
10 black peppercorns
¹/₂ teaspoon cumin seeds
¹/₂ teaspoon coriander seeds
1 teaspoon turmeric powder
1 teaspoon hot mustard powder
1 cup vinegar
¹/₂ cup ghee
2 curry leaves
salt to taste
2 hard boiled eggs   serves 4–6

Clean and prepare the chicken, cut into serving-size pieces and place in a shallow casserole dish. Par-boil the potatoes, then allow to cool and cut into thick slices. Slice the onions. Chop the shallots, garlic and ginger and place in a mortar, together with the dried chilies, cinnamon, cloves, peppercorns, cumin seeds, coriander seeds, turmeric, mustard and approximately 2 tablespoons vinegar. Pound to a smooth paste (for ease, a food processor may be used, if preferred), then add another ¹/₄ cup vinegar and stir to blend thoroughly. Pour the mixture over the chicken and place in a refrigerator for 2–3 hours, turning occasionally to ensure an even coating. Then, heat the ghee in a large pot, add the onion and curry leaves and stir-fry for 3–4 minutes until the onion is soft and transparent. Add the chicken together with any remaining marinade and cook for 5 minutes, stirring frequently to avoid sticking. Pour in the remaining vinegar together with an equal amount of cold water and bring to the boil. Lower heat and simmer for 30 minutes, then add the potatoes and season to taste with salt. Continue to simmer over a fairly low heat until the chicken is tender, then transfer to a large serving dish and garnish with quartered, hard-boiled eggs.

India

CHICKEN ALMOND CURRY

1 chicken, about 3 pounds
4 ounces blanched almonds
12 dried red chilies
6 cloves garlic
1 teaspoon poppy seeds
¹/₂ cup ghee
1 cup thin coconut milk
²/₃ cup thick coconut milk
2 tablespoons tamarind water
salt to taste
chopped coriander leaves   serves 4–6

Place the chicken in a saucepan, cover with cold water (or light stock if preferred) and bring to the boil. Cook until the chicken is tender, then cut into eight pieces and set aside. Reserve the cooking stock. Pound the almonds, chilies, garlic and poppy seeds together with a small quantity of cold water to produce a smooth thick paste. Heat the ghee in large pan and stir-fry the spice-paste for 5 minutes, then add ²/₃ cup of reserved stock and boil until all the liquid has evaporated. Pour in the thin coconut milk and bring to the boil, then add the chicken and lower heat immediately. Simmer gently for 5 minutes, pour in the thick coconut milk and tamarind water and season to taste with salt. Bring back to the boil, stir to blend thoroughly and cook for another 3 minutes. Transfer to a serving dish and garnish with chopped coriander leaves.

Malaysia

KORMA AYAM

1 fresh chicken, about 3 pounds
2 tablespoons light soy sauce
2 brown onions
2 large tomatoes
4 shallots
³/₄ inch knob fresh ginger
2 cloves garlic
2 stems lemon grass
2 tablespoons peanut oil
2 tablespoons coriander powder
1 teaspoon cumin powder
1 teaspoon anise powder
1 teaspoon cinnamon powder
¹/₂ teaspoon white pepper
¹/₂ teaspoon cardamom seeds
4 cloves
¹/₂ cup ghee
2 cups thick coconut milk
¹/₄ cup yoghurt
salt to taste
pinch monosodium glutamate
3 fresh red chilies   serves 4–6

Cut the chicken into serving-size pieces and season with soy sauce. Slice the onions and tomatoes. Finely chop the shallots, ginger, garlic and lemon grass, mix with half the peanut oil and pound to a smooth paste. Pound together the coriander, cumin, anise, cinnamon, white pepper, cardamom seeds and cloves with the remaining peanut oil. Heat the ghee in a large pan and stir-fry the pounded vegetables until lightly brown, then add the spice-paste and continue to fry for another 3 minutes. Add the chicken and cook for 2 minutes, stirring frequently to ensure the chicken is evenly coated with the spices. Pour in the coconut milk and the yoghurt, stir to blend thoroughly and season with salt and monosodium glutamate. Chop the chilies coarsely and add to the pan, together with the onion and tomato, lower the heat and simmer until the chicken is tender. Serve with plain rice.

Thailand

GAENG PHED GAI
(Curried Chicken)

1¹/₄ pounds chicken meat
3 shallots
2 cloves garlic
1 inch knob fresh khaa (Siamese ginger)
1 inch stem lemon grass
2 teaspoons chopped coriander root
10 dried chilies
¹/₄ teaspoon chopped mace
¹/₂ teaspoon chopped nutmeg
¹/₂ teaspoon chopped lime peel
1 teaspoon roasted coriander seeds
1 teaspoon roasted cumin seeds
2 tablespoons blachan (shrimp paste)
1 teaspoon salt
¹/₂ teaspoon black pepper
¹/₂ cup cooking oil
¹/₂ cup bamboo shoot
2¹/₂ cups thick coconut milk   serves 4–6

Remove the skin and cut the chicken meat into small pieces. Chop the shallots, garlic, ginger and lemon grass and pound together with the coriander root, dried chilies, mace, nutmeg, lime peel, coriander seeds, cumin seeds, blachan, salt and pepper. Heat the oil in a large pan and stir-fry the spice-paste for 4–5 minutes. Add the chicken meat and cook for another minute. Cut the bamboo shoot into shreds and add to the pan, then pour in the coconut milk, stir to blend thoroughly and bring slowly to the boil. Continue to cook over a moderate heat for another 10–15 minutes.

103

Overleaf: **Gaeng Phed Gai**

Taiwan

DRUNKEN CHICKEN
(Marinated in Chinese Wine)

1 young fresh chicken, about 2½ pounds
¾ inch knob fresh ginger
2 spring onions
3½ cups chicken stock
2 teaspoons salt
1 teaspoon white pepper
pinch monosodium glutamate
1½ cups Shao Hsin
(Chinese rice wine)   serves 4

Clean and prepare the chicken and place in a large saucepan. Slice the ginger and spring onions and add to the pan. Pour in the stock and bring to the boil. Lower heat and allow to simmer for 20 minutes, then remove the pan from the heat and allow the chicken to cool in the broth for 3 hours. Take out the chicken, cut into eight pieces and arrange in a shallow glass dish. Season with salt, freshly ground white pepper and monosodium glutamate. Combine 1 cup of the broth with the wine and pour this over the chicken. Cover the dish with foil and refrigerate for 48 hours, turning the chicken occasionally during that time. Serve cold.

Pakistan

CHICKEN JALFRAZI
(Spicy Chicken with Tomatoes)

1 chicken, about 3½ pounds
1 large brown onion
¾ inch knob fresh ginger
2 cloves garlic
3 tomatoes
½ cup ghee
1 teaspoon chili powder
2 teaspoons coriander powder
2 teaspoons turmeric powder
½ teaspoon salt
2 teaspoons garam masala
finely chopped parsley
for garnish   serves 4–6

Skin and de-bone the chicken and cut the meat into bite-size pieces. Chop the onion, ginger and tomato and crush the garlic. Heat the ghee in a pan and sauté the chicken for 3–4 minutes, then add the onion, ginger, garlic, chili, coriander and turmeric and cook slowly for 5 minutes, stirring frequently. Season with salt and garam masala, add the tomatoes and ¼ cup of cold water and stir to blend. Continue to cook until most of the liquid has reduced, then transfer to a serving plate and garnish with finely chopped parsley.

Singapore

CHICKEN WITH DRIED RED CHILIES

1 fresh chicken, about 2 pounds
4 cups dried red chilies
3 spring onions
1 inch knob fresh ginger
2 cloves garlic
4 points star anise
10 black peppercorns
½ cup peanut oil
2 tablespoons Chinese wine
2 teaspoons light soy sauce
2 teaspoons dark soy sauce
2 teaspoons vinegar
2 teaspoons sugar
½ teaspoon salt
1 tablespoon cornstarch
½ teaspoon sesame oil   serves 4–6

Prepare the chicken, remove all the bones and cut the meat into small pieces. Cut the chilies into 1 inch lengths, chop the onions, ginger and garlic and crush the star anise and peppercorns. Heat the oil in a wok and stir-fry the chicken for 2–3 minutes, then remove and set aside. Place the chilies in the wok and sauté for 2 minutes, then add the onion, ginger, garlic, anise and pepper and continue to cook over a fairly high heat, stirring frequently until the chilies begin to blacken. Next, add the Chinese wine, soy sauce, vinegar, sugar and salt and stir to blend thoroughly. Mix the cornstarch with a small quantity of cold water and stir into the mixture, then replace the pieces of chicken and cook slowly for another 4–5 minutes, stirring occasionally. Finally, transfer to a serving dish and sprinkle hot sesame oil on top.

Singapore

HAINANESE CHICKEN RICE

1 fresh chicken, about 3 pounds
1 teaspoon salt
2 cups long-grain rice
3 inch piece cucumber
2 tomatoes
6 shallots
4 fresh red chilies
3/4 inch knob fresh ginger
2 cloves garlic
sprig fresh coriander leaves
freshly ground black pepper   serves 4

Prepare the chicken, season both the inside and outside with salt and set aside for 1 hour. Wash the rice under cold running water, then drain thoroughly. Cut the cucumber and tomato into tiny dice, chop the shallots, chilies and ginger and crush the garlic. In a saucepan, bring 4 cups of water to the boil, add the ginger and garlic and allow to boil rapidly for 3–4 minutes. Then, add the chicken and the coriander leaves, cover the pan, and cook slowly until the chicken is tender. Remove a little oil from the surface of the cooking stock and set this aside. Remove the chicken, cut into small slices and arrange on a serving platter. Heat the reserved oil in a fresh saucepan and sauté the shallot for 3–4 minutes, then pour in half the cooking stock, add the cucumber, tomato and chili, season with freshly ground black pepper and bring to the boil. Cover the pan, lower heat and allow to simmer for 20 minutes. Meanwhile, bring the remaining stock back to the boil, add the rice, cover the pan and cook until the rice is tender and fluffy. Transfer the soup and rice to individual serving bowls and place the platter of chicken in the center of the table. Serve with side dishes of ginger and garlic sauce, chili sauce and soy sauce.

Burma

KHAUKSWE
(Spiced Sautéed Chicken with Noodles)

1/2 cup split yellow peas
1 1/4 pounds boned chicken meat
2 brown onions
2 tomatoes
2 cloves garlic
1/2 cup vegetable oil
1 teaspoon paprika
1 teaspoon chili powder
1 teaspoon turmeric powder
salt to taste
freshly ground black pepper
1 2/3 cups thick coconut milk
12 ounces egg noodles   serves 4

Soak the peas overnight, then drain and cook in rapidly-boiling water for 1 hour. Boil the chicken for 20 minutes, then chop into bite-size pieces. Chop the onions and tomatoes and crush the garlic. Pour boiling water over the noodles and drain in a colander. Heat the oil in a pan and sauté the onion and garlic until the onion is transparent, then add the paprika, chili and turmeric, stir well, and cook for 2 minutes. Add the chicken and tomato and cook for 3–4 minutes, stirring frequently, then pour in the stock, add the split peas and bring to the boil. Cover the pan, lower the heat and simmer for 15 minutes, then add the coconut milk, stir to blend thoroughly, and cook slowly for another 5 minutes. Meanwhile, cook the noodles for 3–4 minutes, until soft, then drain thoroughly. To serve; arrange the noodles in a serving dish and pour the chicken on top. Garnish with hard boiled egg and lemon wedges and serve with side dishes of chili sauce.

CHICKEN BIRIYANI

Sri Lanka

1 chicken, about 3 pounds
1 brown onion
½ cup fresh cashewnuts
2 fresh red chilies
2 tablespoons grated coconut
2 cloves
2 cardamom seeds
½ inch cinnamon stick
4 hard boiled eggs
½ teaspoon turmeric powder
½ teaspoon salt
⅓ cup tomato paste
⅓ cup plain yoghurt
1 teaspoon chili powder
1 teaspoon paprika
1 teaspoon curry powder
2 teaspoons curry paste
⅓ cup vegetable oil
¼ cup raisins

Rice:
1½ cups basmati rice
1 small brown onion
½ stem lemon grass
3 cardamom seeds
3 cloves
¼ cup vegetable oil
3 curry leaves
¾ inch cinnamon stick
½ teaspoon turmeric powder
2 cups chicken stock   serves 4–6

Prepare and joint the chicken. Chop finely the onion, chilies and half the cashewnuts. Grind together the cloves, cardamoms and cinnamon. Shell the eggs, prick with a fork and dust with turmeric and a little salt. Place in a blender, the chopped nuts, ground spice powder, coconut, tomato paste, yoghurt, paprika, chili powder, curry powder, curry paste and remaining salt and blend to produce a smooth paste. Coat the chicken with the spice-paste and set aside for 15–20 minutes. Heat some oil in a large pan and sauté the onion and fresh chili, then add the chicken and cook for 8–10 minutes, stirring frequently. Add about ⅓ cup of water to the marinade, stir and pour this over the chicken. Bring to the boil, then lower heat and cook slowly until the chicken is tender. Meanwhile, fry the whole eggs in a little oil until they become light brown, then remove and drain and, in the same oil, stir-fry the raisins and remaining nuts for 1 minute. To serve; arrange the chicken in the center of a small plate, surround with the eggs and prepared rice and garnish with raisins and remaining cashewnuts.

To prepare the rice; wash under cold running water, then drain thoroughly. Chop the onion and lemon grass and crush the cardamoms and cloves. Heat the oil in a large pan, add the onion, lemon grass and curry leaves and stir-fry for 3–4 minutes, then add the ground spices, cinnamon stick and turmeric and cook for another 2–3 minutes. Next, add the rice and cook for a few minutes, until it starts to 'crackle', then pour in the stock, cover and cook slowly until the rice is tender and fluffy and the liquid has been absorbed.

CHICKEN BADUN

Sri Lanka

1 chicken, about 3 pounds
2 brown onions
1 stem lemon grass
3 cardamom seeds
3 cloves
½ teaspoon salt
¼ teaspoon white pepper
3 tablespoons curry powder
¼ cup vinegar
1 inch cinnamon stick
⅓ cup vegetable oil
2 curry leaves
½ cup chicken stock
3 tablespoons Worcestershire sauce   serves 4

Prepare and joint the chicken. Chop one onion and cut the other into rings. Chop finely the lemon grass and crush the cardamoms and cloves. Place the chicken in a saucepan, add the ground spices, salt, pepper, curry powder, ginger and cinnamon stick and pour in about ⅓ cup of water. Bring to the boil and cook until the liquid has been absorbed. Heat the oil in a frying pan, add the chopped onion and lemon grass and sauté for 3–4 minutes, then add the pieces of chicken curry leaves and half the stock and cook over a medium heat until the chicken is tender, approximately 40 minutes. Then, add the onion rings, pour in the Worcestershire sauce and remaining stock and bring back to the boil. Stir well, then lower heat and simmer for another 5 minutes before serving.

Taiwan

BAKED STUFFED PIGEONS

4 small pigeons
1 teaspoon salt
1/2 teaspoon Chinese five-spice powder
freshly ground black pepper
6 dried Chinese mushrooms
oil for frying
2 large brown onions
2 cloves garlic
1 inch knob fresh ginger
4 spring onions
3/4 cup canned bamboo shoots
1/4 pound fresh shrimp
2 eggs
2 tablespoons light soy sauce
2 teaspoons dark soy sauce
2 tablespoons Chinese wine
2 tablespoons oyster sauce
2 teaspoons cornstarch
1/2 cup butter   serves 4

To prepare the pigeons; cut along the backbone, remove the carcass and spread the birds open. Season the insides with salt, five-spice powder and freshly ground black pepper. Soak the mushrooms in warm water for 40 minutes then discard the hard stems. Shell and de-vein the shrimp and chop into small pieces. Chop finely the mushroom caps, brown onions, garlic, ginger, spring onions and bamboo shoots. Heat the oil in a wok, add the chopped shrimp and vegetables and stir-fry for 3–4 minutes. Remove, drain off excess oil, mince the mixture in a food processor, place in a mixing bowl. Beat the eggs lightly, then add to the mixture together with the soy sauce, Chinese wine, oyster sauce and cornstarch. Stir to blend thoroughly, then spread the mixture evenly over the inside of the pigeons. Re-shape the birds and secure with strips of heat-proof, parchment paper. Heat the butter in a clean wok and when it starts to 'sizzle' add the pigeons and cook for 4–5 minutes, turning frequently to ensure the skin is evenly golden and crispy. Finally, place a lid on the pan, lower heat and cook fairly slowly until the birds are tender. Check during the later stage, and add a little more butter if necessary.

Note: If preferred, the final stage of cooking may be done in a steamer, but be sure to brown the birds in butter first.

Hong Kong

MINCED PIGEON IN LETTUCE LEAVES

2 pigeons
4 dried Chinese mushrooms
3/4 cup bamboo shoot
3 spring onions
1 inch knob fresh ginger
1/8 pound cooked chicken liver
2 eggs
2 teaspoons cornstarch
2 tablespoons light soy sauce
1 teaspoon dark soy sauce
1 teaspoon sugar
1/2 teaspoon salt
1/4 teaspoon white pepper
pinch monosodium glutamate
1/4 cup peanut oil
2 tablespoons Chinese wine
1 teaspoon oyster sauce
8 lettuce leaves
1/4 cup sweet plum sauce   serves 4

Prepare the pigeons and boil until tender (approximately 30 minutes), then de-bone and mince the meat. Soak the mushrooms in warm water for 40 minutes, then remove and discard the hard stems. Finely chop the mushrooms, bamboo shoot, spring onions, ginger and chicken liver. Beat the eggs in a large bowl and add the cornstarch, soy sauce, sugar, salt, pepper and monosodium glutamate. Place the minced pigeon and chopped chicken liver in the bowl and allow to stand for 20 minutes. Heat the oil in a wok, add the meat and stir-fry for 2–3 minutes. Remove and drain. Place the mushrooms, bamboo shoot, onion and ginger into the wok and stir for 2 minutes, then replace the meat, add the Chinese wine, oyster sauce and marinade and stir over medium heat for another 3 minutes. Adjust seasonings to taste and, if necessary, thicken with a little extra cornstarch mixed with cold water. Transfer to a serving dish and place on the table together with a plate of lettuce leaves and a dish of plum sauce.

Note: Traditionally, this dish is eaten with the hands, each diner spooning a little meat onto a lettuce leaf, adding some sauce and rolling up the leaf.

Hong Kong

PIGEONS BAKED IN SALT

2 pigeons, about ³/₄ pound each
4 shallots
4 spring onions
³/₄ inch knob fresh ginger
1 clove garlic
¹/₄ cup Chinese wine
2 tablespoons light soy sauce
2 tablespoons dark soy sauce
¹/₂ teaspoon anise powder
salt to taste
freshly ground white pepper
monosodium glutamate
2 sheets aluminum foil
4 pounds rock salt   serves 2

Clean and prepare the pigeons. Chop finely the shallots, spring onions, ginger and garlic and mix with the Chinese wine, soy sauce, anise powder, salt, white pepper and monosodium glutamate. Rub the mixture over the outside of the pigeons and stuff the remainder inside. Set aside for 1 hour, then wrap the birds individually in sheets of well-greased aluminum foil. Heat the rock salt in a wok until it is extremely hot, then bury the birds in the salt, place a cover on the wok and leave on a low heat for 10–12 minutes. Remove the birds and reheat the salt, then repeat the cooking process for another 10 minutes. To serve; unwrap the pigeons, remove the stuffing, and chop the meat into bite-size pieces.

Taiwan

STEAMED PIGEON IN BAMBOO CUPS

2 plump pigeons
¹/₂ pound fat pork belly
¹/₂ cup canned water chestnuts
2 tablespoons light soy sauce
2 teaspoons dark soy sauce
freshly ground white pepper
pinch monosodium glutamate
²/₃ cup chicken stock   serves 4

De-bone the pigeons and cut the meat into small chunks. Chop the pork and chestnuts, mix with the pigeon and pass both through a coarse grinder. Season with soy sauce, white pepper and monosodium glutamate and add the stock. Stir to blend thoroughly, divide the mixture and place into 4 bamboo cups. Place the cups in a tightly sealed container and steam over rapidly boiling water for 25–30 minutes.

Singapore

SLICED PIGEON WITH BAMBOO SHOOTS

³/₄ pound cooked pigeon meat
¹/₂ teaspoon salt
freshly ground black pepper
¹/₂ teaspoon sugar
pinch meat tenderizer
3 dried Chinese mushrooms
³/₄ cup bamboo shoot
¹/₄ cup vegetable oil
2 tablespoons Chinese wine
¹/₄ cup chicken stock
2 teaspoons light soy sauce
1 teaspoon oyster sauce
pinch monosodium glutamate
2 teaspoons cornstarch
1 teaspoon sesame oil   serves 4

Cut the pigeon meat into small, thin slices, season with salt, freshly ground black pepper, sugar and meat tenderizer and allow to stand for 30 minutes. Soak the mushrooms in warm water for 40 minutes, discard the hard stems and cut the caps into thin slices. Cover the bamboo shoot with cold water, bring to the boil, cook for 3–4 minutes, then drain and cut into small pieces. Heat the oil in a wok and sauté the pigeon for 5 minutes, turning occasionally, then remove and set aside. Pour off most of the oil from the wok, add the mushroom and bamboo shoot and stir for 30 seconds. Then, replace the pigeon, add the Chinese wine, chicken stock, soy sauce, oyster sauce and monosodium glutamate and continue to cook for another 3 minutes. Mix the cornstarch with a small quantity of cold water, add to the pan and stir until the sauce thickens. Place onto a serving dish and sprinkle with hot sesame oil.

HIN'S SMOKED DUCK

Singapore

1 duck, approximately 4 pounds
1 teaspoon Chinese five-spice powder
1 teaspoon sugar
1/2 teaspoon salt
1/2 teaspoon white pepper
2 tablespoons honey
1 teaspoon fresh lemon juice

Sauce:
1/4 cup chili sauce
1/2 teaspoon grated fresh ginger
1 teaspoon dark soy sauce
dash garlic juice
1 teaspoon sugar   serves 4

Prepare the duck, clean thoroughly and secure the wings in order that they will not open during cooking. Mix the Chinese five-spice powder, sugar, salt and white pepper and rub the mixture inside the duck. In a saucepan bring 1/2 cup of water to the boil, add the honey and lemon juice and stir until the honey has completely dissolved. Allow the syrup to cool slightly, then rub all over the outside of the duck. Tie a string around the duck's neck and hang in a warm and drafty place to dry. Preferably the duck should then be cooked in a charcoal oven but if this is not available, place on a spit and cook over an open charcoal fire, turning frequently. Serve with a side dish of spiced sauce made by mixing together the chili sauce, fresh grated ginger, soy sauce, garlic juice and sugar.

DUCK IN LEMON SAUCE

Hong Kong

6 breasts of duck
2 shallots
³/₄ inch knob fresh ginger
4 egg-yolks
2 tablespoons light soy sauce
3 tablespoons cornstarch
oil for deep frying
2 fresh lemons, sliced

Sauce:
2 tablespoons rice flour
2 tablespoons butter
¹/₂ cup fresh lemon juice
¹/₂ cup chicken stock
2 tablespoons Chinese wine
2 teaspoons sugar
salt to taste
freshly ground black pepper
2 teaspoons cornstarch   serves 4–6

Remove the skin from the duck breasts and cut away the bones. Slice the meat into bite-size strips and place in a shallow dish. Chop the shallots and ginger very finely. Beat the egg-yolks and mix with the soy sauce, ¹/₄ cup of water and one-third of the cornstarch. Add the finely chopped shallot and ginger, stir to blend thoroughly, then pour over the duck. Set aside in the refrigerator for 1 hour, then coat the duck with the remaining cornstarch. Heat the oil in a wok until it begins to smoke, then deep fry the duck until tender and golden brown. Remove from the oil, drain thoroughly and arrange on a serving plate. Pour the hot sauce over the duck and garnish with fresh lemon slices.

To make the sauce; place the flour and butter in a saucepan and blend over a moderate heat. Add the lemon juice and stock and bring to the boil. Add the Chinese wine, sugar, salt and freshly ground black pepper and stir to blend thoroughly. Mix the cornstarch with a small quantity of cold water and stir into the sauce to thicken slightly.

113

Hong Kong

PEKING DUCK

1 fat duck, about 5 pounds
1 cup golden syrup
3/4 cup boiling water
1 tablespoon soy sauce
1 heaping teaspoon five-spice powder
6 spring onions cut into thin sticks
3 tablespoons sweet plum sauce

Pancakes:
5 cups all-purpose flour
1/2 teaspoon salt
2 cups boiling water
sesame oil   serves 8

Clean and prepare the duck and dry thoroughly inside and out. Melt golden syrup in the boiling water, then bring back to the boil. Rub the duck inside and out with five-spice powder. Holding the duck over a large bowl, pour the boiling syrup over the duck and into the cavity. Place a string around the neck and hang the duck in a cool drafty place, or in front of an electric fan, for about 5 hours. Brush the bird with any remaining syrup and roast in a pre-heated moderate oven for 1 hour. Turn the duck and roast for another 3/4 hour. Test if done by inserting a skewer into the thickest part of the thigh. If the juice runs clear the bird is done.

To make the pancakes; sift the flour and salt into a mixing bowl and make a well in the center. Pour in the boiling water a little at a time and gradually mix into the flour to form a soft dough. Knead gently for 10 minutes until the dough becomes pliable, then cover and allow to stand for 20 minutes. Roll into a cylindrical shape approximately 2 in. in diameter and cut into circles, approximately 1/4 in. thick. Brush one side of each circle with sesame oil and place two together with the oiled sides facing, then roll each out until approximately 6 in. in diameter. Heat a heavy pan and cook each pair of pancakes for approximately 1 minute, turning to cook on both sides. When cooked peel the pancakes apart and stack on a warm plate.

To serve; first, slice off the skin and then the meat and arrange on a serving platter. Serve pancakes and spring onions on another plate and serve individual small bowls of sauce.

Malaysia

ITEK BERSANTAN
(Duckling in Coconut Milk)

1 duckling, about 2 1/2 pounds
4 shallots
1 inch knob fresh ginger
2 cloves garlic
2 stems lemon grass
1/4 cup vegetable oil
2 tablespoons coriander powder
2 teaspoons cumin powder
1/2 teaspoon anise powder
2/3 cup thick coconut milk
salt to taste
freshly ground black pepper   serves 4

Clean and de-bone the duckling and chop the meat into bite-size pieces. Chop the shallots, ginger, garlic and lemon grass and pound together to form a paste. Heat the vegetable oil in a pan and fry this paste for 5 minutes, stirring frequently. Add the pieces of duckling and continue to fry for 3–4 minutes. Then, make a second paste by mixing the coriander, cumin and anise powders with a little coconut milk and add this to the pan. Pour in the remaining coconut milk, and bring to the boil. Lower heat, season with salt and freshly ground black pepper and simmer until the duckling is cooked, approximately 40 minutes.

Note: This dish should not be served dry so, if necessary, add a little extra coconut milk during cooking.

Indonesia

BEBEK BETUTU
(Steamed Stuffed Duckling)

2 young ducklings
1 teaspoon salt
1 teaspoon black pepper
2 shallots
1 inch knob fresh ginger
2 fresh red chilies
1 stem lemon grass
2 lemon leaves
2 cloves garlic
3 candlenuts
⅓ cup vegetable oil
2 teaspoons blachan (shrimp paste)
2 teaspoons turmeric powder
2 teaspoons cardamom powder
1 teaspoon coriander powder
2 tablespoons palm sugar
1 bay leaf
aluminum foil   serves 6

Prepare the ducklings and season, inside and out, with salt and black pepper. Slice the shallots, finely chop the ginger, chilies, lemon grass and lemon leaves, crush the garlic and grind the candlenuts. Heat the oil in a large pan, add the shallot, ginger and garlic and sauté for 3–4 minutes, then add the chili, lemon grass, lemon leaf, candlenut, blachan, spice powders, sugar and bay leaf. Stir-fry for 5 minutes, then remove the mixture from the pan and stuff inside the ducklings. Wrap the ducklings securely in aluminum foil, place in a steamer and cook until very tender, approximately 1¼ hours. Finally, remove the aluminum foil and place the ducklings in a very hot oven, or under a hot grill, until the skins are golden brown and crispy.

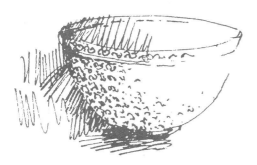

Thailand

GAENG PHED
(Duck and Vegetables)

1 duck, about 3 pounds
1 teaspoon salt
freshly ground black pepper
¼ cup dark soy sauce
4 dried Chinese mushrooms
1 pound squash
2 cloves garlic
1 small brown onion
oil for deep frying
6 cups chicken stock
2 pickled limes
1 tablespoon cornstarch   serves 4

Clean and prepare the duck and cut into large bite-size pieces (with bone). Place in a shallow dish, season with salt, freshly ground black pepper and soy sauce and allow to stand for 40 minutes. Soak the Chinese mushrooms in warm water for 40 minutes, then discard the hard stems and cut the caps in half. Peel the squash and cut into bite-size pieces and chop finely the garlic and onion. Heat the oil in a large saucepan and deep-fry the duck for 3–4 minutes, to brown and seal. Remove the duck and drain thoroughly. Pour away almost all the oil from the pan, then add the garlic and onion and sauté for 3–4 minutes. Replace the duck, pour in the chicken stock and bring to the boil. Cover the pan, lower heat and simmer gently for approximately 30 minutes, until the duck is almost cooked. Remove the lid from the pan, add the mushrooms, squash and pickled limes and continue to cook over a moderate heat for another 10–15 minutes until the duck is tender. Transfer the pieces of duck to a serving plate and surround with the mushrooms and squash. Pour the stock through a strainer into a fresh saucepan and bring back to the boil. Mix the cornstarch with a small quantity of cold water, add this to the pan and stir to thicken before pouring the sauce over the duck.

Barbecues & Hot Pots

The majority of recipes in this section are cooked at tableside, or at specially designed counters, and very often involve the diner's participation in the final cooking process. Preparation, however, should always take place beforehand in the kitchen so that even a table crowded with plates of food and with a steaming cooking utensil in the center still retains an appealing and 'appetizing' appearance. In Japan this style of dining is particularly prevalent and throughout the country can be found restaurants which specialise in **Teppanyaki** (pages 117–118), **Yakitori** (page 122), **Yosenabe** (page 124) and **Sukiyaki** (page 125). In one form or another, the hot pot (or steamboat) occurs in almost every Asian cuisine.

Perhaps the most famous Asian barbecue, claimed as a national dish by both Indonesia and Malaysia, is **Satay** (page 123); a dish where the marinade and sauce are equally, if not more, important than the main meat ingredient. And with Indian **Tandoori** (page 122) it is the marination that makes all the difference and if this is done well, then a very satisfying result will be achieved in spite of the lack of the special ovens used in most professional kitchens.

Teppanyaki Ise-Ebi *Lobster Teppanyaki*	**Tandoori Chicken**	**Mongolian Hot Pot** *Lamb & vegetable hot pot*
Gyruniku Teppanyaki *Beef cooked on griddle*	**Satay** *Skewered meat with hot peanut sauce*	**Chicken Firepot** *Simple chicken hot pot*
Pulgogi *Korean barbecue*	**Yosenabe** *Seafood & vegetables*	**Shabu Shabu** *Beef & vegetable hot pot*
Mongolian Barbecue	**Sukiyaki** *Sliced beef & vegetables*	**Sliced Beef in Vinegar**
Yakitori *Barbecued chicken & vegetable sticks*		

Japan

TEPPANYAKI ISE-EBI
(Lobster Teppanyaki)

1³/4 *pounds fresh lobster meat*
2 large green peppers
1 large brown onion
¹/3 *cup butter*
2 tablespoons Japanese soy sauce
2 tablespoons fresh lemon juice
¹/2 *teaspoon salt*
freshly ground white pepper
¹/4 *cup mirin*

Sauce:
1 small brown onion
1 clove garlic
1 inch knob fresh ginger
2 tablespoons vegetable oil
2 tablespoons Japanese soy sauce
2 tablespoons tomato sauce
2 tablespoons Worcestershire sauce
2 tablespoons fresh lemon juice
¹/2 *cup dashi*
2 teaspoons cornstarch   serves 6

Cut the lobster meat into bite-size chunks and chop the green peppers and onion. Melt half the butter on a large open griddle, add the lobster and cook for 5 minutes, turning frequently. Melt the remaining butter apart from the lobster and fry the green pepper and onion for 2–3 minutes, while the lobster continues to cook separately. Then bring all the food together, add the soy sauce and lemon juice and season with salt and freshly ground white pepper. Mix thoroughly and continue to cook for another 3–4 minutes (the vegetables should still be crispy), then add the mirin, toss well and spoon onto individual plates. Serve with side dishes of the prepared sauce.

To make the sauce; chop the onion, garlic and ginger very finely. Heat the oil in a saucepan, add the onion, garlic and ginger and sauté for 3–4 minutes. Then add the soy sauce, tomato sauce, Worcestershire sauce, lemon juice and dashi and bring to the boil. Lower heat and simmer for 5 minutes. Mix the cornstarch with a small quantity of cold water and stir into the sauce. Allow to simmer for another few minutes until the sauce thickens slightly.

Japan

GYRUNIKU TEPPANYAKI
(Beef Cooked on Griddle)

1¹/2 *pounds fillet steak*
¹/2 *cup mirin*
¹/2 *cup Japanese soy sauce*
freshly ground black pepper
8 cloves garlic
¹/4 *pound bean sprouts*
oil for frying

Sauce:
3 ounces white radish
1 inch knob fresh ginger
¹/4 *cup mirin*
¹/3 *cup Japanese soy sauce*
2 teaspoons sugar   serves 4–6

Cut the beef into thin slices and place in a shallow dish. Pour half the mirin and soy sauce over the beef, season with freshly ground black pepper and set aside for 20 minutes. Chop the garlic finely and trim the bean sprouts. Pour a little oil on to a large open griddle and fry the garlic until it is golden and crispy, then push to one side. Add a little more oil and fry the beef for 3–4 minutes, turning occasionally and adding a little of the remaining mirin and soy sauce during the cooking period. When the meat is almost cooked, pour some more oil on the griddle and add the bean sprouts (cooking separately from the meat). Pour the remaining mirin and soy sauce onto the bean sprouts, toss well and cook for 2–3 minutes. Just prior to serving, add the crispy fried garlic to the beef and mix well. To serve; place portions of beef, bean sprouts and prepared sauce in front of each diner.

To make the sauce; grate the radish and ginger and mix with the mirin and soy sauce then add the sugar and stir until completely dissolved.

Korea

PULGOGI
(Korean Barbecue)

1¼ pounds prime beef
2 spring onions
3 cloves garlic
¾ inch knob fresh ginger
1 teaspoon roasted sesame seeds
⅓ cup soy sauce
2 tablespoons rice wine
1 teaspoon sesame oil
2 teaspoons sugar
freshly ground black pepper

Sauce for dip:
2 spring onions
2 fresh red chilies
2 cloves garlic
1 teaspoon sesame oil
⅓ cup soy sauce
¼ cup rice wine
2 teaspoons sugar
freshly ground black pepper   serves 4–6

Freeze the beef slightly and cut into very thin slices, approximately 3 in. square, and place into a shallow dish. Chop the spring onions, garlic and ginger very finely and crush the sesame seeds. Mix these with the soy sauce, wine and sesame oil and ½ cup of cold water. Add the sugar and freshly ground black pepper and stir to blend thoroughly. Pour the mixture over the beef and allow to marinate for 2 hours. To cook; place a small charcoal burner in the center of the table, and when the coals are red-hot, cook the beef for 2–3 minutes then transfer to individual plates. Serve with a side plate of sauce, plain rice and 'kim chi' (see Salads & Vegetables).

To make the sauce; chop the spring onions and chilies very finely and crush the garlic. Pound these together with the sesame oil to form a smooth paste. Pour the soy sauce into a bowl, add the spice-paste, wine, ¼ cup of cold water, sugar and freshly ground black pepper and stir until the sugar is completely dissolved.

Taiwan

MONGOLIAN BARBECUE

1¼ pounds beef steak
1¼ pounds boneless lamb
1¼ pounds Hunan ham
1¼ pounds chicken meat
2 Chinese cabbage
8 carrots
¾ pound eggplant
4 spring onions
4 shallots
½ pound bean sprouts
2 squares bean curd
oil for frying

Spices:
chili oil
sesame oil
ginger sauce
white vinegar
tomato sauce
chili sauce
oyster sauce
salt & pepper
finely chopped garlic & ginger
light & dark soy sauce
finely chopped red & green chilies
sugar syrup   serves 10–12

Freeze all the meat slightly and cut into paper thin slices. Shred the cabbage, cut the carrots and eggplant into thin strips and chop the spring onions and shallots. Trim the bean sprouts and cut the bean curd into small dice. Arrange all these ingredients along one side of a table as for a buffet and, along the opposite side, arrange bowls of all the spices. Each diner is given a bowl which he fills himself, first with the meats and vegetables and then with the preferred spices. To cook; pour a little oil on to a charcoal-heated griddle, or hot plate, add the ingredients from the bowl and cook for 2–3 minutes, stirring frequently to make sure the spices are all well blended.

Note: Each bowl should be cooked separately as the main point of using the 'buffet' system is that each individual diner chooses just how 'hot' or bland his own meal will be.

Japan

YAKITORI
(Barbecued Chicken & Vegetable Sticks)

Yakitori bars are to be found all over Japan offering a variety of combinations of chicken and vegetables, threaded on skewers and cooked over hot charcoal. Chicken wings with spring onions; chicken livers with ginger and mushrooms; and minced chicken balls with shiso leaves are just three popular combinations. When preparing at home it's a matter of personal preference using, in addition to the above, white chicken meat, chicken gizzards, chicken skin, asparagus, green peppers and eggplant. To prepare; make the marinade (see below), pour over the chicken and set aside for at least 1 hour. Place a few pieces on to a skewer, alternating the chicken and vegetables. (Each skewer should not hold more than 6 pieces of food at the very most, as the idea is to serve a large variety of sticks, Mix the reserved marinade with a similar quantity of dashi and use this to brush the food while it is being barbecued.

MARINADE

1 shallot
2 cloves garlic
3/4 inch knob fresh ginger
1/2 cup Japanese soy sauce
1/2 cup mirin
2 tablespoons golden honey
2 tablespoons brown sugar
freshly ground black pepper
1/2 cup dashi

Chop the shallot, garlic and ginger very finely and pound together with a small quantity of cold water to produce a smooth paste. Pour the soy sauce and mirin into a small saucepan and bring almost to the boil. Add the spice-paste, honey, sugar and freshly ground black pepper and stir to blend thoroughly. Simmer (but do not allow to come to a rapid boil) until the honey and sugar have completely dissolved. Allow to cool before pouring over the pieces of chicken. After the marinated chicken has been removed, add the dashi, stir to blend thoroughly and use to baste during cooking.

India

TANDOORI CHICKEN

In professional kitchens a special clay oven, known as a tandoor, is used for cooking this dish. The oven, heated by hot coals, opens at the bottom and provides a distinctive flavor that is hard to match at home. However, don't despair. Cooking in a charcoal oven is the next best thing but even without this, if the chicken is tender and well marinated, the results should prove highly satisfying.

2 small chickens, about 800 g each
3 cloves garlic
1 fresh red chili
3/4 inch knob fresh ginger
1/2 teaspoon salt
1/4 teaspoon saffron powder
2 tablespoons fresh lemon juice
1 cup natural yoghurt
2 teaspoons coriander powder
1 teaspoon cumin powder
1/4 teaspoon anise powder
1/4 teaspoon cayenne pepper
1 teaspoon paprika
1/4 cup ghee   serves 4–6

Clean and prepare the chickens and remove the skin. Make sure the chickens are dried thoroughly, then, with a sharp knife, make slits in the thighs and breasts. Chop the garlic, chili and ginger and pound together with the salt, saffron powder and lemon juice to form a smooth paste. Rub this paste into the flesh of the chickens and put them to one side for 30 minutes. In the meantime, mix the yoghurt with the coriander, cumin, anise, cayenne pepper, paprika and any remaining spice-paste. Arrange the chickens in a casserole dish, add the yoghurt mixture and place in a refrigerator to marinate for at least 12 hours. After removing from the marinade baste the chickens with ghee, place on a rotisserie and cook in a moderately hot oven for 15–20 minutes. Then, lower the heat slightly, baste again with ghee and continue to cook until the chickens are tender. Serve with naan (a flat Indian bread) and an onion and tomato salad.

SATAY
(Skewered Meat with Hot Peanut Sauce)

Satay is often claimed as 'the national dish' by both Indonesia and Malaysia and, certainly, it is served throughout both countries, at all times of the day, in the finest restaurants and at the simplest road-side stalls. There are many varieties including beef, lamb, pork (popular with the Chinese community but naturally never served in a Muslim restaurant), chicken and shrimp. The meat is cut into fine slices, marinated, skewered on thin wooden sticks and cooked over charcoal. It is served with a bowl of spicy sauce and accompanied by slices of onion, wedges of cucumber and little cakes of glutinous rice. The secret is in the marinade and the sauce and, while a number of ingredients are common to all recipes, each satay cook claims to know that little 'extra' which makes his or her satay just that much tastier than the others. The recipes here are a combination of a number of sources and have been tried, tested and well-received on many occasions, but as with all dishes which involve the use of many spices, personal taste is all-important so don't be afraid to experiment and perhaps you will be yet another to find the 'perfect' satay.

MARINADE

2 small red onions
2 cloves garlic
1 fresh red chili
1/2 inch knob fresh ginger
1/2 inch knob galangal
1 stem lemon grass
1 teaspoon coriander powder
1 teaspoon cumin powder
1 teaspoon anise powder
3 tablespoons sugar
2 tablespoons fresh lime juice
2 tablespoons tamarind water
2 tablespoons light soy sauce
salt to taste
1 teaspoon sesame oil
1/2 cup thick coconut milk

Chop the onions, garlic, chili, ginger, galangal and lemon grass and pound together with the coriander powder, cumin powder, anise powder, sugar, lime juice, tamarind water, soy sauce and salt. Add the oil, coconut milk (and the meat being used) and allow to stand for approximately 30 minutes. Arrange the meat on skewers and cook over an open fire, using the marinade to baste frequently.

SAUCE

8 dried red chilies
4 shallots
3 cloves garlic
1/2 inch knob fresh galangal
1 stem lemon grass
2 candlenuts
3/4 inch piece cinnamon stick
1 teaspoon coriander powder
1 teaspoon cumin powder
1 teaspoon turmeric powder
2 tablespoons peanut oil
1 teaspoon fresh lime juice
2 tablespoons tamarind water
2 tablespoons sugar
salt to taste
3/4 cup ground roasted peanuts
1/2 cup thick coconut milk

Soak the dried chilies in cold water for 30 minutes until soft. Chop the chilies, onions, garlic, galangal, lemon grass, candlenuts and cinnamon stick and pound together with the coriander, cumin and turmeric powders. Heat the peanut oil in a pan and stir-fry the spice-paste for 5 minutes. Add the lime juice, tamarind water, sugar and salt and continue to stir over a medium heat for another 2–3 minutes, then add the ground peanuts and the coconut milk and bring to the boil. Lower heat and boil gently until the oil rises to the surface, then transfer to a serving bowl. Dip the skewers of cooked meat into the sauce to allow plenty to stick to the meat.

Note: The above recipes should allow for approximately 1 pound of meat.

YOSENABE
(Seafoods & Vegetables)

Japan

2 lobster tails
¾ pound red snapper fillets
¾ pound halibut fillets
⅓ pound cuttlefish
6 oysters
6 clams
4 ounces transparent noodles
1 small square kombu (dried kelp)
½ small Chinese cabbage
2 carrots
4 spring onions
3 cups dashi
6 mushrooms
2 tablespoons Japanese soy sauce
2 tablespoons mirin

serves 6

Prepare the seafood and cut into bite-size pieces. Soak the noodles in cold water until soft, then cut into short lengths. Soak the kombu in cold water for 30 seconds. Shred the cabbage and slice the carrots. Cut the spring onions into 1 inch lengths. Pour the dashi into a cooking pot in the center of the table and bring to the boil. Add the kombu and noodles and simmer for 3–4 minutes, then add the cabbage, carrots and mushrooms and continue to cook for another 2 minutes. Add the soy sauce and mirin and stir to blend thoroughly, then add all the seafood and allow to simmer until cooked. Add the spring onion at the last minute. To serve; ladle a little stock into individual bowls to use as a dip and allow each diner to take from the cooking pot. Alternatively, serve the seafood and stock directly into individual soup bowls.

SUKIYAKI
(Sliced Beef & Vegetables)

Japan

1¼ pounds prime beef steak
1 large brown onion
6 large white mushrooms
4 ounces bean curd
1½ cups canned bamboo shoots
6 spring onions
small Chinese cabbage
3 cups bean sprouts
4 ounces transparent noodles
1 piece beef fat (or suet)
3 teaspoons sugar
½ cup sake (Japanese rice wine)
1 cup Japanese soy sauce
4 fresh eggs (for dip)   serves 4

Freeze the beef slightly so that it may be cut into very thin slices. Slice the brown onion, mushrooms, bean curd and bamboo shoots. Cut the cabbage into bite-size pieces and cut the spring onions into 1 inch lengths. Wash, trim and blanch the bean sprouts. Cook the noodles for 1 minute, then cut into short lengths. Arrange all the above ingredients on to one or more plates and place on the table. Preheat an iron pan over a flame in the center of the table. Rub the fat all over the bottom of the pan to grease well. Place a few slices of meat into the pan and cook for 1–2 minutes, turning once. Sprinkle the sugar over the meat and add a few of the vegetables. Cook for 1 minute, stirring continuously, then pour in the sake and half the soy sauce and add the bean curd and noodles. Allow each diner to serve himself directly from the pan and cook the remaining meat and vegetables as required, adding the remaining soy sauce a little at a time. The eggs should be broken into small individual side-bowls, lightly beaten with the chopsticks and used as a dip for the beef.

Taiwan

MONGOLIAN HOT POT
(Lamb & Vegetable Hot Pot)

1¾ *pounds lean boneless lamb*
⅓ *pound lamb liver*
1 small Chinese cabbage
1 lettuce
1 large brown onion
5 ounces transparent noodles
2 spring onions
2 cloves garlic
1¼ *inch knob fresh ginger*
2 tablespoons vegetable oil
6 cups chicken stock
2 tablespoons dark soy sauce
2 tablespoons Chinese wine
salt to taste
freshly ground white pepper
pinch monosodium glutamate

Sauce:
3 fresh red chilies
2 cloves garlic
1 inch knob fresh ginger
2 teaspoons Chinese wine
2 tablespoons light soy sauce
1 teaspoon sesame oil
½ *cup chicken stock*
2 tablespoons soft brown sugar
freshly ground white pepper   serves 6

Freeze the lamb slightly then cut into thin slices. Blanch the liver in boiling water, then remove skin and membranes and cut into thin slices. Trim the ends of the cabbage and lettuce and separate the leaves. Cut the brown onion into thin slices. Arrange the cabbage and lettuce on individual plates, place the meat on top and surround with slices of onion. Soak the noodles for 1 minute, then drain thoroughly and place in a large bowl. Chop the spring onions, garlic and ginger. Heat the oil in a large saucepan, add the garlic and ginger and stir-fry for 2–3 minutes, then pour in the stock and bring to the boil. Add the spring onion, soy sauce, Chinese wine, salt, white pepper and monosodium glutamate and stir to blend thoroughly. Lower heat and allow to simmer for 3 minutes. Place a hot-pot cooker in the center of the table and fill the chimney with hot charcoal. Arrange plates of meat and vegetables in front of each diner together with a small side bowl of prepared sauce (see below) and an empty soup bowl.

Place the bowl of noodles on the table and transfer the simmering stock to the hot-pot cooker. Each diner cooks his own meat and vegetables in the stock and dips in the sauce before eating. (Note that sometimes a side dish of beaten egg is used as a secondary dip.) After all the meat has been cooked, add the noodles to the stock and cook until tender. Transfer the noodles, together with some stock, to the soup bowls and sprinkle a little of the remaining sauce on top.

To prepare the sauce; chop the chilies, garlic and ginger very finely and place into a mixing bowl. Add the Chinese wine, soy sauce, sesame oil, stock, sugar and white pepper and stir to blend thoroughly.

Korea

CHICKEN FIREPOT
(Simple Chicken Hot Pot)

1 pound white chicken meat
2 eggs
2 tablespoons light soy sauce
2 tablespoons Chinese wine
freshly ground black pepper
¼ *pound bean sprouts*
3 spring onions
6 fresh white mushrooms
¼ *cup vegetable oil*
2 cups chicken stock   serves 4

Cut the chicken into bite-size pieces and place in a shallow dish. Beat the eggs, mix with the soy sauce, Chinese wine and pepper and pour over the chicken. Blanch the bean sprouts in boiling water and cut into ½ in. lengths. Cut the spring onions into similar lengths and slice the mushrooms. Place a heavy based pan over a burner in the center of the table and heat the oil. Sauté the mushrooms for 2–3 minutes then add the chicken and stir-fry for another 2 minutes. Bring the stock to the boil and pour into the pan. Add the spring onion and bean sprouts and adjust seasonings. Allow each diner to serve himself directly from the pan.

Japan

SHABU SHABU
(Beef & Vegetable Hot Pot)

1¹/₂ pounds lean beef steak
small Chinese cabbage
6 small carrots
¹/₄ pound spinach leaves
4 large white mushrooms
4 squares bean curd
6 spring onions
5 cups chicken stock

Sesame seed dip:
1 shallot
2 anchovy fillets
¹/₂ cup roasted sesame seeds
¹/₂ cup roasted cashewnuts
¹/₄ cup vinegar
¹/₄ cup Japanese soy sauce
2 teaspoons sugar
¹/₄ teaspoon salt   serves 4–6

Freeze the beef slightly then cut into thin slices. Discard the stem and outer leaves from the cabbage and slice the carrots lengthways. Parboil the cabbage, spinach and carrots separately and drain well. Slice the mushrooms and bean curd and cut the spring onions into 1 inch lengths. Arrange the cabbage and spinach leaves on a large plate, placed the sliced beef on top and surround with the remaining vegetables and bean curd. Place a shabu shabu cooker (or steamboat) in the middle of a table and fill the chimney with hot charcoal. Pour the stock into the cooker and bring to the boil. (The stock should remain simmering while each diner selects from the serving plate and cooks his own food.) Serve with a prepared sesame seed dip.

To make the dip; chop the shallot and anchovy very finely and grind together with the roasted sesame seeds and cashew nuts to produce a smooth paste. Add the vinegar, soy sauce, sugar and salt and blend thoroughly.

Vietnam

SLICED BEEF IN VINEGAR

³/₄ pound lean prime beef
4 spring onions
¹/₄ cup light soy sauce
2 teaspoons rice wine
²/₃ cup white vinegar
1 teaspoon sugar
¹/₂ teaspoon salt
¹/₂ teaspoon white pepper
¹/₄ cup finely shredded carrot   serves 4

Cut the beef into very thin slices and arrange on a serving dish. Chop the spring onions finely and sprinkle over the beef, then add the soy sauce and rice wine and set aside for 30 minutes. In a saucepan, bring 1¹/₄ cups water to the boil, add sugar, salt, white pepper and three-quarters of the vinegar. Stir to blend thoroughly, then lower heat and simmer gently for 15 minutes. Transfer the liquid to a fireproof pot and place over a low flame in the center of the table. (Note that the liquid should remain on a low boil.) Place the marinated beef on the table, cook in the seasoned stock, piece by piece, and serve with a side dip of the shredded carrot mixed with the remaining vinegar.

Meats

The range and variety of meat dishes in Asian cooking appears endless although the roasted joint, so much a part of Western cuisine, is seldom found. It is more usual for meat to be sliced, shredded or cut into chunks and braised, stir-fried or 'stewed', with spices and vegetables, rather than cooked on its own. Marination is a very regular practice and sauces are more often part of the cooked dish (as with casseroles) rather than being served separately as a gravy.

Care must always be taken when serving meat courses in Asia, for both religion and custom impose certain restrictions. In the predominately Muslim areas, beef and mutton are eaten regularly but to the Hindu, where the cow is sacred, beef is naturally strictly forbidden. Pork is the most popular meat with the Chinese but considerable beef is also eaten. Mutton is enjoyed in the North of China but its strong flavor is generally repellent to the Southerners. Venison and other game animals are seldom used in Asian cooking.

Capsicums with Spiced Beef Filling	**Beef Embul**	**Lechon** *Barbecued suckling pig*
Sliced Beef with Spring Onions	**Neau Pad Prik** *Sautéed beef with chilies*	**Crispy Pata** *Deep fried pig's feet*
Shredded Beef in Taro Nest	**Dendeng Ragi** *Beef with shredded coconut*	**Sweet & Sour Pork**
Sanchok *Skewered beef with vegetables*	**Daging Bumbu Bali** *Balinese style sautéed beef*	**Pad Luk Chin** *Deep-fried pork balls with vegetables*
Kalbi Chim *Boiled beef ribs with chestnuts*	**Daging Rendang** *Spicy beef chunks*	**Kofta Curry** *Minced lamb balls in curry sauce*
Bola Curry *Minced beefball curry*	**Teochew Satay** *Pork liver in satay sauce*	**Gulai Kambing** *Spicy lamb*
Daging Besengek *Beef stew*	**Babi Panggang** *Roast belly of pork*	**Lamb Madras**
Kustilyas *Braised beef ribs*		**Lamb Apple Korma**
Daging Belano *Crispy beef with sauce*		

Recipe for **Shredded Beef** (photographed opposite) is on page 131.

Sri Lanka

CAPSICUMS WITH SPICED BEEF FILLING

2 medium size capsicums (green peppers)
½ pound ground beef
2 brown onions
1 inch knob fresh ginger
2 cloves garlic
2 fresh green chilies
3 boiled potatoes
½ cup vegetable oil
3 curry leaves
1 teaspoon salt
½ teaspoon white pepper

Sauce:
1 brown onion
1 clove garlic
2 fresh green chilies
½ teaspoon cumin powder
½ teaspoon cinnamon powder
1 teaspoon coriander powder
1 teaspoon red chili powder
1 cup thick coconut milk
salt to taste   serves 4

Cut the capsicums in half lengthways, remove the seeds and wash under running water. Chop the onions, ginger, garlic and chilies and cut the potatoes into small dice. Heat one third of the oil in a pan and, when very hot, add the curry leaves, onion and garlic and stir-fry for 3–4 minutes. Add the beef, chilies and the ginger and continue to cook, stirring frequently, until the beef is well browned, then add the potato, season to taste with salt and white pepper and cook for another 5 minutes. Remove from the heat, discard the curry leaves, and allow to cool slightly before spooning the mixture into the capsicums. Next, heat the remaining oil in a shallow pan and fry the stuffed capsicums for a few minutes, basting occasionally with the oil. Then, remove and drain off excess oil. Bring the sauce to the boil. Add the capsicums and simmer for 3 minutes, then transfer the capsicums to a serving dish.

To make the sauce; chop the onion, garlic and chili. Heat the oil and sauté the onion and garlic for 3 minutes, then add the chili and all the spice powders and continue to cook for another 4–5 minutes, stirring frequently. Mash with a wooden spoon, then add the coconut milk, season with salt and bring to the boil. Stir to blend, lower heat and allow to simmer for 3 minutes.

Hong Kong

SLICED BEEF WITH SPRING ONIONS

½ pound lean beef
1 tablespoon cornstarch
2 tablespoons light soy sauce
½ teaspoon salt
¼ teaspoon white pepper
6 spring onions
½ inch knob fresh ginger
¼ cup peanut oil
1 egg
½ teaspoon sugar
2 tablespoons Chinese wine
1 teaspoon dark soy sauce
¼ cup beef stock   serves 4

Cut the beef into small thin slices and place in a shallow dish. Dust with half the cornstarch, add the light soy sauce and season with salt and white pepper. Allow to marinate for 30 minutes. Cut the spring onions into 1 inch lengths and finely chop the ginger. Heat the oil in a wok and sauté and beef for 1 minute. Add the spring onion and ginger and stir-fry over medium heat for 2 minutes. Beat the egg and mix with the sugar, Chinese wine, dark soy sauce, beef stock and remaining cornstarch. Pour the mixture into the wok and simmer for 3–4 minutes, stirring frequently. Decorate with extra slices of spring onion if desired.

SHREDDED BEEF IN TARO NEST

Hong Kong

³/₄ pound lean beef
¹/₂ teaspoon salt
¹/₄ teaspoon white pepper
2 tablespoons Chinese wine
¹/₂ pound taro*
1 egg
2 tablespoons cornstarch
vegetable oil for deep frying
1 brown onion
1 green pepper
1 inch knob fresh ginger
3 fresh red chilies
2 cloves garlic
1 teaspoon sugar
2 tablespoons light soy sauce
3 teaspoons oyster sauce   serves 4

Cut the beef into fine shreds and place in a shallow dish. Season with salt and white pepper, pour on the Chinese wine and let stand for 20 minutes. Cut the taro into fine shreds and place in a dish. Beat the egg, mix with half the cornstarch and pour over the taro. Mix to coat the taro evenly, then arrange in a frying basket in the shape of a nest. Heat the oil in a large pan until it is almost smoking and deep fry the taro until it is golden and set in the nest shape, approximately 3 minutes. Remove and set aside and pour off most of the oil from the pan. Chop the onion, green pepper and ginger and crush the garlic. Add to the pan, sauté for 2–3 minutes, then add the beef, marinade, sugar, soy and oyster sauce. Mix the remaining cornstarch with a small quantity of cold water, add to the pan and stir for another 2 minutes, then transfer to the taro nest.

*Note: Potato may be substituted for the taro if preferred.

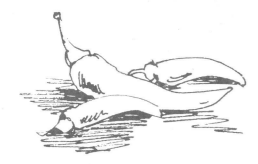

Korea

SANCHOK
(Skewered Beef with Vegetables)

³/₄ pound prime beef steak
4 leeks
4 carrots
6 mushrooms
¹/₂ cup light soy sauce
¹/₂ cup chicken stock
1 inch knob fresh ginger
3 cloves garlic
2 teaspoons sesame seeds
2 tablespoons sugar
1 teaspoon salt
freshly ground black pepper
oil for frying
2 tablespoons sesame oil   serves 4

Trim excess fat from the beef and cut into thin slices. Boil the leeks and carrots for just a few moments, then cut into short lengths. Halve the mushrooms. Place the meat and all the vegetables in a shallow dish and add the soy sauce and stock. Grate the ginger and crush the garlic. Toast the sesame seeds lightly, then crush and add to the beef marinade together with the ginger, garlic, sugar, salt and freshly ground black pepper. Stir well and set aside for 45 minutes. Then, thread the meat and vegetables in alternating layers onto wooden skewers. Heat the oil in a pan and fry the skewered food, turning occasionally, until cooked on all sides. Transfer to a serving dish and sprinkle hot sesame oil on top.

KALBI CHIM
(Boiled Beef Ribs with Chestnuts)

Korea

2 pounds prime beef ribs
12 water chestnuts
1 brown onion
1 carrot
2 shallots
4 cloves garlic
1 inch knob fresh ginger
2 spring onions
1/4 cup sesame seeds
1/2 cup light soy sauce
2 tablespoons dark soy sauce
1/4 cup rice wine
2 teaspoons sesame oil
3 tablespoons sugar
freshly ground black pepper
1/4 cup vegetable oil
2 teaspoons pine nuts (optional) serves 4–6

Remove excess fat from the ribs and cut into pieces, approximately 2 1/2 in. long. Soak the water chestnuts in warm water for 30 minutes, then remove skin and wash under running water. Boil in a little water for 15 minutes, then remove from heat and allow to cool in the pan. Drain and set aside. Slice the brown onion and carrot and chop finely the shallots, garlic, ginger and spring onions. Toast the sesame seeds lightly, then crush. Place the soy sauce, rice wine and sesame oil in a large shallow dish and add the chopped shallot, garlic, ginger, spring onion, crushed sesame seeds, sugar and freshly ground black pepper. Mix thoroughly until the sugar has completely dissolved, then add the ribs. Refrigerate for 1 1/2 hours, turning ribs occasionally during marination. Heat the oil in a large pan and sauté the sliced onion for 3–4 minutes, then add the carrot and the ribs and continue to cook over a fairly high heat, stirring continuously, until the ribs are well browned. Next, pour in 1/4 cup of the marinade and add just sufficient cold water to cover the ribs completely. Bring to the boil, then cover the pan, lower heat and simmer until the meat is cooked, approximately 1 hour. Remove the lid from the pan, add the chestnuts, stir well, adjust seasonings to taste and boil rapidly for another 5 minutes. To serve; transfer to a large dish and sprinkle the pine nuts on top.

BOLA CURRY
(Minced Beef-ball Curry)

Sri Lanka

1 pound ground rump steak
¹/₂ teaspoon salt
¹/₄ teaspoon white pepper
1 thick slice stale bread
2 tablespoons fresh lime juice
2 eggs
1 small brown onion
¹/₂ inch knob fresh ginger
2 cloves garlic
2 cloves
¹/₄ teaspoon cinnamon powder
2 tablespoons curry powder
oil for deep frying

Sauce:
1 small brown onion
1 stem lemon grass
2 slices fresh ginger
2 cloves garlic
¹/₄ cup oil
3 curry leaves
¹/₄ teaspoon fenugreek powder
¹/₂ teaspoon turmeric powder
1 teaspoon chili powder
¹/₂ teaspoon curry powder
1¹/₂ cups thick coconut milk

serves 4

Take the beef and season with salt and white pepper. Grate the bread and moisten with half the lime juice. Beat the eggs lightly. Finely chop the onion, garlic and ginger and crush the cloves. Mix together the beef, half the beaten egg and all the dry ingredients and shape into small balls, about 1 inch in diameter. Brush the meatballs with the remaining egg. Heat the oil until very hot and deep-fry the meat-balls for 5–8 minutes, until cooked as preferred, then remove and drain off excess oil. Bring the prepared sauce to the boil, add the meat-balls and cook for another 3 minutes, then transfer to a serving dish and sprinkle the remaining lime juice on top.

To make the sauce; chop finely the onion, lemon grass, ginger and garlic. Heat the oil in a pan, add the onion, lemon grass and curry leaves and cook until the onion starts to brown. Then, add all the remaining ingredients and bring to the boil. Lower heat and simmer until the sauce starts to thicken.

Note: Before transferring meat-balls to the serving dish, remove curry leaves from the sauce.

133

Indonesia

DAGING BESENGEK
(Beef Stew)

1¼ pounds lean beef steak
2 onions
3 cloves garlic
¾ inch knob fresh ginger
2 fresh red chilies
4 macadamia nuts
2 stems lemon grass
1 teaspoon blachan
¼ cup butter
2 tablespoons tomato paste
3 cups beef stock
2 salem leaves (substitute curry leaves)
salt to taste
freshly ground black pepper serves 4–6

Cut the beef into bite-size pieces. Chop the onions, garlic and ginger, pound together the chilies, macadamia nuts, lemon grass and blachan. Heat the butter in a large pan and sauté the onion and garlic for 3–4 minutes, then add the beef, ginger, spice-paste and tomato paste. Cook for another 5 minutes, stirring frequently, then pour in the stock, add the salem leaves and season to taste with salt and freshly ground black pepper. Bring to the boil, then lower heat, cover the pan and cook slowly until the beef is tender. Serve immediately.

Philippines

KUSTILYAS
(Braised Beef Ribs)

3 pounds beef spareribs
2 brown onions
1 clove garlic
1 red pepper
10 green olives
½ cup margarine
salt to taste
freshly ground black pepper
pinch monosodium glutamate
2 teaspoons lime juice
4 cups beef stock
¼ cup London dry gin serves 4–6

Cut the beef into individual ribs approximately 3 in. in length. Chop the onions and the garlic, cut the red pepper into julienne strips, halve the olives and remove stones. Heat the margarine in an ovenproof pot and brown the ribs, then remove and sauté the onion and garlic for 3–4 minutes, replace the ribs, season with salt, freshly ground black pepper and monosodium glutamate and pour in the lime juice and beef stock. Cover the pot with a tightly fitting lid and cook in a pre-heated moderately hot oven until the meat is tender, approximately 1 hour. Remove the ribs, place the pot over a high heat and reduce the sauce by half, then lower heat, pour in the gin and continue to simmer for another 2 minutes. To serve; arrange the ribs on a plate, pour the sauce on top and garnish with the olives and strips of red pepper.

Malaysia

DAGING BELANO
(Crispy Beef with Sauce)

1¼ pound top round steak
1 teaspoon salt
½ teaspoon white pepper
2 onions
2 tomatoes
4 fresh red chilies
2 cloves garlic
2 stems lemon grass
½ cup vegetable oil
2 teaspoons brown sugar
¼ cup chicken stock serves 4–6

Cut the beef into thin slices, season with salt and white pepper and arrange on a wire rack. Chop the onions, tomatoes, chilies, garlic and lemon grass. Cook the meat in a low oven until it is fairly dry. Heat the oil in a frying pan, add the partially cooked beef and fry until crispy, then remove, drain off excess oil and arrange on a serving dish. Pour away most of the oil from the pan, add the vegetables and stir-fry for 5 minutes. Add the brown sugar, pour in the stock and bring to the boil. Adjust seasonings to taste, allow to simmer for 2 minutes, then pour over the beef and serve immediately.

Sri Lanka

BEEF EMBUL

1 pound beef steak
1 small brown onion
1 clove garlic
1 stem lemon grass
2 tablespoons tamarind water
$^1/_3$ cup beef stock
1 teaspoon chili powder
1 teaspoon turmeric powder
salt to taste
freshly ground white pepper
1 inch cinnamon stick

serves 4

Cut the beef into bite-size chunks. Chop finely the onion, garlic and lemon grass. Combine the tamarind water and stock in a saucepan and bring to the boil. Add the onion, garlic, lemon grass, chili, turmeric, salt, pepper and cinnamon stick and stir well, then add the beef and cook over a moderate heat until the meat is tender and the sauce has reduced by two-thirds, approximately 30–40 minutes. Remove the cinnamon stick and transfer to a serving dish.

Note: Although the sauce is reduced considerably and should be very thick when served, the dish is not meant to be too dry, so add a little extra water (or stock) if necessary.

Thailand

NEAU PAD PRIK
(Sautéed Beef with Chilies)

1 pound beef fillet
$^1/_2$ teaspoon salt
freshly ground black pepper
pinch monosodium glutamate
3 dried Chinese mushrooms
1 brown onion
1 clove garlic
4 fresh red chilies
$^1/_4$ cup vegetable oil
$^1/_3$ cup beef stock
2 tablespoons light soy sauce
2 teaspoons oyster sauce
2 teaspoons rice wine

serves 4

Cut the beef into bite-size pieces and season with salt, freshly ground black pepper and monosodium glutamate. Soak the mushrooms in warm water for 40 minutes, discard the hard stems and slice the caps. Chop the onion and garlic and cut the chilies into fine julienne strips. Heat the oil in a frying pan and sauté the onion and garlic for 3–4 minutes, then add the beef and chilies and continue to cook for another 2 minutes, stirring frequently. Pour in the stock and bring to the boil. Add the mushrooms, soy sauce, oyster sauce and wine and adjust seasonings to taste. Lower heat and continue to cook over a moderate heat until the beef is tender, approximately 5–7 minutes. Serve with steamed rice or fresh green vegetables.

Indonesia

DENDENG RAGI
(Beef with Shredded Coconut)

1$^1/_2$ pounds top round steak
1 onion
2 cloves garlic
2 stems lemon grass
$^1/_4$ cup vegetable oil
1 teaspoon coriander powder
1 cup thick coconut milk
2 tablespoons tamarind water
2 salem (or curry) leaves
salt to taste
freshly ground black pepper
$^3/_4$ cup shredded coconut
2 tablespoons butter
$^1/_2$ cup ground peanuts

serves 4–6

Cut the beef into bite-size pieces. Chop the onion, garlic and lemon grass. Heat the vegetable oil in a pan and sauté the onion, garlic and lemon grass for 3 minutes, then add the coriander powder and the beef and stir-fry until the meat is completely sealed. Pour in the coconut milk and tamarind water, add the salem leaves and season to taste with salt and freshly ground black pepper. Cook over a low heat until the liquid has reduced by half then add the shredded coconut and continue to cook, stirring frequently, until the liquid has almost completely been absorbed. Transfer to a serving dish and keep warm. Finally, heat the butter in a small pan, stir-fry the ground peanuts for 2 minutes and sprinkle over the beef.

135

DAGING BUMBU BALI
(Balinese Style Sautéed Beef)

Indonesia

1¼ pounds top round steak
2 shallots
¾ inch knob fresh ginger
2 fresh red chilies
2 cloves garlic
3 candlenuts
2 tablespoons oil
2 teaspoons ground ginger
2 teaspoons turmeric powder
1 teaspoon cardamom powder
1 teaspoon coriander powder
½ teaspoon black peppercorns
½ teaspoon blachan (shrimp paste)
2 bay leaves
⅔ cup thick coconut milk
salt to taste   serves 4–6

Cut the beef into bite-size pieces. Finely chop the shallots, ginger, chilies and garlic and grate the candlenuts. Heat the oil, add the beef and sauté until well browned. Remove the beef and set to one side. Reheat the oil and sauté the chopped vegetables for 3–4 minutes, then add the grated candlenut, spice powders, peppercorns, blachan and bay leaves. Stir-fry for another 3 minutes, then replace the beef and pour in the coconut milk. Add salt to taste and bring to the boil. Lower heat and allow to simmer until the meat is cooked, approximately 1 hour, and the sauce has reduced by half. Remove bay leaves and serve with steamed rice and green vegetables.

DAGING RENDANG
(Spicy Beef Chunks)

Indonesia

1¼ pounds lean beef
4 shallots
7 fresh red chilies
½ inch knob fresh ginger
½ inch knob fresh langkuas (local ginger)
4 cloves garlic
1¼ cups thin coconut milk
¼ cup vegetable oil
1 teaspoon coriander powder
½ teaspoon cumin powder
salt to taste
freshly ground black pepper
1¼ cups thick coconut milk

serves 4

Chop the meat into chunks and place in a bowl. Chop the shallots and place half to one side. Chop the chilies, ginger, langkuas and garlic and grind these together with half the shallot and ¼ cup of thin coconut milk. Pour this paste over the meat and stir to ensure an even coating. Set aside for 30 minutes, then heat the oil in a large frying pan and sauté the remaining shallot until it softens. Add the meat and the marinade and season with coriander, cumin, salt and freshly ground black pepper. Pour in the remaining thin coconut milk and bring to the boil, stirring continuously, then lower heat and allow to simmer until the meat is tender, approximately 1¼ hours. Finally, add the thick coconut milk and continue to cook, over a medium heat, until the liquid has been almost completely reduced.

Malaysia

TEOCHEW SATAY
(Pork Liver in Satay Sauce)

1 pound pork liver
1 teaspoon salt
1/2 teaspoon white pepper
1/2 pound bean sprouts
1/4 cup satay sauce (see below)
1/3 cup sugar
2 teaspoons cornstarch
4 celery leaves

Satay sauce:
1 pound roasted peanuts
8 shallots
3/4 inch knob fresh ginger
4 cloves garlic
2 stems lemon grass
8 dried red chilies
1/3 cup sambal blachan
1/2 cup dried shrimp
1/3 cup dried salted fish
3 macadamia nuts
1 teaspoon celery seeds
1/2 teaspoon five spice powder
1 teaspoon salt
1/4 cup sesame oil
1 cup peanut oil　　serves 6–8

Slice the liver and season with salt and white pepper. Bring approximately 2 cups of water to the boil and blanch the bean sprouts for 2 minutes, then remove, drain and place in the bottom of a large serving dish. Keep the same water boiling rapidly and cook the liver for 3–4 minutes, then arrange on top of the bean sprouts. Add the satay sauce and sugar to the same water, bring back to the boil and stir until the sugar is completely dissolved. Mix the cornstarch with a small quantity of cold water and stir into the sauce to thicken slightly. Pour the sauce over the liver and bean sprouts and sprinkle with finely chopped Chinese parsley. Serve with small chunks of white bread to dip into any remaining sauce.

To make the sauce; shell the peanuts and chop the shallots, ginger, garlic, lemon grass and chilies. Pound all the dry ingredients together with the sesame oil to form a rich smooth paste. Heat the peanut oil and fry the spice-paste for 30–40 minutes over a low heat, stirring frequently. After cooling, the sauce may be placed in a jar with a tightly fitting lid and stored in a refrigerator for use as required.

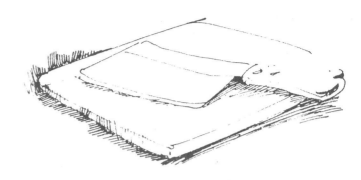

Indonesia

BABI PANGGANG
(Roast Belly of Pork)

2 pounds belly of pork (with skin)
2 cloves garlic
salt
freshly ground white pepper
2 tablespoons dark soy sauce
4 shallots
1 inch knob fresh ginger
3 tablespoons sugar
2 tablespoons coriander powder
1/2 teaspoon five-spice powder
2 tablespoons Chinese wine
2 tablespoons light soy sauce　　serves 4

Place the belly of pork on a flat surface with the skin side down. With a sharp knife make slits in the pork, about 1/2 inch apart and to within about 1/8 inch of the skin. Rub the garlic into the pork and season further with salt, freshly ground white pepper and half the dark soy sauce. Chop the shallots and ginger finely and pound together with the sugar, coriander powder, five-spice powder, Chinese wine and all the remaining soy sauce. Place the pork in a large roasting pan, skin up, and roast in a pre-heated moderate oven for 15–20 minutes. Then remove, jab the skin all over with a fork and rub well with salt. Place under a hot grill until the skin crackles and turns a deep golden brown. Now place the pork back in the roasting pan, this time with the underside uppermost, and cover with the prepared spice paste. Turn the oven up to moderately hot and cook for another 15 minutes. Serve immediately.

Philippines

LECHON
(Barbecued Suckling Pig)

whole suckling pig, about 10 pounds
¹/₂ cup vinegar
¹/₂ cup coarse salt crystals
3 tablespoons sugar
¹/₄ teaspoon red coloring powder
oil for basting

Liver sauce:
¹/₄ pound liver pâté
¹/₃ cup vinegar
2 tablespoons fresh lime juice
³/₄ cup stale white breadcrumbs
3 tablespoons sugar
1 teaspoon salt
freshly ground black pepper
3 cloves garlic
3 shallots
¹/₄ cup lard   serves 12–16

Clean and prepare the pig, scraping off all the bristles. In a large saucepan bring 3 quarts of water to the boil, add the vinegar, salt, sugar and red coloring powder and stir until the salt and sugar have completely dissolved. Rub the mixture into the skin of the pig, then pour the remainder on top. Stretch the pig and secure on skewers; one through the center and two small ones holding the fore and hind legs. Hang in a drafty place for 2–3 hours to allow the skin to stretch, then place on a spit and cook over a hot charcoal fire, basting frequently with the oil. When fully cooked, (approximately 5–6 hours) chop the meat into rough serving pieces and use the liver sauce as a side dip.

To make the sauce; chop the liver pâté into small pieces and place in a bowl. Add the vinegar, lime juice, breadcrumbs, sugar, salt and freshly ground black pepper. Pour 1²/₃ cups of cold water into the bowl and stir to blend all the ingredients. Chop the garlic and shallots finely. Heat the lard in a large pan and sauté half the garlic until golden and crispy, then remove and set aside. Add the shallot and remaining garlic to the pan and sauté until soft and translucent, then add the pâté mixture, including the liquid, and bring to the boil. Boil rapidly for 1 minute, then lower heat and allow to simmer for 10 minutes, stirring occasionally. Finally pour the sauce into a dish and top with the crispy fried garlic.

Philippines

CRISPY PATA
(Deep Fried Pig's Feet)

4 pig's feet
1 teaspoon salt
¹/₂ teaspoon white pepper
¹/₄ teaspoon monosodium glutamate
oil for deep frying

Sauce:
3 cloves garlic
¹/₂ cup light soy sauce
2 teaspoons fresh lime juice
freshly ground black pepper
pinch monosodium glutamate   serves 4

Wash the pig's feet under running water, then place in a large pan and cover completely with cold water. Bring to the boil and season with salt, white pepper and monosodium glutamate. Cover the pan with a tightly fitting lid, lower the heat, and simmer gently for 2¹/₂–3 hours, then remove and drain. Heat the oil in another large pan until it is almost smoking, then deep-fry the feet for a few minutes until the skin is golden and crispy. Serve with a side dish of Crispy Pata sauce.

To make the sauce; crush the garlic and mix with the soy sauce. Add the lime juice, season with freshly ground black pepper and monosodium glutamate and stir to blend thoroughly.

SWEET & SOUR PORK

1 pound pork tenderloin
½ teaspoon salt
¼ teaspoon white pepper
½ teaspoon Chinese five-spice powder
2 eggs
2 tablespoons light soy sauce
2 tablespoons cornstarch
oil for deep frying

Sauce:
1 brown onion
1 green pepper
1 large tomato
2 carrots
1½ inch length cucumber
3 fresh red chilies
¾ inch knob fresh ginger
1 clove garlic
1 cup chicken stock
2 tablespoons Chinese wine
2 tablespoons light soy sauce
2 tablespoons dark soy sauce
2 tablespoons vinegar
2 tablespoons fresh lemon juice
3 tablespoons sugar
¾ cup canned pineapple chunks
1 teaspoon cornstarch   serves 4–6

Cut the pork into bite-size pieces and season with salt, white pepper and five-spice powder. Beat the eggs lightly, mix with the Chinese wine and soy sauce and pour over the pork. Allow the meat to marinate for 30 minutes, then remove and dust with cornstarch. Heat the oil in a wok until it starts to smoke, then deep-fry the pork for 4–5 minutes until it is well cooked and the outside is golden and crispy. Remove the meat, drain off excess oil and arrange on a serving dish. Pour the prepared sauce on top and serve immediately.

To make the sauce; chop the onion, green pepper and tomato coarsely, slice the carrots and cucumber, cut the chilies and ginger into julienne strips and crush the garlic. Place wok over a high heat, add the oil and stir-fry the vegetables for 2 minutes, then add the stock, Chinese wine, soy sauce, vinegar, lemon juice and sugar and bring to the boil. Lower the heat, add the pineapple chunks and continue to cook for another 3 minutes, stirring frequently. Finally, mix the cornstarch with a small quantity of cold water and stir into the sauce to thicken slightly. Pour over the pork immediately.

PAD LUK CHIN
(Deep-fried Pork Balls with Vegetables)

Thailand

1½ pounds finely ground pork
1 clove garlic
½ teaspoon chopped coriander root
2 teaspoons fresh lime juice
1 teaspoon sugar
salt to taste
freshly ground black pepper
1 egg
¼ cup all-purpose flour
1¼ cups finely chopped vegetables
(water chestnuts, bamboo shoots,
Chinese mushrooms and onion)
oil for deep frying
sauce for glazing   serves 4

Make sure the butcher trims the fat before grinding. Chop the garlic finely and pound together with the coriander root, lime juice, sugar, salt and pepper. Beat the egg lightly. Place all these ingredients into a mixing bowl, stir to blend thoroughly and set aside for 30 minutes. Then, add the flour and finely chopped vegetables, mix well and shape into small balls, approximately 1 inch in diameter. Heat the oil in a large pan until it is very hot, then deep-fry the meat-balls for 6–8 minutes until cooked. Remove from the oil, drain thoroughly and place on top of a dish of freshly cooked vegetables. Brush the top with a light sauce and serve with steamed rice.

Note: If preferred, the meat balls may be steamed instead of fried.

141

Malaysia

KOFTA CURRY
(Minced Lamb Balls in Curry Sauce)

1 pound lamb
1 large brown onion
1 sprig Chinese parsley
1 teaspoon turmeric powder
1 teaspoon coriander powder
1 teaspoon cumin powder
2 teaspoons chili powder
½ teaspoon salt
¼ teaspoon white pepper
2 eggs
2 tomatoes

Sauce:
4 shallots
4 fresh red chilies
¾ inch knob fresh ginger
3 cloves garlic
2 stems lemon grass
2 teaspoons coriander powder
1 teaspoon turmeric powder
1 teaspoon cumin powder
¼ teaspoon salt
2 tablespoons vegetable oil
1 cup thick coconut milk   serves 4

Chop the meat, onion and parsley, pass them together through a fine grinder and season with turmeric, coriander, cumin, chili, salt and pepper. Beat the eggs lightly and add to the meat. Blend thoroughly and shape the mixture into small 'balls', about 1 inch in diameter. Cut the tomatoes into small wedges. In a large saucepan, bring the prepared sauce to the boil, add the meat balls and tomato and stir well. Then, lower the heat and cook slowly for approximately 30 minutes.

To make the sauce; chop finely the shallots, chilies, ginger, garlic and lemon grass. Pound these together with the spice powders, salt and a small quantity of cold water to produce a smooth paste. Heat the oil in a saucepan and stir-fry the spice-paste for 6 minutes, then add the coconut milk, bring to the boil and simmer for 2–3 minutes.

Indonesia

GULAI KAMBING
(Spiced Lamb)

1¾ pounds fresh lamb
2 onions
3 fresh red chilies
¾ inch knob fresh ginger
½ inch knob lemon root
1 stem lemon grass
2 cloves garlic
8 macadamia nuts
2 ripe tomatoes
⅓ cup vegetable oil
½ teaspoon ground cardamom
½ teaspoon cumin powder
½ teaspoon turmeric powder
¼ teaspoon fennel powder
1 cinnamon stick
4 cloves
salt to taste
freshly ground black pepper
4 cups thick coconut milk   serves 4–6

Cut the lamb into bite-size chunks. Chop the onions, chilies, ginger, lemon root and lemon grass, crush the garlic and grind the macadamia nuts. Skin the tomatoes and cut the flesh into small dice. Heat the oil in a large pan, add the onion, chilies and garlic and sauté until the onion becomes translucent. Then, add the lamb, ginger, lemon root, lemon grass and tomato and cook for another 3 minutes, stirring frequently. Add the spice powders, cinnamon stick and cloves and season to taste with salt and freshly ground black pepper. Pour in the coconut milk and bring to the boil, stirring continuously, then lower heat and allow to simmer until the meat is very tender, approximately 45 minutes. Serve immediately with steamed rice.

India

LAMB MADRAS

1 pound boneless lamb
1 teaspoon salt
1/2 teaspoon white pepper
2/3 cup yoghurt
1 large brown onion
2 tomatoes
2 boiled potatoes
2 fresh red chilies
1 shallot
1 inch knob fresh ginger
2 cloves garlic
1/4 cup ghee
1 teaspoon cumin powder
2 teaspoons coriander powder
1 teaspoon turmeric powder
1 teaspoon hot mustard powder
10 black peppercorns
2 tablespoons vinegar
2 tablespoons tomato paste
2 tablespoons fresh lemon juice
1/2 cup cooked green peas
fresh coriander leaves   serves 4

Chop the meat into small pieces and place in a shallow dish. Season with salt and freshly ground white pepper and pour the yoghurt over the meat. Place in a refrigerator for 45 minutes, stirring occasionally. Chop the brown onion, tomatoes, potatoes and red chilies. Chop very finely the shallot, ginger and garlic. Heat one third of the ghee in a pan and sauté the shallot, ginger and garlic until soft, then add the cumin, coriander, turmeric and mustard powders and black peppercorns. Stir-fry over a fairly high heat for another 5 minutes then allow to cool. Transfer to a mortar, add the vinegar and pound to a smooth paste. Add the remaining ghee to the pan and, when very hot, add the lamb together with the marinade and cook for 3 minutes, stirring continuously. Then, add the chili, tomato, spice-paste, tomato paste and lemon juice and stir to blend thoroughly. Lower heat and simmer for 8–10 minutes until the lamb is cooked, then add the potato and peas and cook for another 3 minutes. Transfer to a serving dish and sprinkle chopped coriander leaves on top.

Singapore

LAMB APPLE KORMA

1 1/4 pounds boned lamb
2 cooking apples
2 large brown onions
2 large ripe tomatoes
3 cloves garlic
1/4 cup ghee
2 teaspoons coriander powder
2 teaspoons cumin powder
1 teaspoon chili powder
1/4 cup ground cashew nuts
1/3 cup plain yoghurt
salt to taste
freshly ground white pepper
1/4 cup fresh cream   serves 4

Trim excess fat from the lamb and cut into cubes. Peel and dice the apples and onions, mash the tomatoes and finely chop the garlic. Heat the ghee in a frying pan, add the onion and fry until golden. Then, add the tomato, garlic, coriander and cumin and stir-fry for 5 minutes. Add the chili powder and ground cashew nuts and cook for another 3 minutes, then pour in the yoghurt and season to taste with salt and freshly ground white pepper. Simmer for 5 minutes, stirring frequently, then add the lamb, pour in 1 cup of cold water and bring to the boil. Lower heat and cook slowly until the lamb is tender, approximately 45 minutes, then add the apple and cook for another 5 minutes. Finally, remove from heat, stir in the cream and serve immediately.

Vegetables & Salads

In Asian restaurants many of the menu items are seasonal, for freshness is all-important in Eastern cooking. The same approach is taken in the domestic kitchen and no traditional housewife would resort to the frozen 'T.V. Dinners', ever-present in the Western supermarket. And nowhere is this principle of freshness more strictly adhered to than when it comes to selecting the vegetables to be used for either the salads or cooked dishes.

Vegetables are used a lot in soups and as part of a meat dish but most meals will consist of a vegetable dish in its own right. The cooking process can be steaming, stir-frying or boiling but in the latter case only a small amount of water is used and always the cooking time itself is minimal so that the goodness and flavors are retained.

Salads are usually quite substantial (seldomed served as a small side-dish) and are often topped with a tasty and spicy sauce.

Mixed Vegetable Curry	**Lo Han Tsai Choy** *Buddhist vegetable stew*	**Pak Dong** *Pickled vegetables*
Dal Curry		
Nimono *Mixed braised vegetables*	**Eggplant in Hot Garlic Sauce**	**Kim Chi** *Pickled cabbage*
	Braised Assorted Mushrooms	
Tumis Goreng *Balinese style spinach*	**Yaki-Nasu** *Grilled eggplant*	**Thanatsone** *Broccoli salad*
Sayur Goreng *Sautéed mixed vegetables*	**Matsutake Tsutumi-Yaki** *Grilled mushrooms*	**Charmorro Bean Salad**
Brinjal Moju *Spiced eggplant*	**Gado Gado** *Mixed salad with peanut sauce*	
Ala Badun *Fried potato & onion*	**Sunomono** *Vegetable salad*	
Curried Leeks		

Recipes for **Indian Vegetables** (photographed opposite) are on pages 146.

India

MIXED VEGETABLE CURRY

2 potatoes
2 tomatoes
4 carrots
¼ pound green beans
1 small cauliflower
2 shallots
¾ inch knob fresh ginger
2 cloves garlic
2 fresh red chilies
¼ cup ghee
½ teaspoon turmeric powder
½ teaspoon coriander powder
¼ teaspoon cumin powder
½ cup yoghurt
salt to taste
freshly ground black pepper   serves 4–6

Wash and prepare all the vegetables. Parboil the potatoes and cut into medium-size dice. Slice the tomatoes, carrots and beans and break the cauliflower into florets. Chop finely the shallots, ginger, garlic and chilies. Heat the ghee in a large pan and sauté the shallot, ginger and garlic for 3–4 minutes, then add the chili and turmeric powder and continue to cook over a moderate heat for another 3 minutes. Add the coriander and cumin powder and stir well, then add the potato, carrot and beans and stir-fry for 2–3 minutes over a high heat. Pour in the yoghurt and bring to the boil. Add the tomato and season to taste with salt and freshly ground black pepper. Lower heat, stir to blend thoroughly and allow to simmer until the vegetables are cooked and most of the liquid has been absorbed.

Note: Take care not to overcook the vegetables.

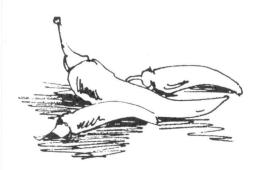

India

DAL CURRY

1 pound red dal (lentils)
3 brown onions
1 teaspoon turmeric powder
2 fresh red chilies
¾ inch knob fresh ginger
2 cloves garlic
2 tomatoes
½ teaspoon coriander seeds
½ teaspoon cumin seeds
2 tablespoons vinegar
⅓ cup ghee
1 teaspoon garam masala
½ teaspoon salt
1 teaspoon freshly
chopped coriander   serves 4–6

Place the dal in a saucepan. Chop 1 of the onions finely and add to the dal. Cover with cold water and bring to the boil. Add the turmeric powder, lower heat, and simmer until the dal is soft, then remove from heat and set aside. Slice the remaining 2 onions and chop finely the chilies, ginger and garlic. Chop the tomatoes. Grind the chili, ginger garlic, cumin and coriander seeds and blend with the vinegar to form a smooth spice paste. Heat the ghee in a pan and sauté the sliced onion until soft and translucent, then add the spice-paste and cook for 5 minutes, stirring frequently. Add the mixture to the dal and place over a moderate heat. Add the chopped tomato and season with garam masala and salt. Stir to blend thoroughly and allow to simmer for 3–4 minutes, then transfer to a serving dish and sprinkle the chopped coriander on top.

Japan

NIMONO
(Mixed Braised Vegetables)

½ cup bamboo shoots
¼ pound yams
¼ pound turnips
1 long white radish
6 carrots
4 small onions
4 fresh mushrooms
4 cups dashi
⅔ cup mirin
2 tablespoons Japanese soy sauce
salt to taste   serves 4

Prepare all the vegetables, cutting into appropriate serving-size pieces and cook each separately until partially cooked. Then place all the vegetables into a large pan, add the dashi, mirin, soy sauce and salt and bring to the boil. Lower heat and cook slowly for approximately 10 minutes. Drain vegetables thoroughly before serving.

Malaysia

TUMIS GORENG
(Balinese Style Spinach)

1 pound spinach
4 shallots
1 small tomato
2 fresh red chilies
1 clove garlic
2 tablespoons vegetable oil
2 curry leaves
1 teaspoon sugar
½ teaspoon salt
freshly ground black pepper
2 tablespoons light soy sauce
2 teaspoons dark soy sauce
⅔ cup chicken stock   serves 4–6

Wash the spinach under cold running water, shake dry, then wash again. Cut into short lengths and cook in a steamer until tender. Chop the shallots, tomato, chilies and garlic. Heat the oil in a large pan and sauté the shallot, chili and garlic for 3–4 minutes, then add the tomato, curry leaves, sugar, salt, freshly ground black pepper, soy sauce and stock. Bring to the boil and add the spinach, then lower heat and cook for a few minutes, turning frequently with a slotted spoon, until the spinach starts to wilt. Remove curry leaves before serving.

Indonesia

SAYUR GORENG
(Sautéed Mixed Vegetables)

1 brown onion
4 shallots
2 cloves garlic
1 cauliflower
6 carrots
3 fresh red chilies
1 green pepper
12 small corncobs
20 long green beans
¼ cup peanut oil
⅓ cup tomato ketchup
⅓ cup chili sauce
salt to taste
freshly ground black pepper
pinch monosodium glutamate   serves 8

Chop the onions, shallots and garlic and pound together to form a smooth paste. Break the cauliflower into florets, slice the carrots, chilies and green pepper and cut the beans into short lengths. Heat the oil in a large pan and sauté the onion-paste for 3–4 minutes, then, add the vegetables and stir-fry for 5–6 minutes. Add the ketchup and chili sauce, season to taste with salt, freshly ground black pepper and monosodium glutamate and continue to cook for another 2–3 minutes, stirring frequently. Serve immediately.

BRINJAL MOJU
(Spiced Eggplant)

Sri Lanka

1 pound eggplant
1 green pepper
4 shallots
½ inch knob fresh ginger
2 cloves garlic
1 teaspoon mustard seeds
⅔ cup vegetable oil
¼ cup vinegar
½ teaspoon turmeric powder
½ teaspoon salt
1 teaspoon sugar   serves 4

Slice the eggplant lengthwise. Cut the green pepper into thin strips, chop finely the shallots and ginger and crush the garlic. Grind the mustard seeds. Heat the oil in a frying pan and fry the eggplant for 3–4 minutes, then remove and set to one side. In the same oil, stir-fry the green pepper and shallot for 2 minutes, then remove and pour off most of the oil from the pan. Place the pan back over heat and sauté the ginger and garlic for 1 minute, then add the vinegar, turmeric powder, mustard and salt and continue to cook, stirring frequently for another 3 minutes. Replace the eggplant, pepper and shallot, stir well and cook for another 5 minutes. Finally, stir in the sugar and transfer to a serving dish.

ALA BADUN
(Fried Potato & Onion)

Sri Lanka

1 pound potatoes
¼ teaspoon salt
¼ teaspoon turmeric powder
1 teaspoon curry powder
½ teaspoon paprika
2 large brown onions
½ teaspoon mustard seeds
½ cup vegetable oil
3 curry leaves
¾ inch cinnamon stick
1 teaspoon fresh lime juice   serves 4

Boil the potatoes, cut into bite-size chunks and season with salt, turmeric powder, curry powder and paprika. Slice the onions and grind the mustard seeds. Heat the oil and when very hot, add the curry leaves, onion, mustard and cinnamon stick. Stir-fry until the onions are golden brown, then add the potato. Continue to cook, stirring frequently, until the potato is brown and hot. Remove the cinnamon stick, transfer to a serving dish and sprinkle the lemon juice on top.

CURRIED LEEKS

Sri Lanka

1 pound leeks
1 brown onion
2 green chilies
¼ teaspoon salt
¼ teaspoon turmeric powder
3 curry leaves
⅔ cup thin coconut milk
½ cup thick coconut milk
¼ teaspoon curry powder   serves 4

Wash the leeks and chop into small pieces. Chop the onion and green chilies. Place all the vegetables in a saucepan, add the salt, turmeric powder, curry leaves and thin coconut milk and bring to the boil. Cook slowly until the liquid has almost completely reduced, then add the thick coconut milk and bring back to the boil. Cook for another minute, then transfer to a serving dish and sprinkle the curry powder on top.

Hong Kong

LO HAN TSAI CHOY
(Buddhist Vegetable Stew)

6 black Chinese mushrooms
½ cup black fungus
½ cup white fungus
2 large carrots
¼ pound kale (or broccoli)
4 ounces canned bamboo shoots
4 ounces canned water chestnuts
2 ounces canned button mushrooms
2 ounces canned straw mushrooms
2 squares fresh bean curd
¼ cup vegetable oil
¼ cup light soy sauce
2 teaspoons dark soy sauce
10 gingko nuts
2 teaspoons sesame oil
2 teaspoons sugar
salt to taste
freshly ground black pepper
1 tablespoon cornstarch   serves 4

Soak the Chinese mushrooms in warm water for 40 minutes, then drain thoroughly and retain the water. Discard the hard stems from the mushrooms and set the caps to one side. Soak the black and white fungus (separately) in warm water for 15 minutes, then drain and cut into narrow strips. Wash and drain the fresh vegetables and drain the canned vegetables. Slice the bamboo shoots, water chestnuts and carrots and chop the bean curd into small pieces. Heat the oil in a wok, add the Chinese mushrooms and the bean curd and stir-fry for 3 minutes. Then, add ⅓ cup of the reserved mushroom-water together with the soy sauce and bring to the boil. Lower heat immediately and allow to simmer for 10 minutes, then add the remaining vegetables and pour in a little more of the mushroom-water. Bring back to the boil, add the gingko nuts, sesame oil, sugar, salt and freshly ground black pepper. Lower heat and allow to simmer for another 5–6 minutes, then add the strips of fungus. Mix the cornstarch with a small quantity of cold water and add to the pan. Stir to blend thoroughly, cook for 1 minute longer, then transfer to a serving dish.

Taiwan

EGGPLANT IN HOT GARLIC SAUCE

1 large long eggplant
4 cloves garlic
2 spring onions
1 inch knob fresh ginger
3 fresh red chilies
⅔ cup peanut oil
½ cup shredded beef
2 tablespoons light soy sauce
2 teaspoons dark soy sauce
2 tablespoons Chinese wine
½ cup chicken stock
2 tablespoons sugar
½ teaspoon salt
½ teaspoon white pepper
2 teaspoons vinegar
1 teaspoon sesame oil   serves 4

Wash the eggplant and cut, on a bias, into thin slices. Chop the garlic, spring onions, ginger and chilies. Heat the oil in a wok and fry the eggplant over a low heat for 3–4 minutes until soft, then remove and drain off excess oil. Pour most of the oil from the pan, add the garlic, onion, ginger, chili and shredded beef and stir-fry for 5 minutes, then add the soy sauce, Chinese wine and stock and bring to the boil. Season with salt and freshly ground white pepper and cook until the liquid has reduced by two-thirds. Then, add the vinegar, stir to blend thoroughly and transfer to a serving dish. Heat the sesame oil and sprinkle on top.

Malaysia

BRAISED ASSORTED MUSHROOMS

8 ounces canned golden mushrooms
4 ounces canned straw mushrooms
4 ounces canned button mushrooms
¹/₂ cup cooked ham
4 ounces canned abalone
¹/₄ cup vegetable oil
¹/₂ cup snow peas
2 teaspoons dark soy sauce
salt to taste
freshly ground black pepper
2 teaspoons Chinese wine   serves 6

Drain the mushrooms and reserve ¹/₃ cup of the liquid. Shred the ham and cut the abalone into thin slices. Heat the oil in a wok and sauté the ham and abalone for 30 seconds, then add the mushrooms, snow peas, soy sauce, salt and pepper. Stir-fry for 1 minute, then add the reserved liquid and Chinese wine and bring to the boil. Stir well and serve immediately.

Japan

YAKI NASU
(Grilled Eggplant)

2 small eggplants
¹/₂ teaspoon salt
¹/₄ teaspoon white pepper
¹/₃ cup vegetable oil
2 teaspoons bonito flakes

Dip:
³/₄ inch knob fresh ginger
¹/₂ cup Japanese (sweet) soy sauce
2 tablespoons mirin   serves 4

Wash the eggplants under cold running water, then dry thoroughly. Halve lengthwise, but do not remove the skin. Score the flesh with a sharp knife, season with salt and white pepper and set aside for 30 minutes. Then, brush the eggplants with a little oil and cook under a moderately hot grill until tender, approximately 20–25 minutes (baste occasionally with the remaining oil). Slice and arrange on a serving plate. Sprinkle the bonito flakes on top and serve with a side-dip.

To make the dip; cut the ginger into very fine shreds and mix with the soy sauce and mirin.

Japan

MATSUTAKE TSUTSUMI-YAKI
(Grilled Mushrooms)

12 large dried Japanese mushrooms
2 teaspoons light soy sauce
¹/₄ cup Japanese (sweet) soy sauce
¹/₄ cup mirin
2 teaspoons fresh lemon juice
2 tablespoons sugar
salt to taste
freshly ground white pepper
pinch monosodium glutamate
2 teaspoons cornstarch   serves 4

Wash the mushrooms under cold running water, then place in a saucepan and cover with cold water. Allow the mushrooms to soak for 45 minutes, then remove, dry thoroughly and discard the hard stems. Reserve ¹/₄ cup of the water. Sprinkle a little light soy sauce over the mushrooms, wrap each, individually, in foil and cook under a hot grill for 10–12 minutes. Meanwhile, combine the reserved water, Japanese soy sauce, mirin and lemon juice in a small saucepan and bring to the boil. Add the sugar, salt, pepper and monosodium glutamate and allow to simmer for 2–3 minutes. Mix the cornstarch with a small quantity of cold water and add to the sauce to thicken slightly. To serve; unwrap the mushrooms, arrange on a serving plate and pour the sauce on top.

Overleaf: **Gado-Gado** (recipe page 154)

Indonesia

GADO-GADO
(Mixed Salad with Peanut Sauce)

½ small cabbage
½ pound beansprouts
¼ pound green beans
2 potatoes
¼ pound spinach leaves
¼ pound bean curd
¼ cup peanut oil
1 small cucumber
2 hard-boiled eggs
½ cup crumbled shrimp crisps

Sauce:
2 shallots
2 cloves garlic
2 fresh red chilies
¾ cup roasted peanuts
1 teaspoon blachan (shrimp paste)
2 tablespoons peanut oil
1 cup tamarind water
2 tablespoons dark soy sauce
2 tablespoons soft brown sugar
salt to taste
freshly ground black pepper   serves 4–6

Wash and prepare all the vegetables. Separately, steam the cabbage, beansprouts, green beans, potatoes and spinach until barely cooked (they should be tender but still crispy). Cut the bean curd into thin slices and fry in the oil until golden, then remove and drain off excess oil. Peel and slice the cucumber and quarter the hard-boiled eggs. Arrange the cucumber and egg around the edge of a dinner plate, place all the vegetables in the center and add the slices of fried bean curd. Pour the peanut sauce over the salad and sprinkle the crumbled shrimp crisps on top.

To make the sauce; chop finely the shallots, garlic and chilies and grind the peanuts. Chop the blachan into tiny pieces. Heat the oil in a pan and sauté the shallot, garlic, chili and blachan for 4–5 minutes, then pound into a smooth paste. In a fresh saucepan, bring the tamarind water to the boil, add the peanuts and cook, over a moderate heat, for 15 minutes. Then, add the spice-paste, soy sauce, sugar, salt and freshly ground black pepper. Stir to blend thoroughly and cook for another 10–12 minutes, until the sauce is thick. Allow sauce to cool before pouring over salad.

Japan

SUNOMONO
(Vegetable Salad)

1 small cucumber
½ small Chinese cabbage
¼ pound white radish
¼ cup rice vinegar
½ cup dashi
¼ cup Japanese soy sauce
2 tablespoons mirin
2 teaspoons fresh lemon juice
2 teaspoons sugar
1 egg-yolk
salt to taste
freshly ground black pepper   serves 4

Wash the vegetables and dry thoroughly. Slice the cucumber, shred the cabbage and radish and place in a bowl. Combine the vinegar, dashi, soy sauce, mirin and lemon juice in a small saucepan and bring to the boil. Lower heat, add the sugar and allow to simmer for 3–4 minutes. Whisk the egg-yolk lightly, then add to the simmering stock. Season to taste with salt and freshly ground black pepper and continue to cook over a low heat, stirring frequently, until the sauce thickens. Remove the pan from heat and allow to cool before pouring over the vegetables. Place in refrigerator for 30 minutes, then serve into individual bowls.

Thailand

PAK DONG
(Pickled Vegetables)

1 small cabbage
1 small cucumber
1 small cauliflower
1 shallot
1 fresh red chili
2 cloves garlic
2 cups vinegar
2 teaspoons sugar
1 teaspoon salt
2 cups sweetcorn kernels
1 cup oil
¼ cup roasted sesame seeds   serves 4–6

Prepare the vegetables. Chop the cabbage and cucumber into bite-size pieces and break the cauliflower into florets. Chop finely the shallot, chili and garlic and pound these together with a little cold water to produce a smooth paste. Bring the vinegar to the boil, add the sugar and salt and partially cook all the vegetables, including the sweetcorn, then drain thoroughly. Heat the oil in a large pan and stir-fry the spice-paste for 3–4 minutes, then add the vegetables, adjust seasonings to taste and cook over a moderate heat for another 2 minutes. Transfer to a serving dish and sprinkle the sesame seeds on top.

Note: Alternatively, allow to cool, place in a jar with a tightly-fitting lid and store in the refrigerator.

Korea

KIM CHI
(Pickled Cabbage)

1 large Chinese cabbage
4 tablespoons common salt
¼ teaspoon saltpetre
2 tablespoons sugar
1 small white radish
3 cloves garlic
¾ inch knob fresh ginger
2 spring onions
4 fresh red chilies
2 tablespoons light soy sauce
2 tablespoons chicken stock   serves 12

Cut the base from the cabbage and slice into quarters. Mix the salt, saltpetre and half the sugar with approximately 4 cups of water. Stir to blend thoroughly then place the cabbage in the brine, cover and set aside for 36 hours. Turn the cabbage occasionally during that time, then rinse well under cold running water. Squeeze out most of the excess liquid and chop the cabbage into smaller pieces. Chop finely the radish, garlic, ginger, spring onion and chilies and mix with the soy sauce, stock and remaining sugar. Place a layer of cabbage in the bottom of a preserving jar and cover with a little of the other mixture, then add another layer of cabbage and continue that way until the jar is full. Place a tightly fitting cover on the jar and set aside in a cool place for at least 4 days before serving.

Burma

THANATSONE
(Broccoli Salad)

1¼ pounds broccoli
2 onions
4 cloves garlic
1 cup vegetable oil
2 tablespoons sesame oil
½ teaspoon turmeric powder
¼ cup white vinegar
salt to taste
½ cup toasted sesame seeds   serves 4–6

Cut the broccoli into bite-size pieces and cook in rapidly-boiling water for 1–2 minutes, until tender but still crisp. Drain in a colander and rinse under cold running water. Slice the onions and garlic. Combine the vegetable and sesame oils in a saucepan and place over a high heat. When the oil is very hot, add the onion, garlic and turmeric powder and stir-fry until the onion begins to turn brown, then remove the pan from the heat, continue to stir until the onion and garlic are crispy and set aside. When the oil is cool, add the broccoli, vinegar and salt and toss well. Remove the broccoli, drain off excess oil and arrange on a serving plate, then sprinkle the sesame seeds on top.

Philippines

CHARMORRO BEAN SALAD

½ pound fresh green beans
1 small brown onion
¼ cup light soy sauce
2 tablespoons fresh lemon juice
1 teaspoon olive oil
few drops tabasco sauce
freshly ground black pepper
½ teaspoon freshly
chopped mint   serves 4

Trim the beans and parboil, then place in a salad bowl. Cut the onion into very thin slices and add to the beans. Add the soy sauce, lemon juice, olive oil, tabasco sauce and freshly ground black pepper and toss well. Place in a refrigerator for 45 minutes, then sprinkle the freshly chopped mint on top just prior to serving.

Breads, Rice & Noodles

It was a matter of 'layout' which decided the order of recipes in this section and is certainly not a true indication of their importance or precedence in the Asian culinary scene. For, without any doubt, rice is the most important single ingredient in the overall-all regional diet. From Japan to Sri Lanka and from Pakistan to the Philippines the ubiquitous bowl of plain rice (steamed or boiled) will appear at some stage in every meal, whether a simple family repast or a banquet at a fine restaurant. In addition, rice is often cooked with a variety of other ingredients to make up a main dish. Indeed, **Nasi Goreng** (literally, fried rice) (page 164) is served in Indonesia and Malaysia with shrimp crackers and a sambal (and often topped with a fried egg) as a complete meal.

Noodles are also prepared in a variety of ways and are used to make delicious soups as well as 'dry' dishes. It is generally agreed that the best noodles are served at the more simple eating places and many hawkers and food stalls have a very successful business by specialising in, and serving, just one particular dish.

The popularity of bread is not so widespread throughout the region but usually with an Indian or Pakistani meal there will be an accompanying **Naan, Chapatis, Puri** (pages 157, 158 & 159) or Pappadam and tasty **Steamed Buns** (page 159) are often served with Northern Chinese dishes.

Naan *Baked leavened bread*	**Kahu Buth** *Yellow rice*	**Nasi Goreng** *Special fried rice*
Chapatis *Unleavened whole wheat bread*	**Nasi Kuning** *Rice cooked in coconut milk*	**Bami Goreng** *Fried noodles*
Steamed Buns	**Khao Pad Prik Gaeng** *Fried curried rice*	**Khao Soi** *Curried noodles*
Masala Puri *Deep-fried spiced bread*	**Moo Yong** *Fried rice in pineapple*	**Laksa Asam** *Sour soup noodles*
Baked Sesame Buns	**Kitsune Domburi** *Rice with fried bean curd*	**Pancit Luglog**
Biriyani *Mixed fried rice*	**Boiled Rice**	**Hokkien Fried Noodles**
Bringe *Mixed rice in leaves*		

India

NAAN
(Baked Leavened Bread)

1 package dried yeast
5 cups white flour
½ teaspoon salt
3 eggs
½ cup yoghurt
½ cup ghee
2 teaspoons sesame seeds   makes 10

Dissolve the yeast in a little warm water and set aside for 20 minutes. Sift the flour and salt into a mixing bowl, break in the eggs and add the yoghurt, yeast and just sufficient water to produce a firm, sticky dough. Mix thoroughly and shape into a ball then turn on to a lightly-floured, cold surface and knead for 15 minutes. Place the dough back into the bowl, cover with a damp cloth and set aside for 1 hour. Again, transfer to a cold surface and divide the mixture into 10 pieces. Flatten each piece with the hands and form into rough circles, approximately ½ inch thick, then stretch one side slightly so that the naans have an elongated shape. Place the naans on a lightly greased baking tray, coat with a little ghee and sprinkle sesame seeds on top. Place in a moderately hot pre-heated oven and bake for 10–12 minutes until golden brown.

Note: Traditionally this bread is cooked in a tandoor, or clay oven, which gives it a most distinctive flavor. A charcoal oven will give a similar result and should be used wherever possible.

India

CHAPATIS
(Unleavened Whole Wheat Bread)

2¼ cups whole wheat flour
½ teaspoon salt
¼ cup vegetable oil
½ cup ghee   makes 12

Sift the flour and salt into a mixing bowl and add the oil. Rub with the fingers until the oil and flour are thoroughly blended. Add warm water, just a little at a time, and continue to mix until the dough is firm but not too stiff (Between ⅓ cup and ½ cup of water should be sufficient). Transfer the dough to a lightly-greased surface and knead well for 10–15 minutes, then cover with a cloth and set aside for 1 hour. Next, divide the dough into 12 portions and, on a lightly-floured surface, roll each into a thin circular shape. Heat a heavy-based, or nonstick, frying pan until it is very hot, add one of the chapatis and cook for approximately 45 seconds then turn with a spatula, press around the edges with a folded tea towel and cook for another 45 seconds. (At this point the chapati should be a golden brown and slightly swollen but if necessary, turn again and cook for a little longer on each side.) Cook all the chapatis in a similar manner and, after removing from the pan, and while still hot, coat each with ghee.

Taiwan

STEAMED BUNS

1 package dried yeast
1/4 cup sugar
3 1/2 cups all-purpose flour
1/4 teaspoon salt
2 tablespoons lard　　　makes 12

Dissolve the yeast and sugar in 1/2 cup of warm water and set aside for 5 minutes. Sift the flour and salt into a mixing bowl, make a well in the center, and slowly add the fermented yeast. Melt the lard, add to the dough and stir to blend thoroughly. Turn on to a lightly-floured surface and knead for 10 minutes until the dough is firm and smooth. Cover with a damp cloth and set aside for 20 minutes, then shape into a roll, approximately 2 1/2 in. in diameter and cut into circles of 1 inch thickness. Flatten each piece of dough, fold in half and pinch the edges together to form a bun, leaving a small opening at the top. Place on a bamboo rack in a steamer and cook over rapidly boiling water for 8–10 minutes.

India

MASALA PURI
(Deep-Fried Spiced Bread)

2 1/4 cups whole wheat flour
1/4 teaspoon salt
1/2 teaspoon coriander powder
1/4 teaspoon cumin powder
1/4 teaspoon red chili powder
1/4 teaspoon turmeric powder
2 tablespoons ghee
1/4 cup yoghurt
oil for deep frying　　　makes 10–12

Sift the flour, salt and spice powders into a mixing bowl. Melt the ghee, add to the bowl and rub with the fingers to blend thoroughly. Add the yoghurt and just sufficient water to produce a firm dough. Turn the dough onto a lightly-greased surface and knead for 10–15 minutes then cover and set aside for 30 minutes. Divide the dough into equal portions and roll into small circles (puris). Heat the oil in a deep pan until it is very hot then add the puris, 2 or 3 at a time. When they rise to the surface of the oil and are slightly puffed, turn with a slotted spoon and continue to cook until golden brown on both sides. Remove and drain on absorbent paper before serving.

Hong Kong

BAKED SESAME BUNS

2 tablespoons peanut oil
1 3/4 cups all-purpose flour
1/2 teaspoon dried yeast
2 tablespoons sugar
2 tablespoons dark soy sauce
2 teaspoons light soy sauce
2 teaspoons sesame seeds　　　makes 6–8

Heat the oil in a small pan, add one quarter of the flour and mix to blend thoroughly. Set aside and allow to cool. Dissolve the yeast in 1/4 cup of warm water, sift in the remaining flour and mix well. Cover with a damp cloth and set aside for 30 minutes, then transfer to a lightly greased surface and shape into a rectangle of approximately 1/2 inch thickness. Spread the first mixture of flour and oil on top and roll lengthways. (The roll should be about 2 1/2 in. in diameter.) Cut the roll into 1/2 in. slices and place on a baking tray. Dissolve the sugar in a little warm water, add the soy sauce and brush the buns with the mixture. Sprinkle the sesame seeds on top, place in a pre-heated moderate oven and bake until the buns are golden brown in color and have risen slightly, approximately 12–15 minutes.

159

BIRIYANI
(Mixed Fried Rice)

3 cups long-grain rice
³/₄ pounds fresh lamb
4 brown onions
1 inch knob fresh ginger
2 cloves garlic
³/₄ inch length cinnamon stick
4 cloves
2 candlenuts
2 points star anise
¹/₂ teaspoon turmeric powder
10 black peppercorns
¹/₄ cup ghee
salt to taste
¹/₄ teaspoon saffron powder
2¹/₄ cups chicken stock
mint leaves
coriander leaves

serves 6

Boil the rice until half cooked, then drain and set aside. Chop the lamb into tiny pieces. Chop the onion, ginger and garlic. Pound together the cinnamon, cloves, candlenuts, star anise, turmeric powder and peppercorns with just sufficient cold water to form a thick paste. Heat the ghee in a large frying pan and sauté the onion, ginger and garlic for 3–4 minutes, then add the lamb and continue to cook for 45 minutes, stirring frequently to avoid sticking. Add the spice-paste and salt to taste and stir to blend thoroughly, then transfer the mixture to a large casserole. Sprinkle a little saffron on top and cover with the half-cooked rice. Pour in the stock and bring to the boil. Chop the mint and coriander leaves and place on top of the rice. Lay a slightly dampened cloth over the rice and place a tightly-fitting lid on the casserole. Place in a pre-heated moderate oven until the rice is tender and all the liquid has been absorbed, approximately 30 minutes.

160

BRINGE
(Mixed Rice in Leaves)

Philippines

³/₄ pound chicken meat
³/₄ pound lean pork
salt to taste
freshly ground black pepper
2 brown onions
1 inch knob fresh ginger
3 cloves garlic
¹/₄ cup vegetable oil
1¹/₄ cups rice
¹/₃ cup chicken stock
2 tablespoons patis (fish sauce)
1¹/₂ cups thick coconut milk
¹/₂ cup cooked peas
2 hard-boiled eggs, sliced   serves 4–6

Cut the chicken and pork into small pieces and season with salt and freshly ground pepper. Finely chop the onions and ginger and crush the garlic. Heat the oil in a large pan and sauté the onion, ginger and garlic for 3–4 minutes, until the onion is translucent, then add the chicken, pork, rice, chicken stock and patis and continue to cook, stirring frequently, for another 5 minutes. Pour in the coconut milk, adjust seasonings to taste and bring to the boil, then lower heat and simmer slowly until most of the liquid has been absorbed. Add the peas, cover with banana leaves and cook very slowly for another 4 minutes. To serve; cover a platter with banana leaves (or any large leaves), spoon the mixed rice on top and garnish with slices of hard boiled eggs.

Note: Aluminum foil can be substituted for the leaves.

Sri Lanka

KAHU BUTH
(Yellow Rice)

2¾ cups basmati rice
1 small onion
1 inch stem lemon grass
6 cloves
6 black peppercorns
4 cardamom seeds
sprig curry leaves
½ teaspoon turmeric powder
salt to taste
½ inch cinnamon stick
3½ cups thick coconut milk   serves 4

Soak the rice for 2 hours, then rinse under running water and drain thoroughly. Slice the onion, chop the lemon grass and grind the cloves, peppercorns and cardamoms. Heat the ghee and fry the onion, lemon grass and curry leaves until the onion becomes transparent, then add the rice and stir-fry for 3 minutes. Add the ground spices, turmeric powder, salt, cinnamon stick and coconut milk and bring to the boil. Cook over a high heat for 5 minutes, then lower the heat, cover the pan and allow to cook slowly until the liquid has been absorbed and the rice is light and fluffy.

Indonesia

NASI KUNING
(Rice cooked in Coconut Milk)

2 cups long-grain rice
1 shallot
2 fresh red chilies
1 inch knob fresh ginger
½ inch knob lemon root
2 salem leaves (or bay leaves)
2 cups thin coconut milk
½ teaspoon turmeric powder
salt to taste   serves 4

Soak the rice for 2 hours, then wash under cold running water, drain thoroughly and place in a pan. Chop the shallot, chilies, ginger and lemon root. Pour the coconut milk into a saucepan, add the shallot, chili, ginger, lemon root and salem leaves, and bring to the boil. Lower heat and allow to simmer slowly for 45 minutes, then strain the liquid, through a fine sieve, over the rice. Add turmeric powder and salt to taste and cover the pan with a tightly fitting lid. Place the pan over boiling water and cook until the rice is tender and fluffy.

Thailand

KHAO PAD PRIK GAENG
(Fried Curried Rice)

3 cups long-grain rice
¼ pound cooked chicken meat
¼ pound cooked lean pork
⅓ pound long green beans
¼ pound cooked shrimp
2 shallots
6 fresh red chilies
2 cloves garlic
½ inch knob khaa (Siamese ginger)
2 teaspoons chopped coriander root
½ teaspoon grated lime peel
1 teaspoon chopped lemon grass
1 teaspoon salt
¼ teaspoon white pepper
½ cup vegetable oil
1 teaspoon nam pla (fish sauce)
2 teaspoons sugar   serves 6

Boil the rice and set aside. Cut the green beans into 1 in. lengths and blanch. Cut the chicken and pork into small, thin slices. Shell and de-vein the shrimp and cut in half, lengthwise. Finely chop the shallots, chilies, ginger and garlic and pound these together with the coriander root, lime peel, lemon grass, salt, pepper and 2 tablespoons of oil to form a smooth paste. Heat remaining oil and fry the spice-paste for 5–6 minutes, stirring frequently. Add the chicken, pork, shrimp, rice, nam pla and sugar, mix well and cook for another 2 minutes, then finally add the beans, stir again and transfer to a serving dish.

Note: As an alternative; divide the mixture into equal portions, wrap in aluminium foil and steam for an additional 3 minutes.

Thailand

MOO YONG
(Fried Rice in Pineapple)

2¼ *cups rice*
¼ *pound fresh shrimp*
¼ *pound crabmeat*
¼ *pound Chinese sausage*
2 *shallots*
2 *cloves garlic*
2 *small green chilies*
¼ *cup vegetable oil*
¼ *teaspoon saffron powder*
salt to taste
freshly ground black pepper
pinch monosodium glutamate
4 *medium size pineapples*
⅓ *cup crispy fried onion*   serves 4

First, boil the rice until it is three-quarters cooked, then drain and set aside. Shell and de-vein the shrimp and chop into small pieces. Shred the crabmeat and chop the sausage. Chop the shallots, garlic and chilies very finely. Heat the oil in a frying pan, add the shallots, garlic and chilies and sauté for 3–4 minutes. Add the shrimps and continue to cook for another 3 minutes, then add the crabmeat and sausage and stir to blend thoroughly. Add the rice, pour in ¼ cup of water and season with saffron, salt, freshly ground black pepper and mono-sodium glutamate. Stir well and cook until most of the liquid has been absorbed. Meanwhile, cut the tops off the pineapples about one quarter of the way down and scoop out all the flesh. Chop a little of the fresh pineapple and add to the fried rice. (The remaining flesh should be set aside for another dish, or discarded). Fill the pineapple shells with the rice mixture and sprinkle a little crispy fried onion on top. Place the tops back on the pineapples and bake in a pre-heated, moderate oven for 15 minutes.

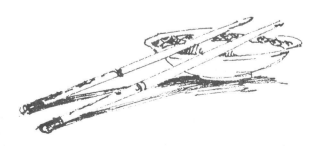

Japan

KITSUNE DOMBURI
(Rice with Fried Bean Curd)

4 *sheets aburage (fried bean curd)*
⅔ *cup dashi (recipe page 30)*
½ *cup Japanese soy sauce*
½ *cup mirin*
2 *tablespoons sugar*
¼ *teaspoon salt*
4½ *cups cooked rice*   serves 4–6

If the aburage is frozen allow time to completely thaw out then rinse thoroughly under hot water, drain and cut into narrow strips. Place the aburage into a saucepan, add the dashi, soy sauce and mirin and bring to the boil. Lower heat, add the sugar and salt and allow to simmer for 10 minutes, stirring occasionally. Slice the spring onions finely, add to the stock and continue to cook slowly for another 2 minutes. To serve; place portions of rice into individual serving bowls and pour the hot soup on top.

Hong Kong

BOILED RICE

2¼ *cups long-grain rice*
½ *teaspoon salt*
2 *tablespoons butter*   serves 4–6

Wash the rice under cold, running water, then drain thoroughly. Place in a saucepan, add just sufficient cold water to barely cover the rice (¼ inch above the level of the rice), add the salt and bring to the boil. Boil rapidly for 1 minute, then lower heat, cover the pan and cook until all the water has been absorbed. In a separate pan bring some water to a rapid boil and pour over the rice, again just barely covering it. Place the lid back on the pan and cook over a moderate heat for 3–4 minutes. Then, remove from the heat and allow to stand for 5 minutes. Remove the lid to make sure the rice is now dry and fluffy. If any liquid remains, replace the lid and set aside for a little longer. To serve; transfer the rice to a large bowl, add the butter and whisk well with a fork.

163

NASI GORENG
(Special Fried Rice)

Indonesia

5¼ cups long-grain rice
¼ pound fresh shrimp
¼ pound chicken meat
¼ pound fresh lamb
3 eggs
2 shallots
2 cloves garlic
4 fresh red chilies
2 teaspoons blachan (shrimp paste)
¼ cup peanut oil
¼ cup sweet soy sauce
salt to taste
freshly ground white pepper   serves 4–6

Wash the rice and drain thoroughly, then steam until tender and fluffy. Shell and de-vein the shrimp and halve, lengthwise. Chop the chicken meat and lamb and beat the eggs lightly. Chop the shallots, garlic, red chilies and blachan and pound together with one third of the peanut oil to produce a smooth paste. Heat the remaining oil in a pan and stir-fry the spice-paste for 3–4 minutes, then add the shrimp, chicken and lamb and season with soy sauce, salt and freshly ground white pepper. Cook over a moderate heat for 8 minutes then increase the heat to high, add the beaten egg and cook, stirring continuously, until the egg begins to set. Finally, add the rice, stir to blend thoroughly, then serve immediately.

BAMI GORENG
(Fried Noodles)

Indonesia

12 ounces fresh noodles
¹/₄ pound shrimp
¹/₄ pound cooked chicken meat
1 cup beansprouts
¹/₄ pound leafy green vegetable
2 cloves garlic
¹/₄ cup vegetable oil
2 eggs
2 tablespoons light soy sauce
salt to taste
freshly ground black pepper   serves 4

Place the noodles into a saucepan of rapidly-boiling water and cook for 3 minutes, then remove from the pan and drain thoroughly. Shell and de-vein the shrimp and shred the chicken meat. Trim and chop the beansprouts and green vegetable and chop the garlic very finely. Heat the oil in a large pan and sauté the garlic for 2–3 minutes, then add the shrimp and stir-fry for another 2 minutes. Break the eggs into the pan and stir, then add the chicken meat, noodles, vegetables, soy sauce, salt and freshly ground black pepper. Stir to blend thoroughly and retain over a medium heat for 2 minutes. Serve with chili sauce and hot pickles.

Thailand

KHAO SOI
(Curried Noodles)

1¼ pound fresh chicken meat
¼ cup vegetable oil
2 tablespoons curry paste*
4 cups thick coconut milk
6 rolls egg-noodles
1 cup concentrated coconut cream
2 fresh red chilies
2 shallots
2 spring onions
2 tablespoons fresh lime juice
2 tablespoons light soy sauce
Curry paste:
1 shallot
2 cloves garlic
½ inch knob khaa (Siamese ginger)
1 teaspoon chopped coriander root
1 teaspoon chopped lemon grass
4 dried red chilies
1 teaspoon roasted coriander seeds
1 teaspoon roasted cumin seeds
2 tablespoons shrimp paste
2 tablespoons curry powder
8 white peppercorns
salt to taste.

serves 6

Remove the skin from the chicken and cut the meat into small slices. Heat the oil in a large pan and stir-fry the curry paste for 5–6 minutes. Add the chicken, pour in the coconut milk and bring to the boil. Lower heat and allow to simmer, stirring frequently, until the chicken is cooked, approximately 20 minutes. Meanwhile cook 5 rolls of noodles rapidly in boiling water, drain well and place in individual bowls. Add portions of chicken and pour a little concentrated coconut cream on top. Fry the remaining noodles until crispy, then crumble these over the curry. Slice finely the chilies, shallots and spring onions and place these on top. Finally, add the lime juice and soy sauce and serve immediately.

To make the curry paste; chop the shallot, garlic, ginger and chilies. Pound these together with all the other ingredients and a small quantity of cold water (or coconut milk) to form a smooth paste.

*Note: The quantity of paste used should be adjusted according to personal preference.

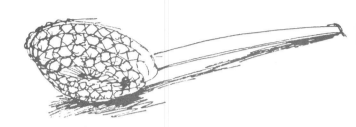

Malaysia

LAKSA ASAM
(Sour Soup Noodles)

1¼ pounds rice vermicelli noodles
1¾ pounds fish pieces, including head
salt to taste
freshly ground black pepper
6 fresh red chilies
1 stem lemon grass
2 teaspoons blachan
3 large brown onions
1 teaspoon turmeric powder
1 small cucumber
4 slices pineapple
2 tablespoons sugar
¼ cup tamarind water
fresh mint leaves

serves 4

Place noodles in a strainer and scald with boiling water, then drain thoroughly and set aside. Place the pieces of fish in a large saucepan, cover with 4 cups of water and bring to the boil. Season with salt and freshly ground black pepper, cover the pan and allow to simmer for 30 minutes. Pour the stock through a sieve into a fresh saucepan and set aside. Discard all the fish bones and skin and cut the remaining flesh into shreds. Chop the chilies, lemon grass, blachan and 2 of the onions and pound together with the turmeric powder and 2 teaspoons of the fish stock to form a smooth paste. Chop the cucumber, pineapple and remaining onion into small pieces. Bring the stock back to the boil, add the spice-paste and sugar and stir to blend thoroughly. Add the shredded fish and tamarind water and adjust seasonings to taste. Allow to simmer for 5 minutes. To serve; place a portion of noodles in individual bowls, add pieces of onion, cucumber and pineapple and pour in the stock. Garnish with mint leaves.

Philippines

PANCIT LUGLOG

³/₄ pound rice noodles
³/₄ pound boiled pork
¹/₂ pound cooked shrimp
1 brown onion
2 shallots
2 cloves garlic
3 squares preserved bean curd
¹/₄ cup peanut oil
¹/₄ cup achuete water (see glossary)
2 teaspoons patis
salt to taste
freshly ground white pepper
2¹/₄ cups beef stock
1 tablespoon cornstarch
2 ounces finely flaked tinapa (smoked fish)
2 spring onions, finely chopped
2 hard boiled eggs, sliced
3 limes   serves 6

Soak the noodles in cold water for 10 minutes, then drain thoroughly and set aside. Chop the pork into small pieces. Shell and de-vein the shrimp. Pound the shrimp heads with a small quantity of cold water, strain through a muslin cloth and reserve the liquid. Chop the onion, shallots and garlic and cut the bean curd into small cubes. Heat the oil in a pan and sauté the onion, shallot and garlic until soft, then add the pork, shrimp and bean curd and cook over a medium heat for 3–4 minutes, stirring frequently. Pour in the achuete water and bring to the boil, then remove the pork and shrimp and set aside. Add the stock to the sauce and bring back to the boil. Add the patis, salt and freshly ground white pepper and allow to boil for a few minutes. Mix the cornstarch with a small quantity of cold water, add to the sauce and stir to thicken slightly. Bring a large pan of water to a rapid boil and cook the noodles for 3 minutes, then pour into a colander and when thoroughly drained serve the noodles into individual bowls. Pour the sauce over the noodles and top with the pork and shrimp mixture. Sprinkle the finely flaked smoked fish and the chopped spring onion on top and garnish with slices of hard boiled eggs and fresh limes.

Singapore

HOKKIEN FRIED NOODLES

1 pound yellow-flour noodles
¹/₂ pound bean sprouts
¹/₂ pound small fresh shrimp
¹/₄ pound boiled squid
¹/₄ pound boiled pork
6 fresh red chilies
2 spring onions
2 cloves garlic
¹/₄ cup peanut oil
¹/₄ cup chicken stock
salt to taste
freshly ground black pepper
2 teaspoons dark soy sauce
2 eggs
2 tablespoons fresh milk   serves 4–6

Soak the noodles in a bowl of very hot water for 30 seconds, pour into a colander and drain thoroughly, then parboil for 2 minutes. Wash and trim the bean sprouts. Shell and de-vein the shrimp and cut in half lengthwise. Cut the squid and pork into thin strips. Chop the chilies and spring onions and crush the garlic. Heat half the oil in a wok and sauté the garlic for 1 minute, then add the chili, shrimp, squid and pork and continue to stir-fry over a moderate heat for another 3 minutes, placing a cover on the wok for the last minute. Then, remove the cover, pour in the stock, add the spring onion and season to taste with salt and freshly ground black pepper. Bring to the boil, add the bean sprouts and stir for 1 minute. Add the remaining oil, the soy sauce and the noodles and stir to blend thoroughly. Replace the cover on the wok and cook for 30 seconds, then transfer to a serving dish. Beat the eggs with the milk and pour into the wok. Place over a moderate heat and when the egg is set cut into thin strips and place on top of the noodles.

Desserts

A t last, and with the final section of this book, is a category of food in which the Chinese fail to predominate. Although there certainly are a number of interesting desserts, particularly from Szechuan and the Northern provinces, the Chinese generally prefer to finish a meal with fresh fruit. Fruit is also favored in Japan and Korea and if a dessert is served at all it is usually extremely simple and indeed, it may be nothing more than a sweet drink. However, in South East Asia and throughout the Indian sub-continent the dessert is an important part of a meal and the majority of recipes that follow originated in those regions.

Lapis Legis
Spiced layer cake

Bibikkan
Coconut cake

Kue Kelepon
Coconut rice balls

Wajik
Rice cake

Biki Ambon
Almond cake

Pandan Layer Cake

Pudding Buahbuahan
Fruit jelly pudding

Sapin Sapin with Fruit Mold

Carrot Halwa
Sweet carrot dessert

Om Ali
Bread & nut pudding

Bo Bo Cha Cha

Guinatan
Sweet potato & fruit

Peanut Pudding

Onde Onde

Pineapple Ice-Cream

Mango Patricia

Halo Halo

Payasam
Sago & fruits

Sri Kaya

Szechuan Pancakes

Meringue with Sweet Bean Paste

Kesari Buth
Semolina & milk dessert

Gula Melaka
Sweet sago pudding

Toffee Apples & Bananas

Almond Jelly with Fruits

Cazuela Moji
Cream cheese pudding

Bodin

Rum Raisin Ice-Cream in Coconut

Woon Wan
Sweet agar agar molds

Ice-Cream Ka Ti
Coconut ice-cream

Khao Niew Mamuang
Sticky rice & mango

Tub Tim Krob
Water chestnuts in coconut syrup

Recipes for **Indonesian Cakes** (photographed opposite) are on pages 170 and 171.

LAPIS LEGIS
(Spiced Layer Cake)

6 egg-whites
1½ cups sugar
10 egg-yolks
1⅓ cups butter
2½ cups all-purpose flour
½ teaspoon vanilla essence
½ teaspoon cinnamon powder
½ teaspoon nutmeg powder
½ teaspoon all-spice powder   serves 4

Beat the egg-whites with one third of the sugar and, in a separate bowl, beat the egg-yolks with another third. Soften the butter and cut into small pieces, then mix this with the remaining sugar and beat until light and creamy. Place the three mixtures into one large bowl, add the flour and vanilla essence and blend thoroughly. Transfer two-thirds of the mixture to another bowl and to this add cinnamon, nutmeg and all-spice powder and stir to blend well. Pour one third of the spiced mixture into a well-greased cake tin and bake in a moderate oven until firm, then add half the plain mixture and bake until this is also firm. Repeat the process three more times; spiced, plain and ending with spiced. Turn out on to a wire rack and allow to cool before serving.

BIBIKKAN
(Coconut Cake)

2 cups coconut
1½ cups palm sugar
½ cup dates
½ cup cashewnuts
½ cup preserved ginger
2 tablespoons candied peel
½ cup semolina
½ teaspoon fennel powder
½ teaspoon cardamom powder
¼ teaspoon cinnamon powder
½ teaspoon baking powder
¼ teaspoon salt
1 egg   serves 8

Grate the coconut and palm sugar. Chop the dates, cashewnuts, preserved ginger and candied peel. In a saucepan, bring 2½ cups of water to the boil, add the palm sugar and stir until it is completely dissolved, then add the coconut and cook for 2–3 minutes. Allow the mixture to cool, then add the dates, cashewnuts, ginger, candied peel, semolina, fennel, cardamom, cinnamon, baking powder and salt and stir to blend thoroughly. Separate the egg, beat the yolk and fold into the mixture, then do likewise with the white. Pour into a lightly-greased, shallow baking dish and cook in a preheated, moderate oven for 1½ hours.

KUE KELEPON
(Coconut Rice Balls)

2¼ cups thick coconut milk
½ teaspoon vanilla essence
¼ teaspoon salt
2 pandan leaves
3½ cups glutinous rice powder
⅔ cup soft brown sugar
¾ cup finely grated coconut   serves 4–6

Pour coconut milk into a saucepan, add vanilla essence, salt and pandan leaves and bring to the boil, then lower heat and allow to simmer for 10 minutes. Remove the pandan leaves and pour liquid into a mixing bowl. Then, add the glutinous rice flour and stir with a wooden spoon until the mixture is smooth and firm (if mixture is not firm enough, add a little more rice flour). Turn the mixture out on to a lightly-floured surface and divide into small portions. Flatten into circles, place a little brown sugar in the center of each and shape into small balls, approximately 1 inch in diameter. Bring a large pan of water to a rapid boil and add the rice balls. After they rise to the surface, leave for 45 seconds, then remove, pat dry and coat with grated coconut. Allow to cool before serving.

WAJIK
(Rice Cake)

3 cups glutinous rice
1/2 cup thick coconut milk
1 cup palm sugar
1/4 teaspoon salt
banana leaves   serves 4

Wash the glutinous rice under cold running water, then place in a bowl of fresh water and allow to soak overnight. Before cooking, rinse again, then steam until well cooked. Pour the coconut milk into a saucepan and bring to the boil. Add the sugar and salt and continue to cook, stirring frequently, until the mixture is thick and oily, then add the rice and blend thoroughly. Allow to simmer over a medium heat until very thick, then pour into a shallow dish that has been lined with banana leaves. Allow to cool slightly, then place in a refrigerator for at least 2 hours. Cut into small wedges to serve.

Note: Aluminum foil may be used instead of the leaves

BIKA AMBON
(Almond Cake)

2 1/2 cups all-purpose flour
1/4 teaspoon salt
1 teaspoon dried yeast
12 egg-yolks
2 cups sugar
1 1/4 cups thick coconut milk
1/2 teaspoon finely chopped lemon grass
1/4 cup sliced almonds   serves 8

Sift the flour and salt into a large mixing bowl and make a well in the center. Dissolve the yeast in warm water and pour into the well. Mix to blend well, then cover with a cloth and set aside for 30 minutes to allow the dough to rise. Beat the egg-yolks and sugar until very creamy, then add this mixture to the dough, together with the coconut milk and very finely chopped lemon grass. Stir to blend thoroughly then pour into a cake tin and place the sliced almonds on top. Bake in a moderate oven for 25–35 minutes. Allow to cool before serving.

PANDAN LAYER CAKE

2 fresh pandan leaves
9 eggs
2 cups castor sugar
2 tablespoons fresh lime juice
1 1/2 cups all-purpose flour
buttercream filling
grated coconut   serves 8

Place the pandan leaves in a small saucepan and cover with 1/4 cup of cold water. Allow to stand for 1 hour, then bring to the boil and simmer for 20 minutes. Pour through a fine muslin cloth and reserve the liquid. Break the eggs and separate the yolks and whites into two mixing bowls. Add half the sugar to the yolks and whisk well for 3–4 minutes, then add the pandan liquid and continue to whisk for another minute. Add the flour, a little at a time, and blend in thoroughly. Next whisk the egg-whites and fold into the yolk mixture. Divide the mixture into three equal portions, place into lightly-greased 8 inch cake tins and bake in a pre-heated moderate oven for 25–30 minutes. Remove from the oven and allow to stand for 1 minute before turning onto wire racks to cool. Finally arrange the layers on top of each other with a generous portion of cream filling between each layer and sprinkle the grated coconut on top of the cake.

Note: If using a pandan essence, add just 3 drops to 1/4 cup of cold water, stir well and use without boiling.

PUDDING BUAHBUAHAN
(Fruit Jelly Pudding)

Malaysia

6 egg yolks
⅓ cup castor sugar
1¼ cups fresh milk
2 tablespoons gelatin powder
½ cup double cream
¼ cup grated coconut
½ teaspoon coconut essence
½ cup small pineapple chunks
½ teaspoon pineapple essence
¼ teaspoon yellow food coloring
¼ cup green pea flour
¼ teaspoon green food coloring
2 teaspoons soft butter
4 pineapple rings, quartered
½ cup papaya balls
½ cup melon balls
8 maraschino cherries, halved

serves 8

Place the egg yolks and sugar in a saucepan, put on to a low heat and beat until creamy. In a separate pan, bring the milk to the boil and slowly add this to the mixture, stirring continuously until the mixture thickens slightly. Dissolve one half of the gelatine powder in a little warm water and add this to the pan. Stir to blend thoroughly, then remove from heat and allow to cool slightly. Whip the cream lightly and fold into the mixture, then divide and transfer to three separate bowls. Add the grated coconut and coconut essense to the first bowl, the pineapple chunks, pineapple essence and yellow coloring to the second and the green pea flour and green coloring to the third. Stir all the mixtures to thoroughly blend the ingredients. Use the butter to lightly grease the sides and bottom of a large mold. Place the pieces of quartered pineapple rings, papaya and melon balls and maraschino cherries in the bottom of the mold. Dissolve the remaining gelatine powder in warm water, pour on top of the fruit and allow to set. Then, carefully add the three different flavored mixtures in layers, allowing each sufficient time to set firmly before adding the next. Place the mold into a refrigerator and chill for at least 4 hours. To serve; turn mold upside-down on to a large flat plate and garnish with additional fruit. The leafy top of a pineapple, if available, makes an excellent top decoration.

172

SAPIN SAPIN WITH FRUIT MOLD

Philippines

3 cups glutinous rice
2 cups sugar
2 cups thick coconut milk
¼ teaspoon red food coloring
¼ teaspoon purple food coloring
¼ teaspoon yellow food coloring

Fruit mold:
2 cups thick coconut milk
½ cup gelatine powder
2½ cups sugar
½ teaspoon vanilla essence
2 bananas
2 mangoes
½ pineapple   serves 10–12

Soak the rice in cold water, then rinse with fresh water and drain thoroughly. Place the rice through a fine grinder into a large mixing bowl and add the sugar and coconut milk. Blend well and divide into three portions. Color one third with the red coloring, one third with the purple and the remainder with the yellow. Line a large cake tin with cheesecloth, pour in the red mixture and steam over boiling water until set. Allow to cool slightly, then pour the purple mixture on top and steam and finally, do likewise with the yellow. Place in a refrigerator to cool, then lift from the cheesecloth and place on a serving plate covered with large leaves.

To make the fruit mold, bring the coconut milk to the boil, add the gelatine powder, sugar and vanilla essence and stir until everything has completely dissolved. Slice the bananas, scoop out pieces of mango into ball shapes and cut the meat of the pineapple into small chunks. Arrange the fruit in an appropriately-sized bowl and add half the coconut jelly mixture. Allow to set slightly, approximately 10 minutes, then add the remaining jelly. Allow to set firmly, then unmold on top of the sapin sapin base. Place in a refrigerator for at least 1 hour before serving.

Singapore

CARROT HALWA
(Sweet Carrot Dessert)

1 pound carrots
1¼ cups fresh milk
1¼ cups sugar
¼ cup melted butter
¼ cup sliced almonds
¼ cup chopped pistachios
¼ cup seedless raisins
¼ teaspoon saffron powder   serves 4

Wash and scrape carrots, then grate finely and place into a saucepan. Add two-thirds of the milk together with three-quarters of the sugar and slowly bring to the boil. Allow to simmer, stirring frequently, until all the milk has been absorbed. Dissolve the remaining sugar with some warm water and add to the mixture. Boil the remaining milk and allow to reduce to one-quarter, then add this to the pan also. Stir well and continue to cook over a low heat for 3–4 minutes, until the mixture is of a very thick consistency. Add the butter, almonds, pistachios and raisins, stir to blend thoroughly and cook until the mixture turns a deep golden brown. Sprinkle a little saffron powder on top and serve immediately.

India

OM ALI
(Bread & Nut Pudding)

4 slices white bread
½ cup chopped walnuts
½ cup chopped pistachios
½ cup sliced almonds
½ cup chopped peanuts
3½ cups fresh milk
1 cup sugar
1 teaspoon grated lemon rind
½ cup fresh cream   serves 4–6

Toast the bread, cut into triangles and arrange on the bottom of a large rectangular casserole dish. Combine all the nuts, set aside two teaspoons full and sprinkle the remainder over the toast. Place the milk, sugar and lemon rind in a separate pan and bring slowly to the boil, stirring until the sugar has completely dissolved. Pour the milk over the toast and allow to cool slightly. Whip the cream until it is very thick then add to the casserole. Smooth the cream with a spatula, then sprinkle the remaining nuts on top. Place in a moderately hot oven for 10–15 minutes, until the top of the pudding is golden. Serve immediately.

Malaysia

BO BO CHA CHA

1 pound yam
¼ cup powdered gelatine
2 cups fine white sugar
½ teaspoon red food coloring
½ teaspoon green food coloring
shaved ice
2 cups thick coconut milk   serves 6

Peel the yams, cut into ½ inch cubes and cook in boiling water for 15 minutes, then drain and set aside to cool. Dissolve the gelatine powder in a small quantity of boiling water. In a saucepan bring 4 cups of water to the boil, add the gelatine and half the sugar and stir until the sugar has completely dissolved. Then pour equal amounts into two separate bowls and mix the red coloring into one and the green into the other. Allow to cool, then place in the refrigerator to set firmly. In a clean saucepan bring another cup of water to the boil, add the remaining sugar, stir to dissolve, then set aside to cool. To serve; cut the jellies into small cubes and place a few of each color into individual tall sundae glasses. Add the yam and then the remaining jelly. Add the syrup, fill up the glasses with shaved ice and pour the coconut milk on top.

Malaysia

PEANUT PUDDING

³/₄ cup fresh peanuts
¹/₃ cup peanut oil
¹/₃ cup cornstarch
¹/₄ cup condensed milk
1 cup granulated white sugar
2 teaspoons soft brown sugar   serves 4

Heat the oil in a pan and stir-fry the peanuts for 3 minutes, then pour into a colander and allow to cool. Remove husks from the peanuts and grind very finely. Mix the cornstarch with a small quantity of cold water. In a saucepan heat 3 cups of water and when just coming to the boil add the ground peanut and stir. Add the cornstarch, condensed milk and sugar and simmer over a moderate heat for 4 minutes, stirring frequently. Transfer to individual serving dishes and sprinkle a little brown sugar on top.

Philippines

GUINATAN
(Sweet Potato and Fruit)

¹/₂ pound yam
¹/₂ pound taro
¹/₂ pound jackfruit
4 small bananas
1 cup thick coconut milk
¹/₂ cup ground rice
3 tablespoons sugar   serves 6

Cut the yam, taro and jackfruit into small dice and slice the bananas. Place the yam and taro in a saucepan, pour in half the coconut milk and bring to the boil. Lower heat, simmer gently for 10 minutes, then add the jackfruit, bananas, ground rice and sugar. Stir well, bring back to a rapid boil and when the ground rice floats to the top pour in the remaining coconut milk and blend thoroughly. Bring back to the boil once again and cook for another minute before pouring into a serving bowl. Allow to cool, then place in the refrigerator for at least 2 hours before serving.

Malaysia

ONDE ONDE

³/₄ pound yam
1¹/₄ cups glutinous rice
¹/₂ teaspoon green food coloring
1¹/₂ cups date-palm sugar
2 tablespoons castor sugar
³/₄ cup grated coconut   serves 4–6

Steam and mash the yam and mix with the rice flour, food coloring and about ²/₃ cup of cold water. Knead well and divide into 12 portions, then shape into balls and make a small 'well' in the center of each. Crumble the date-palm sugar, place in a saucepan and add a small quantity of cold water. Set over a moderate heat and stir until the sugar has completely dissolved, then add the castor sugar and continue to stir for another 2–3 minutes. Remove from heat and allow the thick syrup to cool, then spoon it into the yam-ball cavities, seal the holes and reshape. Bring a large saucepan of water to a rapid boil and add the yam-balls. Retain over a high heat until they rise to the surface, then remove, drain and coat with grated coconut.

PINEAPPLE ICE-CREAM

Philippines

7 egg-yolks
1 cup sugar
4 cups milk
1 cup crushed pineapple
1 teaspoon pineapple essence
½ cup double cream   serves 6–8

Place the egg-yolks in a large heatproof mixing bowl, add the sugar and beat until white and fluffy. In a saucepan bring the milk almost to the boil and slowly pour into the mixing bowl. Place the mixing bowl over a low heat while the milk is being poured in and whisk continuously. Do not allow to come to the boil. Meanwhile, process the crushed pineapple together with the pineapple essence in a blender until a thin-paste consistency is achieved then add this to the milk mixture, stir to blend thoroughly and remove from the fire. Whip the cream to medium thickness, add to the mixture, stir well and allow to cool. When cold, turn in an ice-cream maker until set, then store in the freezer compartment.

Note: If no ice-cream maker is available pour the mixture into a bowl, place in the freezer compartment and stir at frequent intervals until the ice-cream is completely hardened.

MANGO PATRICIA

Philippines

4 mangoes
2 egg-yolks
⅓ cup castor sugar
⅓ cup double cream
2 tablespoons Grand Marnier
6 scoops mango ice-cream
freshly whipped cream
maraschino cherries   serves 4

Cut the mangoes in half, scoop out the flesh with a spoon and retain 4 of the empty 'skins'. Line these with wax paper and set aside. Set half the mango flesh to one side and purée the other half in a food processor. Place the egg-yolks and sugar into a bowl and whip until the mixture is smooth and fluffy. Then, add the cream, Grand Marnier and mango purée and continue to whip to blend thoroughly. Soften the ice-cream and fold into the mixture, then spoon into the prepared shells and add pieces of the remaining mango on top. To decorate; pipe extra whipped cream around the sides and add red and green maraschino cherries. Place in the freezer for at least 1 hour before serving.

HALO HALO

Philippines

¼ cup sweet mango
¼ cup sweet potato
¼ cup jackfruit
1 teaspoon sweet beans
1 teaspoon coconut flesh
1 teaspoon fruit jelly
2 tablespoons syrup
shaved ice
1 scoop vanilla ice-cream   serves 1

Chop all the fruits and the jelly into small pieces and place in the bottom of a tall sundae glass, add the syrup, place a mound of shaved ice on top and finish with a scoop of vanilla ice-cream.

Note: Halo Halo literally means 'mix-mix' and that is exactly the way to eat this dessert, mixing well before each spoonful. Almost anything goes for the ingredients and for variety substitute bananas, melons, pineapple, garbanzos and assorted jams.

177

Singapore

PAYASAM
(Sago & Fruits)

1¼ cups sago
2 ounces thin rice-noodles
¼ cup unsalted cashew nuts
¼ cup sultanas
⅔ cup thick coconut milk
1 cup castor sugar
pinch of salt
1 teaspoon rose essence   serves 4

Wash the sago under cold running water and drain well. Pour 1 cup of water into a saucepan and place over moderate heat. When the water is just at the boil, sprinkle in the sago and simmer until the sago becomes transparent, approximately 8–10 minutes. Add the noodles, cashew nuts and sultanas and continue to simmer for 7–8 minutes. Then, add the coconut milk, sugar and salt, bring back to the boil and stir until the sugar has completely dissolved. Spoon into individual dishes and sprinkle a little rose essence on top of each. Serve either hot or cold.

Malaysia

SRI KAYA

1 cup date-palm sugar
10 eggs
1 cup thick coconut milk   serves 6

Place the date-palm sugar in a saucepan, add 1 cup of cold water and bring to the soil. Stir until the sugar has completely dissolved, then remove from heat and allow to cool. Break the eggs into a large ovenproof bowl and beat lightly. Add the coconut milk and the syrup and stir to blend thoroughly, then place the bowl in a pan with a tightly fitting lid and steam over rapidly boiling water for 30–40 minutes. Serve immediately or allow to cool.

Singapore

SZECHUAN PANCAKES

2 eggs
1 cup all-purpose flour
2 tablespoons melted butter
⅓ cup fresh milk
2 teaspoons fine white sugar
½ teaspoon vanilla essence
peanut oil for frying
1 teaspoon finely ground almonds

Filling:
1 cup Chinese red dates
¾ cup sweet bean paste
1 teaspoon Chinese wine
1 teaspoon fine white sugar   serves 6–8

Break the eggs into a mixing bowl, add the flour, butter, milk, sugar and vanilla essence and beat to blend thoroughly, then add just sufficient cold water to make a thin, creamy batter. Heat some of the oil in a large frying pan until it is very hot, then pour in a little batter and tilt the pan so that the batter spreads out into a large, thin circle. Allow to set slightly, then add a portion of prepared filling, spread out evenly and fold the pancake into a long rectangular shape. Seal the folds with a little batter and continue to cook, turning once, until the outside is golden and crispy, then remove to a wire rack and keep warm. Continue to prepare pancakes until all the batter and filling have been used up, adding a little more oil to the pan each time. To serve; cut the pancakes, crosswise, into small fingers, arrange on a plate and sprinkle the finely ground almond on top.

To prepare the filling; mash the dates with a little cold water, add the bean paste, Chinese wine and sugar and stir to blend thoroughly.

Taiwan

MERINGUE WITH SWEET BEAN PASTE

4 egg-whites
¼ cup custard powder
2 tablespoons sugar
red food coloring
½ cup sweet bean paste
¼ cup cornstarch
oil for deep frying   serves 4–6

Beat the egg-whites until fairly stiff, then add the custard powder, blend thoroughly and continue to beat until a very stiff consistency results. In a shallow dish, mix the sugar with just sufficient coloring to turn it deep pink, then set this to one side. Mix the bean paste with a small quantity of cold water and shape into small balls about the size of walnuts. Dust these with cornstarch and dip into the egg mixture, allowing a considerable amount to stick (the finished meringue should be 1 inch in diameter). Heat the oil in a wok until it starts to smoke and deep-fry the meringues until the outsides are golden, approximately 2 minutes, then remove, drain off excess oil and roll in the colored sugar. Serve immediately.

Sri Lanka

KESARI BUTH
(Semolina and Milk Dessert)

1¼ cups cashewnuts
3 cardamom seeds
⅓ cup ghee
1¼ cups sultanas
2 cups semolina
1 cup milk
¾ cup sugar
3 teaspoons rose water
½ teaspoon rose essence   serves 6

Chop the cashewnuts and crush the cardamoms. Heat the ghee and fry the cashewnuts until golden, then remove and set aside. Fry the sultanas in the same fat for 3 minutes, then remove and put them also to one side. Add the semolina to the pan and stir-fry over a moderate heat until brown. Then, heat the milk in another pan, add the sugar, stir to dissolve and pour over the semolina. Cook until most of the liquid has been absorbed, then add the cashewnuts, cardamom, sultanas, rose water and essence and stir to mix thoroughly.

Malaysia

GULA MELAKA
(Sweet Sago Pudding)

1 cup sago
1 cup date-palm sugar
2 thin slices fresh ginger
1 cup thick coconut milk
¼ teaspoon salt   serves 4

Wash the sago under cold running water, then place in a saucepan and cover with cold water. Bring to the boil and cook for 8–10 minutes, until the sago becomes transparent. Wash again under cold water to remove all the starch, then pour into a mold and place in the refrigerator to set. Crumble the date-palm sugar and place in a small saucepan together with 1 cup of cold water. Bring to the boil, then lower heat, add the slices of ginger and allow to simmer until the sugar has completely dissolved. Discard the ginger, pour the syrup into a jug and place in the refrigerator to chill. Add the salt to the coconut milk and allow this to chill also. To serve; spoon sago into a bowl and add the syrup and coconut milk according to taste.

Note: In Malaysia date-palm sugar is, itself, known as gula melaka and is usually packed in 'cakes' of 6 ounces. An acceptable substitute would be soft brown sugar but it would be necessary to increase the quantity to obtain the same degree of sweetness.

TOFFEE APPLES & BANANAS

Hong Kong

2 large cooking apples
3 bananas
1 cup all-purpose flour
vegetable oil for deep frying
¹/₂ cup peanut oil
1 cup sugar
¹/₄ cup sesame seeds
iced water   serves 6

Peel and core the apples and cut into wedges. Skin the bananas and cut into quarters, first lengthways then across. Mix the flour with sufficient cold water to produce a smooth batter and coat the apple and banana pieces evenly. Heat the vegetable oil in a wok and deep-fry the fruit for 2–3 minutes, until golden in color. In a saucepan heat the peanut oil, add the sugar together with a small quantity of cold water, bring to the boil and stir over a medium heat until the sugar has completely dissolved. Add the apple and banana and stir to coat evenly with the syrup. Remove the pieces of fruit from the pan, sprinkle with sesame seeds and plunge immediately into the iced water so that the syrup sets hard.

ALMOND JELLY WITH FRUITS

Taiwan

2 tablespoons agar-agar powder
3 tablespoons sugar
1 teaspoon almond essence
²/₃ cup sweetened condensed milk
12 ounces canned fruit salad serves 4–6

Place 2¼ cups of water in a saucepan, add the agar-agar and half the sugar. Bring to the boil slowly and allow to simmer for 10 minutes, then add the almond essence, condensed milk and remaining sugar and continue to simmer for another 5 minutes, stirring frequently. Pour the mixture into a shallow, lightly-greased, cake tin and allow to cool, then place in the refrigerator to set firmly. When ready to serve; cut the almond jelly into cubes and place in a large bowl together with shaved ice and the fruit salad.

Philippines

CAZUELA MOJI
(Cream Cheese Pudding)

1 pound cream cheese
4 eggs
1/2 teaspoon grated lemon rind
1/2 teaspoon cinnamon powder
1 apple
1 1/2 cups white breadcrumbs
1/2 cup honey
1 1/2 cups sugar
4 cups milk   serves 6

Press the cream cheese through a sieve into a mixing bowl. Add the eggs, one by one, beating well each time, then add the lemon rind and cinnamon powder and blend together. Peel, core and grate the apple. Mix together the breadcrumbs and honey. Place the sugar in a saucepan, pour in the milk and bring to the boil. Stir until the sugar has completely dissolved, then pour into the cream cheese mixture and beat well. Add the breadcrumbs and honey and the grated apple and blend thoroughly. Pour the mixture into a well-greased baking dish and bake in a pre-heated, moderately hot oven for 45–50 minutes. Allow to cool, then turn out onto a cake platter.

Singapore

RUM RAISIN ICE-CREAM
IN COCONUT

1 fresh vanilla stick
1 2/3 cups fresh milk
1 egg
5 egg-whites
3/4 cup fine white sugar
1/2 cup fresh cream
1/2 cup dark rum
1 1/2 cups seedless raisins
4 young coconuts
1/4 cup grated coconut   serves 4

Slice the vanilla stick and with a knife remove the seeds. Pour the milk into a saucepan, add the vanilla seeds and bring to the boil. Beat the egg and egg-whites together with the sugar and add to the milk. Continue to simmer until the mixture thickens but do not allow to come to the boil again. Remove the pan from the heat, stir in the cream and allow the mixture to cool, then strain through a fine muslin cloth into an ice-cream tray. Place in the freezer compartment and when half set remove and fold in the rum and two-thirds of the raisins. Return to the freezer until completely set. To serve; remove the tops from the coconuts, pour away any liquid and place scoops of ice-cream inside. Sprinkle the grated coconut and the remaining raisins on top.

Philippines

BODIN

6 eggs
1 cup sugar
1/2 teaspoon vanilla extract
1 2/3 cups fresh milk
1 1/4 cups seedless raisins   serves 4

Break the eggs into a mixing bowl and beat lightly, then add the sugar and vanilla extract and continue to beat. Slowly add the milk, fold in the raisins and stir well. Pour the mixture into a mold and place on an oven rack. Place the rack in a pan of water and cook in a pre-heated, moderate oven for 30–40 minutes. Serve hot or allow to cool and serve with fresh local fruits.

Thailand

WOON WAN
(Sweet Agar Agar Molds)

2 tablespoons agar agar powder (gelatine)
1¼ cups sugar
food coloring
coconut cream   serves 4

Bring 2¼ cups of water to simmering point, sprinkle in the agar agar powder and stir to dissolve completely. Add the sugar and continue to stir, then pour the mixture into four bowls and add a few drops of different food coloring into each. Pour into small molds, allow to cool slightly and place in the refrigerator until completely set. Serve with thick sweetened coconut cream.

Thailand

ICE-CREAM KA-TI
(Coconut Ice-cream)

½ cup coconut water
2 sheets gelatine
3½ cups coconut cream
⅓ cup castor sugar
¼ teaspoon salt
1½ grated coconut   serves 4–6

Warm the coconut water in a small saucepan, add the gelatine and stir until completely dissolved, then set aside to cool. Combine the coconut cream, sugar, salt and grated coconut with the liquid gelatine and blend thoroughly. Pour the mixture into ice-cream trays and place in the freezer. Allow to partially set, then remove and stir well. Replace in the freezer and repeat the stirring process three more times at approximately 20 minutes intervals. Finally, leave to set firmly before serving.

Thailand

KHAO NIEW MAMUANG
(Sticky Rice and Mango)

¾ cup glutinous rice
1¼ cups thick coconut milk
¼ cup sugar-syrup
pinch of salt
2 fresh mangoes   serves 4

Soak the rice for at least 12 hours, then cook in a steamer and allow to cool. Combine the coconut milk, syrup and salt. Peel the mangoes and cut the flesh into small chunks. To serve; spoon a little rice into the bottom of individual serving dishs, add the mango and pour the milk on top.

Thailand

TUB TIM KROB
(Water Chestnuts in Coconut Syrup)

6 ounces fresh water chestnuts
½ cup thin coconut milk
¼ cup sugar-syrup
pinch of salt   serves 4

Peel the water chestnuts and place into a pan of rapidly boiling water. When they rise to the surface, remove, set aside to cool, then chop into small pieces. Pour ½ cup of iced water into a serving dish, add the water chestnuts, coconut milk, syrup and salt and stir to blend thoroughly. Serve immediately.

183

Overleaf: **Thai Desserts**

Glossary & Notes

In the editing of the original recipes some alterations have been made and most of the ingredients now listed should be generally familiar and readily available, even outside Asia. The notes below are intended to give, in a very simple form, some useful information on Asian culinary terms, rather than act as a comprehensive glossary for this particular book.

Abalone:
A large shellfish with a particularly hard shell. Can often be seen live in fish tanks outside Chinese seafood restaurants. Fresh abalone can be very expensive at certain times of the year but it is always readily available in canned form.

Achuete Water:
A red coloring liquid obtained by soaking annatto seeds in cold water, then pressing through a fine strainer. Its use is more for the appearance of a particular dish rather than taste and, where annatto seeds are not available, a similar effect can be obtained with a mixture of paprika and turmeric powder.

Agar Agar:
A form of seaweed used as a setting agent. Gelatine is an acceptable substitute but the big advantage to agar agar is that it does not melt so easily and is, therefore, more suitable for use in hotter climates.

Anise Seeds:
Similar in taste to caraway seeds but with a richer and more pungent flavor. Also available in powdered form or as an essence and is used to flavor both sweet and savory dishes. Star Anise is used often in Chinese cooking.

Bak Choi:
Chinese white cabbage with a distinct and mild flavor. Is often added to soups and meat dishes as well as being served as a vegetable.

Bamboo Shoots:
Cream colored, spear-like vegetable often used in Chinese and Japanese cooking. When bought fresh, they must be peeled to remove the hard skin and boiled for some considerable time. Much simpler to use the canned variety which, unlike many other vegetables, retain their fresh flavor.

Bean Curd:
Soy beans treated with an extract of rennet. Sold fresh in slabs it is highly nutritous and very popular with the Chinese and Japanese. Also known as tofu. Comes in a variety of flavors.

Bean Paste:
Available in various forms and made with a base of preserved soy beans. Hot bean paste, used a great deal in Northern Chinese cuisine, is flavored with red chilies while the sweet variety uses sugar and seasonings.

Bean Sprouts:
The sprouts of green mung beans. Sold in markets throughout in Asia. Used as a vegetable in their own right and also popular for mixing with other dishes, particularly in Chinese cooking. Must never be overcooked.

Blachan:
A dried shrimp paste used in the making of sambals. Has a very pungent flavor and has no substitute. Is sold in small slabs and can be stored for lengthy periods in an air-tight container. Used a great deal in Indonesia and Malaysia.

Candlenuts:
An oily nut used a great deal in making Indonesian and Malaysian curries. Macadamia nuts are a good substitute.

Cardamom:
A seed pod of the ginger family and one of the world's most expensive spices. Can be used whole or in powdered form.

Chilies:
Fresh chilies, both red and green, are used a great deal in Asian cooking and the quantities used (despite what any recipe may say) should always be a matter for personal taste. The real 'fire' comes from the seeds and for the more 'tender palates' these should always be discarded. Dried chilies are generally used whole but discarded before serving.

Chinese Mushrooms:
These black mushrooms, dried and soaked in warm

water before using, are an essential ingredients in any Chinese kitchen. Their flavor is unique and there is no substitute. Available worldwide in Chinese grocery stores.

Choi Sum:
One of the most popular Chinese vegetables, it has round green stems, long 'pencil-like' leaves and small yellow flowers. It has a slightly bitter taste and is often served with oyster sauce.

Chopsticks:
The art of using chopsticks may at first appear awkward and difficult but in actual fact they can be mastered with just a minimum of practice. Start by gripping one of the chopsticks in a fixed and firm position in the right hand (see illustration below), then take the second one between the thumb and forefinger and manipulate this as you would a pencil. In no time at all you'll find you can pick up even the smallest morsels with ease. And the added enjoyment of eating Chinese and Japanese food this way will certainly prove to be worth the small effort of learning.

Cinnamon:
A spice used in both savory and sweet dishes. Sometimes powdered but usually added in its 'stick' form.

Coconut Milk:
Where fresh coconuts are available this is obtained by grating the flesh of a mature coconut and squeezing with water. On an average, the flesh of one coconut squeezed with ⅓ cup of water will produce the thick milk often referred to in this book. To make a thinner milk the same process should be repeated one or more times. The liquid from young, immature, coconuts is known as coconut water and is sometimes used in Asian cooking but not as regularly as the milk. Where fresh coconuts are not available the frozen or canned variety of milk should be used.

Coriander:
Grown throughout Asia and also known as Chinese parsley. The seeds have a very aromatic flavor and are used in all curries. The leaves are often recommended as a garnish. Western parsley is, at the best, a very poor substitute.

Cumin:
A small brown aromatic seed, usually ground before being used. Like coriander, is an essential ingredient for curry powders.

Curry:
There are many 'secrets' for the best curry but the normally accepted basic curry powder consists of red chili, coriander, cumin, turmeric, garam masala (see below) and salt. Proportions naturally depend on individual taste. In Pakistan and Northern India, natural yoghurt is used in the making of most curries while in Southern India, Sri Lanka and South East Asia that is generally replaced with coconut milk.

Curry Leaves:
Small, bright aromatic leaves that are available fresh throughout Asia. Also dried and packaged.

Dim Sum:
A collective name for small, delicious Chinese snacks, normally served from breakfast through lunch but also popular with afternoon tea. There are literally hundreds of varieties and, because most people like to taste as many different ones as possible, it's a complicated and time-consuming meal to prepare; so is more likely to be served in a restaurant rather than at home.

Dried Seaweed:
Used a great deal in Japanese cooking and Buddhist vegetarian dishes. Generally available at all Asian food stores.

Fennel:
Also known as sweet cumin, fennel is used in either seed or ground form.

Fenugreek:
Particularly good in fish curries and also as a basic ingredient of curry powders. The seeds have a slightly bitter taste so the stated quantity should not be exceeded.

187

Five Spice Powder:
A strong seasoning used a great deal in Chinese cooking. To prepare; grind to a fine powder, equal portions of black peppercorns, fennel seeds, cinnamon bark, star anise and cloves. Store in an air-tight container.

Galangal:
A member of the 'ginger' family, seldom grown outside Asia. Used widely in South East Asia, often as an additional ingredient to ginger, rather than a substitute.

Garam Masala:
A vital ingredient for all Indian and Pakistani curries. To make 1 cup of garam masala, place into a pan 1/4 cup each of cloves, white and black cumin seeds, nutmeg and black peppercorns and 2 tablespoons of black cardamom and cinnamon bark. Place over a medium heat and dry-fry for 10–12 minutes, stirring frequently. Remove to a stone mortar and pound finely. Sift through a fine sieve before storing in an air-tight container.

Ghee:
Pure butter fat with all the milk solids removed. It can be heated to much higher temperatures than butter and gives a very distinctive flavor. If not available, use clarified butter.

Gingko Nuts:
Used a great deal in Japanese cooking and have no really acceptable substitute. Are readily available canned.

Glutinous Rice:
A particular variety of long-grained rice which becomes sticky and transparent when cooked.

Hoi Sin Sauce:
A sweet, spicy sauce, often served as a side dish with Chinese meat and poultry.

Lemon Grass:
An aromatic grass with a small bulbous root which, when crushed, gives a strong lemon flavor. Commerically packaged in powder form as 'Serai'.

Mirin:
A sweet Japanese sake, or rice wine. If not available, substitute with a pale sherry, using slightly less than the quantity of mirin called for in the recipe.

Nam Pla (fish sauce):
A thin, salty, brown sauce used in Southeast Asian cooking to bring out the flavor in other foods.

Palm Sugar:
A strong flavored, dark sugar obtained from the sap of coconut palms, boiled down until it crystallizes, and sold in round, flat cakes. Western equivalents include unrefined black sugar or refined dark brown sugar.

Pandan Leaves:
The leaves can be used whole in the cooking and removed at some stage or they can be finely chopped and pounded with a little water to form a paste. They give a distinctive taste and also act as a green coloring agent.

Patis:
A salty fish or shrimp sauce, sold under different names in different countries. Is likely to be known in Chinese grocery stores as Shrimp Sauce. Used throughout Asia and is a particularly important ingredient in any Philippine kitchen.

Sago:
An edible starch, like tapioca, which is often used in sweet dessert dishes. Before cooking the tiny white granules are hard, white and opaque. During cooking they expand slightly and become soft and translucent.

Sambal:
Usually served as a side dish and very popular throughout South East Asia. Made from grinding chilies, blachan (see above) and salt and, in that form, can be stored for lengthy periods. Just prior to use the required amount should be blended with sugar and fresh lime juice. All proportions depend on individual tastes but is generally served very hot.

Taro:
A tuber from a leafy tropical plant which can be used interchangeably with the potato for dishes requiring a starch that can be boiled and mashed or fried. Poi is made from taro.

Tamarind Water:
Made by soaking fresh or dried tamarind rind in cold water for 15–20 minutes, then straining the liquid through a fine sieve. Adds a very distinctive sour taste and is only used in small quantities.

Turmeric:
Belongs to the ginger family and, with its orange color, gives curry powders their distinctive appearance.

Water Chestnut:
The bulb of an aquatic plant available in cans in Asian food stores. It has a crisp, clean taste and texture and is widely used in Chinese cooking.

Won Ton Wrappers:
Squares of very thin noodle pastry dough, available frozen at Chinese grocery stores and many Western supermarkets.

Yam:
A root vegetable with a mild, slightly sweet flavor. Can be roasted like potatoes or mashed and used for desserts; particularly good for cakes.

Index

Ikan Acar Kuning	83	**Rellenong Bangus**	76	**Unagi Unatma**	71
Fish with yellow pickle sauce		*Stuffed milkfish*		*Eel with egg*	
Ikan Asam Padeh	90	**Saengson Chim**	86	**West Lake Fish**	85
Fish in sour sauce		*Fish & vegetable stew*		**Zarzuela de Pescado**	70
Ikan Bantut	77	**Saengson Chun**	90	*Mixed seafoods in wine*	
Spicy fish in aluminum foil		*Fried fish fillets*			

Ikan Acar Kuning 83
Fish with yellow pickle sauce

Ikan Asam Padeh 90
Fish in sour sauce

Ikan Bantut 77
Spicy fish in aluminum foil

Jhinga Curry 54
Shrimp curry

Kakuluwo 50
Crab curry

Karee Udang 57
Shrimp curry

Kakejiru 71
Grilled eel

Kinulot 91
Shark meat with coconut milk

Laing 51
Spicy crabs

Lobster with Chinese Wine 63

Lobster Curry 'Pulau Tioman' 62

Lobster Masala 63

Lobster Omelette 62

Machli Curry 79
Curried fillets of pomfret

Miris Malu 87

Mixed Seafoods in Coconut Shell 70

Orr Chien 66
Oyster omelette

Pad Priew Wan Goong 54
Sweet & sour shrimp

Pla Mueg Pad Prik 75
Fried squid with hot sauce

Pla Pad King 87
Sea bass with fresh ginger

Poo Cha 69
Stuffed crab shells

Po Tak 69
Sour seafood pot

Rellenong Bangus 76
Stuffed milkfish

Saengson Chim 86
Fish & vegetable stew

Saengson Chun 90
Fried fish fillets

Sautéed Cuttlefish with Oyster Sauce 75

Sautéed Eel 71

Sautéed Lobster 61

Sautéed Shrimp with Garlic 55

Shredded Abalone with Vegetables 67

Shrimp in Hot Garlic Sauce 55

Sliced Fish in Wine Sauce 90

Smoked Pomfret 80

Sotong Ayam 75
Stuffed cuttlefish

Spiced Shrimp with Okras 58

Spicy Fried Cockles 67

Spicy Shrimp 58

Steamed Garoupa with Ham & Vegetables 89

Steamed Garoupa with Ginger 86

Steamed Pomfret Rolls 88

Steamed Shrimp 59

Stuffed Red Snappers 81

Sweet & Sour Shrimp 56

Szechuan Stir-Fried Shrimp 59

Tahong Filipina 66
Mussels in spicy sauce

Tempura 64
Deep-fried seafood & vegetables

Thakkali Isso 50
Shrimp & tomato curry

Tinuktok 70
Seafoods in cabbage leaves

Tod Man Pla 83
Fried fish cakes with hot sauce

Unagi Unatma 71
Eel with egg

West Lake Fish 85

Zarzuela de Pescado 70
Mixed seafoods in wine

POULTRY

Almond Chicken with Pineapple 99

Ayam Bakakak Bumbu Bali 98
Balinese style barbecued chicken

Ayam Bumbu Rujak 101
Spiced chicken in coconut milk

Ayam Golek 97
Chicken in spiced coconut sauce

Baked Stuffed Pigeons 110

Bebek Betutu 115
Steamed stuffed duckling

Beggar's Chicken 95

Chicken Adobo 99

Chicken Almond Curry 102

Chicken Badun 108

Chicken Buriyani 108

Chicken & Cashew Nuts 98

Chicken with Dried Red Chilies 106

Chicken Jalfrazi 106

Chicken Livers Baked in Salt 94

Chicken Vindaloo 102

Drunken Chicken 106

Duck in Lemon Sauce 113

Gaeng Phed 115
Duck & vegetables

Gaeng Phed Gai 103
Curried Chicken

Hainanese Chicken Rice 107

Hin's Smoked Duck 112

Itek Bersantan	114
Duckling in coconut milk	

Kari Kering Hati Ayam	94
Dried chicken liver curry	

Khaukswe	107
Spiced sautéed chicken with noodles	

Korma Ayam	103

Minced Pigeon in Lettuce Leaves	110

Paper Wrapped Chicken	95

Peking Duck	114

Pigeons Baked in Salt	111

Rellenong Manok	100
Stuffed chicken	

Rendang Padas Hati Ayam	94
Chicken liver & heart curry	

Sliced Pigeon with Bamboo Shoots	111

Tom Kem Gai	96
Chicken casserole	

BARBECUES & HOT POTS

Chicken Firepot	126

Gyruniku Teppanyaki	118
Beef cooked on griddle	

Mongolian Barbecue	119

Mongolian Hot Pot	126
Lamb & vegetable hot pot	

Pulgogi	119
Korean barbecue	

Satay	123
Skewered meat with hot peanut sauce	

Shabu Shabu	127
Beef & vegetable hot pot	

Sliced Beef with Vinegar	127

Sukiyaki	125
Sliced beef & vegetables	

Tandoori Chicken	122

Teppanyaki Ise-Ebi	118
Lobster Teppanyaki	

Yakitori	122
Barbecued chicken & vegetable sticks	

Yosenabe	124
Seafood & vegetables	

MEATS

Babi Panggang	138
Roast belly of pork	

Beef Embul	135

Bola Curry	133
Curried beef balls	

Capsicums with Spiced Beef Filling	130

Crispy Pata	139
Deep fried pig's feet	

Daging Belano	134
Crispy beef with sauce	

Daging Besengek	134
Beef stew	

Daging Bumbu Bali	136
Balinese style sautéed beef	

Daging Rendang	137
Spicy beef chunks	

Dendeng Ragi	135
Beef with shredded coconut	

Gulai Kambing	142
Spiced lamb	

Kalbi Chim	132
Boiled beef ribs with chestnuts	

Kofta Curry	142
Minced lamb balls in curry sauce	

Kustilyas	134
Braised beef ribs	

Lamb Apple Korma	143

Lamb Madras	143

Lechon	139
Barbecued suckling pig	

Neau Pad Prik	135
Sautéed beef with chilies	

Pad Luk Chin	141
Steamed pork balls with vegetables	

Sanchok	131
Skewered beef with vegetables	

Shredded Beef in Taro Nest	131

Sliced Beef with Spring Onions	130

Sweet & Sour Pork	140

Teochew Satay	138
Pork liver in satay sauce	

VEGETABLES & SALADS

Ala Badun	149
Fried potato & onion	

Braised Assorted Mushrooms	151

Brinjal Moju	149
Spiced eggplant	

Charmorro Bean Salad	155

Curried Leeks	149

Dal Curry	146

Eggplants in Hot Garlic Sauce	150

Gado Gado	154
Mixed salad with peanut sauce	

Kim Chi	155
Pickled cabbage	

Lo Han Tsai Choy	150
Buddhist vegetable stew	

Matsutake Tsutumi-Yaki	151
Grilled mushrooms	

Mixed Vegetable Curry	146

Nimono	147
Mixed braised vegetables	

Pak Dong	154
Pickled vegetables	

Sayur Goreng	147
Sautéed mixed vegetables	